ACROSS THE IRISH SEA

Promenade Deck of *Ulster Monarch* **alongside at Belfast. (Author)**

ACROSS THE IRISH SEA

Belfast–Liverpool Shipping since 1819

Robert C Sinclair

CONWAY
MARITIME PRESS

© Robert C Sinclair 1990

First published in Great Britain by
Conway Maritime Press Ltd,
24 Bride Lane, Fleet Street,
London EC4Y 8DR

British Library Cataloguing in Publication Data
Sinclair, Robert C.
Across the Irish Sea: Belfast-Liverpool shipping since 1819.
1. Belfast. Shipping company, history
I. Title
387.5'065416'7
ISBN 0 85177 524 1

Designed by Tony Garrett
Typeset by Swanston Graphics Ltd, Derby
Printed and bound in Great Britain by
Butler & Tanner Ltd, Frome.

Contents

But everything that floats and is built by man ...
has a way of its own, and that way is certainly,
in all its variations, past finding out.

Frank T Bullen
A Sack of Shavings

Foreword

It is an honour and a privilege to be asked to write an introduction to a book written by my friend, Robert Sinclair. The pages bear witness to the amount of patient enquiry, research and investigation carried out by the author in producing a volume which will bring great pleasure to those who remember the splendid days of the coasting and short-sea trades and the people who operated them, and it is to be hoped it will prove to be of considerable interest to a younger generation wishing to learn something of sea transport in more spacious days.

It is difficult to realise that an organisation such as Coast Lines, which at one time operated a fleet of 120 ships ranging from passenger vessels to trawlers, no longer exists. With the advent and growth of road haulage the writing was on the wall, spelling out the end of the coastal trade; similarly, the introduction of air services made serious inroads into the successful operation of cross channel passenger vessels, just as the competition from transatlantic air services brought to an end the activities of the magnificent passenger liners sailing to the USA, Canada, South Africa, South America, India and the Far East.

The author has dealt faithfully with all aspects, not only with regard to the various services but particularly the individuals concerned.

I have enjoyed every moment spent in reading this book and I am certain it will achieve the success it so richly deserves.

R W Berkeley

Preface

To chronicle the century and a half and more of steam and diesel navigation between Belfast and Liverpool implies a lengthy voyage of discovery.

For most of the time on our voyage we shall be absorbed by the story of the Belfast Steamship Company which traded for 123 years on the Irish Sea. Quirkily, that distinguished Belfast institution limited its pedigree to 1824, the year when the Belfast Steam Packet Company commenced business, even though its lineage could not in any way be traced back to the short-lived Steam Packet Company. Instead, had it wished, it could so easily have claimed an even older origin for in 1859 it had bought the assets and goodwill of the Liverpool trade conducted by the surviving sons of George Langtry. The 'Great Improver and Promoter of Commercial Marine', with his partner, William Herdman, had despatched the pioneering PS *Waterloo* down the shallow, winding Lagan to the open sea in 1819 and so commenced steam communication with the great Mersey port, which the Belfast Steamship Company carried on and developed over the years.

We shall on our voyage keep friendly company with Coast Lines Limited whose Group the Belfast Steamship Company joined in 1919, as well as with associated Group companies such as Burns and Laird Lines and the British and Irish Steam Packet Company but in no way shall we pretend to a detailed history of these concerns.

Whilst a member of the Coast Lines Group, it was the Belfast Steamship Company's destiny on two different occasions to be part of two even larger international shipping combines, both of which sailed into financial storms. From the death agonies of the first, the Belfast Steamship Company extricated itself but it perished in the successful struggle for life of the other.

Five decades of membership of the Coast Lines Group, however, does mean that we shall have to scrutinise relatively closely Coast Lines' activities on the Irish Sea. In the nineteenth century railway companies found a surprising ally in the reforming politician, John Bright, who did not hesitate to praise them for the services they had rendered and deplore the lack of gratitude which was their lot. On a more limited scale, the Coast Lines Group needed a twentieth-century John Bright for it received much criticism in its day and little appreciation of its enormous contribution to the maintenance of high standards of safety, efficiency and comfort on the Irish Sea with a minimal share of the mail subsidies that its competitors enjoyed. Where it deserves criticism, this will be given in full measure.

The Group was astonishingly resilient. It overcame the serious investment mistakes of the 1950s and had it remained independent of P&O it would have overcome the design shortcomings of the *Ulster Prince* and *Ulster Queen* of 1967 which so handicapped the Belfast Steamship Company at the dawn of the ro-ro revolution. Simplistic criticism has attributed the demise of the Belfast/Liverpool route in 1981 almost entirely to these ships. They were a large contributory factor but far outweighed in blameworthiness by the financial difficulties of P&O and by the self-imposed inactivity of Government.

Now Belfast Ferries has a solitary ship ploughing her lonely way backwards and forwards between Belfast and Liverpool, supported afloat and ashore by many former employees of the Belfast Steamship Company. Soon a tunnel between the Continent and the English mainland will be an accomplished fact. There will be a premium placed on adequate and efficient links between Northern Ireland and the English mainland. It would be unthinkable if the Belfast/Liverpool route were ever to be placed in doubt again.

Accountants and economists cannot take away from us imagination nor nostalgia for times past. On our frontispiece, the *Ulster Monarch* still lies at her berth. From her foremast flies the Blue Peter with its insistent message, '... All persons are to repair on board as the vessel is about to proceed to sea'. In fancy let us now go on board. May the voyage bring interest and pleasure.

R C S

I
Anger in Belfast

The year 1852 dawned to the angry strains of Belfast's merchants meeting in the town's Chamber of Commerce.

In other less fortunate parts of Ireland some might have wondered why these Northern men of business were so enraged. They dwelt and worked in a town through whose port exports of linen had more than trebled between 1810 and 1852. A town which fifty years before had a population of little more than 19,000 now had one of more than 70,000 and the numbers were soaring each year. Whilst Dublin languished, Belfast stood confident and assured at the threshold of a shipbuilding and engineering revolution which, before the century's end, would make her the largest city in Ireland.

Already, the Port of Belfast handled a greater number of vessels and a greater tonnage than any other in the country. Down its recently straightened and deepened channel went the bulk of Ulster's burgeoning linen exports and, of these, £1,500,000-worth were destined for Liverpool. Communication with the great Mersey port, the only deep water haven on the western shores of England, then rapidly rising to its pre-eminent position in the American trade, was essential for Belfast linen merchants intent on trading with the New World. It was vital also to those seeking home markets, for Liverpool money and enterprise had made the port a keystone of the expanding English railway system.

Belfast men were angry when they saw the merchants of Dublin, Cork, Waterford, Limerick, Wexford, Dundalk and Drogheda trading with Liverpool in ships owned by local steam packet companies composed of their own people. With a solitary exception, there was not a single steamship trading in and out of Belfast which was locally owned so

William Herdman. (Ulster Museum)

that these independently minded Ulster men were largely indebted to strangers for carrying their goods.

Of course, there were other steamers sailing to English ports and to Liverpool but this was not the point. Let us then first retrace our steps to a fine Sabbath forenoon in June 1819 when watchers on the green hills bordering Belfast Lough beheld the awesome spectacle of an approaching vessel belching smoke.

The usual reports spread of a ship on fire but instead of disaster a new epoch in the shape of the Clyde-built paddle steamer *Rob Roy* from Greenock was arriving in Belfast. Uncharacteristically, but excusably, the God-fearing townspeople of Belfast 'permitted curiosity to overcome their religious leanings and went off sightseeing.'

The *Rob Roy* snatched the distinction of being Belfast's first steamship from the locally owned *Waterloo* which sailed just over a month later on 21 July 1819 for Liverpool. This schooner-rigged paddle steamer, built of English oak at Greenock in 1816, has the greater distinction, however, of being the first cross-channel steamer ever to enter the Mersey, which she did after a voyage of 24 hours. Of 201 tons burthen with two low pressure engines of 30hp each, 98ft in length by 37ft in beam, she offered comfortable saloon accommodation with a dining room capable of seating all her passengers at one sitting. There was a ladies' cabin, described as 'neatly decorated' and two state rooms for families. The single fare was £1 11 6d and that for the steerage was 10/6d. The *Waterloo* commenced a saga of steam and diesel on the Belfast/Liverpool service which continues with the *Saint Colum I*, five times the length of the diminutive pioneer of 1819.

The *Waterloo* was owned by the firm of Langtry & Herdman of Belfast. She did not carry cargo and landed her passengers in the Mersey wherever was convenient to time and tide. Sailings were advertised from Liverpool on Mondays and Fridays but despite good intentions there were frequent lapses.

George Langtry was born in Lurgan, Co Armagh, in 1764, becoming a general merchant in Belfast where he lived in 'a large, gloomy looking mansion' beside his place of business in the commercial heart of eighteenth-century Belfast. The site is now occupied by the head offices of the Ulster Bank. Money from his wife's family enabled George Langtry to escape from the prosaic affairs of starch and hair powder, indigo, liquorice ball, gunpowder, castor oil, tea, prunes, shovels, nails and irons and puncheons of strong Jamaica rum to become 'the great improver and promoter of (Belfast's) commercial marine,' by way of the romantic world of shipowning.

Undoubtedly, the rapid expansion of the Ulster linen trade was the catalyst for Langtry's shipping venture. For example, in 1791 only four small sloops traded to Liverpool and four brigs to London. Yet twenty years later eight brigs were in the Liverpool trade and ten in that to London. By 1813 George Langtry could boast of nine brigs sailing to London, Liverpool, Greenock, Bristol and Chester, 'with as much regularity as the winds permitted', whilst in 1809 he had become Master of the Fort William demesne overlooking Belfast Lough on the outskirts of the town.

Willam Herdman, Langtry's partner, was a great-great grandson of a man who had fought in King William's army at the Battle of the Boyne, John Herdman of Tullynewbank, Glenavy, Co Antrim. His immediate forebears had owned the Millfield Tannery in Belfast. The business of Langtry & Herdman (later described as Langtrys and Herdman, presumably as George's sons joined the business) was at first carried on separately from that of George Langtry who continued to own brigs sailing to Liverpool and other ports carrying merchandise and who bade 'gentlemen who have linens to forward' to please send them to him. He also advertised Liverpool coals for sale. The *Waterloo* was joined in the following year, 1820, by the Belfast built PS *Belfast* which like her consort carried passengers only, for whom there were now four sailings per week each way between Belfast and Liverpool.

The absence of cargo facilities and the example of steam packet companies elsewhere, such as the St George Steam Packet Company established in Liverpool in 1821 with much Irish capital for the Irish trade and the Dublin firm of Charles Wye Williams & Company, founded in 1823 and soon to be the genesis of the City of Dublin Steam Packet Company, doubtless led to dissatisfaction among Belfast's merchants. The upshot was that several of Belfast's men of business came together in 1824 and formed the Belfast Steam Packet Company with a capital divided into shares of one guinea each.

The PS *Shamrock* was built for the new steam packet company. She was said to be a handsome vessel and more practically was the first steamer on the station to cater for cargo as well as passengers and set sail on her maiden voyage from Belfast on Sunday, 5 December 1824. Her Liverpool loading berth was in Prince's Basin, later to be reconstructed as Prince's Half Tide Dock and foreshadowing the close connection of Prince's Dock with the Irish trade later in the century. Though the *Shamrock* sailed regularly each week she was said to have been too small for the trade. On the other hand, the port of Belfast at the time was scarcely adequate for anything larger.

Looming ever larger in the Irish cross channel scene at the time was the selfsame Charles Wye Williams whom we have already noted. As managing director of the City of Dublin Steam Packet Company, created from the firm of Charles Wye Williams & Company, he had acquired the Dublin and Liverpool Steam Navigation Company on 1 February 1826 and now headed a puissant undertaking with a capital of £250,000. As a younger man Williams had spent his early business career in the linen industry in the Lagan Valley where he is said to have introduced the beetling process. It is more than likely that he would have been well known to the merchants of Belfast where his ships seem to have traded as early as 1825.

Despite its title, the Steam Packet Company, lacking a royal charter or a special Act, did not enjoy corporate status, being no more than a trading syndicate with each member having unlimited liability for its debts. Maybe they decided after all that running their own steam packet company was not the unmixed blessing that these wily merchants had anticipated and that a sale to Williams would be more to their advantage. Perhaps, also, the abrupt ending of the first known stock exchange 'boom' in 1825 with its trail of bank failures frightened them. Whatever the reason, the disposal of their assets, including the *Shamrock*, to the City of Dublin Steam Packet Company seems to have included an undertaking by Williams that the Belfast merchants would continue to have an influence on the Belfast/Liverpool trade in return for their support.

An immediate consequence of the sale was the transfer of the unsuitable *Shamrock* to the Belfast/Dublin trade and her replacement by the City of Dublin's *Sheffield*. Hill, Charley & Company became agents for both ships at Belfast.

In reply to this dangerous new foe, Langtry & Herdman replaced their *Waterloo* and *Belfast* by the *Chieftain* which came from John Ritchie's shipyard on the south side of Belfast's Pilot Street in 1826. Victor Coates of Belfast built her 150hp engines and she was said to have been both 'a costly ship' and 'a very splendid but very slow vessel'. At the time she was the largest steamer trading to and from Liverpool but her size prevented her from berthing at Belfast except at high water and passengers, at other times, were obliged to come ashore in a small boat. The following year she was joined by the Port Glasgow built *Corsair*, commanded by Captain John Gowan. Like her older consort, to which she is said to have been superior, she carried general cargo and cattle as well as passengers.

Until peace was restored and an 'amicable arrangement' was entered into, the steerage passenger could command a passage to Liverpool for threepence from either of the warring rivals and have bread and meat thrown in to sustain him on the voyage. Langtry & Herdman undertook to maintain two-thirds of the sailings and the City of Dublin Steam Packet Company the remaining one-third. This arrangement lasted for two decades.

During this period Langtry & Herdman replaced the *Chieftain* and the *Corsair* with the *Falcon* and the *Reindeer* in 1835 and 1838. Neither vessel was fast enough for the trade. Both were replaced in 1845 by the 600 ton 350hp *Sea King* built that year by Tod and McGregor at a cost of £24,000. Chartered vessels supplemented her sailings. One such vessel in the years 1846–48 was the Isle of Man Steam Packet Company's PS *Tynwald* built by Napier and Sons of Glasgow in 1846, complete with a figurehead of a Manx-Scandinavian monarch in full armour. While on this service, in December 1846, she was damaged in collision in dense fog with the Liverpool/Kingstown mail steamer *Urgent*.

It was fog which cruelly claimed a victim in the *Sea King* on 4 July 1847. She had left

Clarence Dock, Liverpool, on Saturday 3 July with twenty cabin passengers, a number of deck passengers and cargo under the command of Captain Gowan. In dense fog at 2am next morning, while proceeding with all care and using the lead, she struck on Mew Island at high water. All passengers and crew were landed at Donaghadee but the ship's position soon became hopeless. Despite this, the Langtrys asked Alexander Bremner, who was salvaging the *Great Britain* in Dundrum Bay, to come. He refused but sent his son. Alas, no one could save the *Sea King*.

As a replacement, in 1848 Langtry & Herdman commissioned the fine iron paddle steamer *Blenheim*, also from the yard of Messrs Tod and McGregor. She was to serve Langtry & Herdman until the end of their Belfast/Liverpool service in 1859 and, as we shall see, for a period was to be the only steamer sailing between the two ports. She was of 400hp and took on average 12 to 15 hours on passage. She was notable in having one master, Captain George Fitzsimons, who commanded her from December 1851 until the vessel joined the fleet of the Belfast Steamship Company eight years later. Possibly emboldened by their new acquisition, Langtry & Herdman described themselves as the Belfast Steam Packet Company.

Meanwhile, the opposition City of Dublin Steam Packet Company employed various vessels from their large fleet on the Belfast/Liverpool station. One of these which became particularly associated with the service was the PS *Athlone*.

A London bound traveller, Charles Stewart, joined her in Belfast on a fair April evening in 1837 and has left behind a picture in words of the darkening river, of land which was merely a faint outline of darkness against the skyline and of vessels looking picturesque in the light of the stars as they were towed past the *Athlone*'s berth. As the town receded, Stewart watched the Long Bridge (replaced in 1842/43 by the present Queen's Bridge) with its lamps stretching across the top of the harbour 'like a row of stars fallen from the sky' and 'swimming like ducks in the bosom of the Lagan'. James Walker's scheme for cuts across the bends of the river to make a straight channel from the town to Garmoyle

was only authorised by statute in 1837 so the *Athlone* was an hour threading the tortuous windings of the channel and it was only when she reached the Holywood buoy 'that the helm relapsed from a state of perpetual motion into something like steadiness'. Stewart enjoyed a sound night's rest in his berth and soon regretted leaving it, for the *Athlone* had passed the Isle of Man and was being tossed about upon the waste of waters with no land in sight. He is less picturesque about the state of his digestion soon after unwisely taking breakfast and was clearly glad to approach the Mersey with 'sandy hillocks devoid of vegetation on both sides' and berth in Clarence Dock, 14 hours 20 minutes after sailing from Belfast.

Signs that the 'amicable arrangement' was not entirely pleasing to shipper and passenger became clear towards the end of the 1840s. Though the *Tynwald* (Langtry & Herdman) and *Windsor* (City of Dublin) were on the station, the Whitehaven Steam Navigation Company, with Robert Henderson as Belfast agent, were advertising in 1847 their Royal Mail steamer *Queen* as sailing every Friday from Belfast to Whitehaven and proceeding from that port to Liverpool where her berth was in Trafalgar Dock.

A quarrel in the southern Irish Sea trades finally called the 'amicable arrangement' into serious question. The British and Irish Steam Packet Company and the City of Dublin Steam Packet Company became embroiled in disputes with the Waterford Steamship Company which resulted in the Waterford Company appearing on the Belfast/Liverpool station in 1850 and before the year was out the Cork Steamship Company had succeeded the Waterford Company as competitor with the City of Dublin Steam Packet Company. Again, as in 1826, the customers enjoyed a short lived bounty until April 1851 when Joseph Malcolmson, influential chairman of the Waterford Steamship Company and a large shareholder in the Cork Steamship Company, arranged a meeting between himself and a director of the City of Dublin Steam Packet Company. The outcome was entirely satisfactory to the contestants. Secure from competition on their valuable Kingstown Station, the City of Dublin Steam

Packet Company could afford to be generous to their adversaries. Their Belfast and Liverpool trade was expendable and was transferred to the Cork Company.

The merchants of Belfast were enraged that their trade and port should be regarded as a mere incidental arrangement in an overall settlement among companies without any financial and territorial commitment to Belfast. 'Great was their discontent and loud their expressions of dissatisfaction', so ran a contemporary account. Belfast men were learning bitterly that those who bear the financial responsibility for vital sea communications dictate present and future policy.

More irritation was caused soon after the Cork Steamship Company arrived on the station. At first, their PS *Minerva* maintained the service. She had a splendid saloon, a very fine second class cabin, was schooner rigged and had a figurehead of a woman. On her withdrawal for repairs, the company proposed to replace her with a screw vessel. Screw propulsion had been introduced in the Cork Steamship Company's fleet in 1846 when the steamer *Blarney* was built in Cork by Messrs R J Lecky & Company and her owners were enlightened enough to see that the paddle must soon give way to the screw. This attitude was not shared at the time by the people of Belfast who, it was said, were unaccustomed to screw vessels and disliked them, as did much misguided contemporary opinion. Captain H C Denham RN, for example, reporting on the steamers between Ireland and Liverpool, had a low opinion of them.

The passengers on the *Minerva*'s last trip before her repairs were so disgruntled that they subscribed to a protest. The substitute vessel was unpopular and to make matters worse, soon after sailing from Belfast it broke down off Holywood and was off service for five days. The precise date of this incident is unrecorded but in Belfast, where memories of past wrongs linger long, it was a major grievance in 1852.

Since the *Minerva* had been long restored to the station by her owners and joined by their paddle steamers *Sabrina*, *Ajax* and *Nimrod* at the time when the Belfast merchants' frustrations had spilled over into anger at the Chamber of Commerce annual meeting, there were clearly other reasons at the root of their discontent.

One grievance aired in the chamber was the inadequacy of the mail service to Liverpool which failed to reflect the growing importance to Belfast of the rising port and town on the Mersey. The mail went via Fleetwood and sometimes even to Manchester before a belated delivery in Liverpool. Another was the strong feeling that the buoyant passenger traffic caused by the Great Exhibition of 1851 would inevitably diminish and there would be an overreaction by the steamship owners who might disproportionately reduce facilities.

Yet the main impetus for action was surely the Belfast men's complacent reliance on the empathy existing between Charles Wye Williams and his successors and themselves, which had given way to outraged betrayal as the familiar Dublin men withdrew in favour of strangers from Cork.

Since 1847 Belfast port had a new dynamic authority, the harbour commissioners, a widened and extended Donegall Quay and from it, at last, a fine new straight channel to the sea. Instead of fulminating, the time was ripe for the Belfast merchants to match this enterprise.

Ever cautious towards financial risks, the possible worries of the Northern men of business had been alleviated a little by the Joint Stock Companies Act of 1844. A corporate existence of a sort was conferred upon 'companies' registered under the Act but the liability of partners for corporate debt remained unlimited and the modern notion of a company was still far into the future.

It was the Chamber of Commerce which had provided a forum for the indignation of Belfast merchants; now it was their turn again to take the initiative and appoint a provisional committee with the object of forming a steam packet company. The chairman of the committee was the Mayor of Belfast, Alderman Samuel Fenton, who had been one of the first directors of the Ulster Railway Company.

The Belfast Steamship Company was registered on 25 May 1852 with an authorised capital of £50,000 divided into shares of £50 each. The company's office was at 33 Donegall Quay and the first secretary was George

McTear who was to be agent for the company's vessels until 1861.

The first chairman was Robert Stewart Lepper, a cotton spinner, whose great mill and family have long since disappeared from the Belfast scene. Although members of the Lepper family had belonged to the United Irishmen in 1798, Robert himself was a prominent Conservative member of Belfast Corporation. Only forty years of age, he brought not only youth but affluence and respect in the community to his office.

Among the directors were William Valentine, a harbour commissioner and managing partner in Richardsons, the greatest of the Lagan Valley bleachers and later to be a director of the Northern Bank, and David Grainger. Grainger came from a family of merchants and shipowners in Belfast. Soon after becoming a director, Grainger moved to Liverpool and in association with other Belfast men founded the firm of Grainger, Bristow & Johnston who were to be agents for the Belfast Steamship Company for over forty years and play a major part in establishing its success in the Irish Sea.

Grainger's partner, Samuel Bristow, was the son and brother of directors of the Northern Bank which had been founded in 1824 following the ending by statute of the banking monopoly enjoyed by the Bank of Ireland in 1821. The Northern Bank had originated as the Belfast banking house of Orr, McCance, Montgomery and McNeil who had provided valuable short term credit facilities for the linen masters, including the Richardsons. Thus closely intertwined were linen, banking and the infant Belfast Steamship Company.

These men were a fair sample of the early proprietors of the Belfast Steamship Company, enterprising enough to risk their own personal capital and reputations, courageous enough to have as security only their position in the mercantile community and their trust in each other. Their enterprise and courage were put to the test at once.

The *Telegraph*. (P&O)

II
Strife at Home and Abroad

On 17 April 1852, the directors reported that they had entered into a contract with Messrs J & G Thompson of Clydebank Foundry to build an iron paddle steamer of 880 gross tons. She was to be 243ft in length, 27ft in beam with a depth of 15ft, have accommodation for eighty cabin class passengers and her loaded draught was not to exceed 9ft. She was to have two beam engines developing 440hp, each supplied with steam by tubular boilers with brass tubes and delivery was to be on 31 December 1852. The contract price was £25,000 minus stewards' furnishings, payable in four instalments of £6,250, the first to be paid when the keel was laid and the stem and keel post were up, the second when the vessel was fully framed, the third when she was launched and the last on delivery in the Clyde after satisfactory trials.

Unfortunately, the delivery date proved too optimistic. The shareholders' meeting on 7 March 1853, was told that the delay was due to the wet season and difficulty in getting iron.

At last the new vessel was launched on 26 February 1853 and named *Telegraph*. Her name was doubtless a sly allusion to a topic in which Belfast's merchants had shown an interest as far back as 1830 when the electric telegraph was still in a purely experimental stage. The possibility of a line from points along the coast to report ship movements to the News Room in Belfast's Waring Street had been seriously discussed in the Chamber of Commerce. In fact, it would be 1856 before the English and Irish Magnetic Telegraphic Company was able to establish itself in the town.

Since the short-lived Belfast Steam Packet Company of 1824, there had been striking developments in the port of Liverpool where the new Clarence Dock had been opened in 1830 specially to accommodate steamships. To minimise the risk of fire to other shipping, it was situated some distance to the north of Prince's Dock and was the first in the port to be equipped with covered sheds. The Belfast Steamship Company was allocated a berth at the southeast corner of the dock.

Furthermore, since 1836 it had been possible for most ships to enter and leave Liverpool at most states of the tide as the result of the work of the port's first marine surveyor, Lieutenant H C Denham RN, a brilliant hydrographer before whom lay further distinction in the Navy and an admiral's flag. From his 'New Channels' of 1836 evolved the improved Victoria Channel of 1846, the forerunner of the modern channel used today.

Vast improvements at Belfast and Liverpool and a fine new vessel commanded by Hugh Leitch, lately chief mate of the Cunard liner *Africa*, with James Johnston, formerly mate of Langtry's *Blenheim*, as his chief mate, bid fair for the success of the new company.

The *Telegraph* sailed on her maiden voyage from Belfast to Liverpool on 25 June 1853, and was said to have come up fully to the expectations of the directors. Insured for £30,000 and with a fair cargo, she had a draught of 10ft and, being a fast and powerful vessel, made average passages of 10 hours. But despite their publicly expressed satisfaction, the directors would soon have cause to ponder the wisdom of their earlier determination to provide Belfast with its own steam packet company.

The shareholders were told in September 1853 that a second vessel was needed but high prices (a familiarly modern ring to this) prevented an order from being placed. The new company had to cut its coat according to its cloth.

The Cork Steamship Company and Langtry & Herdman were still on the station.

Ebenezer Pike visited Belfast and saw the Belfast Steamship Company's directors, generously acknowledging the right of the people of Belfast to supply themselves with additional 'steam accommodation'. In furtherance of this, the Belfast Steamship Company courteously applied to the Cork company for their tariff and met with a refusal but Langtrys were more accommodating and supplied theirs which was, in any case, the same as the Cork company's. The *Telegraph* was discreetly sailed three times a fortnight in each direction so as not to interfere with the sailings of the other vessels. To this ironical gesture, the Cork company reacted with open hostility.

Could all this have forced the directors possibly to have second thoughts about running to Liverpool? The *Telegraph* made a special sailing on 14 September 1854 with a party to Cairnryan who were interested in establishing a service to Loch Ryan in connection with railway developments being proposed. Nothing more was heard from the directors of this.

Fares and freights were slashed. The cabin return fare was reduced to 15/-, the former single rate, and down went the fare for deck passengers from 4/- to 3/-.

This could not go on and George McTear, director and agent for the Belfast Steamship Company, went to see the chairman of the Cork Steamship Company, Ebenezer Pike JP, but found him in uncompromising mood. There was a hint of concession and McTear was told that provided the Cork company was guaranteed the earnings which they had enjoyed on the Belfast to Liverpool line during the first year in which they were on that station, then in return the Belfast company could charge what rates and fares they pleased. By now, however, the Belfast Steamship Company's directors were wary of Cork men bearing gifts and it was not lost on them that the year to which Pike was referring, 1851, was the year of the Great Exhibition when cross channel passenger traffic was altogether exceptional. There was correspondence but Glover, the Cork secretary, would only reiterate Pike's proposal.

With peace apparently far away, the situation became nastier and merchants using the *Telegraph* were threatened by Pike's representatives whilst he himself taunted the upstart Belfast company with a disparaging sneer, saying, 'You have only a capital of £50,000 and you have only one vessel. You are without means to purchase others and cannot, therefore, help yourselves or retaliate'. But the Cork man had misjudged the mettle of Robert Lepper. On 9 January 1854. a meeting of the shareholders of the company was called and told by Lepper that the *Telegraph* had commenced sailing from Liverpool for Cork in opposition to the service of the Cork Steamship Company.

Lepper proposed carrying the war even further into the enemy's camp by placing steamers on the London to Cork and Liverpool to Rotterdam lines. McTear assured incredulous shareholders that he had an offer of two first class steamers. Another shareholder raised the spirits of the meeting by declaring that, 'a just war was to be preferred before an unhallowed peace'. From the canny Ulster Scots town of Ballymena came words of warning that shareholders in that town would accept the directors' decision but 'disapproved of going into opposition'. In the meantime, the Company bought the paddle steamer *Sea Nymph* to maintain the Belfast to Liverpool sailings in the *Telegraph*'s absence.

Earning a reputation of being a splendid and very powerful boat, sailing from Cork each Wednesday and Saturday, the *Telegraph* succeeded, where diplomacy had failed, in bringing Pike back to the conference table. In fact a very friendly but protracted meeting took place between Pike and Glover on the one hand and Lepper and Valentine on the other and it was agreed that the *Telegraph* would be withdrawn from Cork and the *Minerva* likewise from Belfast. News of the peace terms was given to the Belfast Steamship Company's shareholders on 26 January 1854 and it was further reported that the Cork company's *Minerva* would be purchased by the Belfast Steamship Company in which a financial interest would be taken by the Cork company. In fact, neither of these decisions was put into effect.

The *Minerva* went back to her owners though her return was to be brief. On 29 August 1854, on passage Liverpool to Cork under the command of Captain Rochfort, laden with a valuable cargo and 130 passengers, she struck the Victoria Rock in the Skerries Islands, off Anglesey, in dense fog, heeled over and sank in a calm sea. Fortunately, all her passengers and crew were saved.

With the Cork competition ended, the company found itself with two ships available for its Belfast to Liverpool service. The directors believed that a daily service to Liverpool would be an advantage and were anxious for harmonious relations with Langtrys who had their fine paddle steamer *Blenheim* on the station, despite the sense of grievance that the Belfast Steamship Company felt over the failure of Langtrys to assist in the recent rates war with the Cork company. It was known that Langtrys had suffered financially from the competition and they had every reason to feel surprise, then anger when the family firm chose the path of competition rather than co-operation.

George Langtry, the pioneer of steam navigation from Belfast, had died in 1846. His eldest son and heir, Robert, was one of the first Belfast harbour commissioners to be appointed when the new harbour body was established in 1847. He had resigned as a commissioner in 1848 and quit the Belfast business scene. There is no evidence to say why but it seems almost certain that it must have been connected with the grievous loss of the *Sea King* the previous year. For a time he lived in Islay with his youthful bride and young family. He died in 1859, the precise time and place wrapped in mystery as impenetrable as the last five years of his life after leaving his island home.

On Robert's departure, his three brothers, George, Richard and Charles, were left in control of the firm but George died in 1849. The three brothers had been determined to pick themselves up after the *Sea King* disaster. The commissioning of the *Blenheim* in 1848 was one example. In answer to the *Telegraph* they chartered the Dundalk Steam Packet Company's *Dundalk* and fought back vigorously, pending the completion of their brand new PS *Waterloo*. She was larger than the *Blenheim* and came from Denny's yard on the Clyde.

Then there was trouble from the North

Robert Langtry. (Ulster Museum)

Lancashire Steam Navigation Company's Belfast/Fleetwood steamers which had been offering a nightly service since 1853. This company was closely associated with the London and North Western and Lancashire and Yorkshire railway companies who were later to acquire the service. The L&NWR was offering fourteen day return fares to English stations at the rate of single fare and a half. The Belfast Steamship Company's secretary wrote to the L&NWR asking for similar concessions but these were peremptorily declined.

William Valentine and Samuel Fenton were directors of Irish railway companies. They set the tone which was to be the keynote of the Belfast Steamship Company's future commercial success, ie close co-operation with railway companies on both sides of the Irish Sea from a steamship company which had been conceived and born in the railway age. They were not abashed by the rebuff from Euston for the Great Western Railway, already at Chester, was reaching up to the Mersey and would reach Birkenhead in

The *Blenheim*. (Belfast Harbour Commissioners)

September 1854 over the rails of the Birkenhead, Lancashire & Cheshire Junction Railway. In 1860, the Great Western Railway would become joint proprietor of the local company's line and such would be the warmth of its alliance with the Belfast Steamship Company that the latter would agree to represent the Great Western Railway in Belfast and Derry, an association that was destined to endure for eighty-seven years. Later, would come fruitful associations with the Midland, Manchester, Sheffield and Lincolnshire and Great Northern Railways of England.

These better times lay in the future; the contemporary world was bleak.

The developing crisis in the Balkans at the end of 1853 caused a trade depression which adversely affected cross channel traffic, the more so after the British declaration of war on Russia on 28 March 1854.

It was no surprise that heavy losses were incurred in 1854 but trade depression was not the only reason. The paddle steamers could not be worked economically in the competitive situation then existing, especially with the Fleetwood steamers. Many might have decided that excessive competition, trade depression and uneconomical ships were too much and cut their losses, leaving shipping and its uncertainties to others, but not these dogged and determined men.

Instead, they decided to square up to adversity. Wisely, they resolved to sell the *Sea Nymph* and order a screw steamer. Unwisely, they took the small paddle steamers *Newcastle* and *Lyra* on short charters but this only made the situation worse, incurring further losses, and their charters were terminated.

Even war clouds have silver linings, however, and before putting the *Sea Nymph* up for sale she was taken off their hands by the government in July 1854 who chartered her for service in the Black Sea.

The company's bankers may not have been as sanguine as the directors in their determination to withstand potential calamity by courageous development for the Northern Bank was replaced by the Belfast Bank towards the end of 1854. This change of banker was followed by the placing of a contract on 1 December 1854, with Messrs Alexander Stephen & Sons for the construction of a screw steamer.

The obscurantism of the Admiralty had delayed the widespread introduction of the screw and their Lordships insisted on paddles for steamers carrying Her Majesty's mails. Unembarrassed by a mail contract and sailing to and from Liverpool with its deep water channels, the Belfast Steamship Company had no reason to stay with the uneconomical and vulnerable paddle wheel. Instead they could enjoy the advantages of a greater cargo capacity on a deeper draught ship, the greater sea kindliness and economy in working which screw propulsion would allow.

The new ship was to be of 568 tons gross, have condensing engines with $45\frac{1}{2}$ in diameter cylinders and accommodation for thirty-six passengers. Messrs Tod and McGregor built the engines sometime previously as it seems that they were displayed at the Great Exhibition in 1851.

Better fortune awaited Lepper and his fellow directors in the new year. On 19 January 1855 the uneconomical *Telegraph* was time chartered to the government at 55/- per month per ton, or £2,253 per month, and set sail for the Black Sea never to return to her owners' service. To replace her the company arranged an eight weeks' charter of the Drogheda Steam Packet Company's PS *Brian Boroimh* from 20 January 1855. This avoided leaving Langtry & Herdman's *Waterloo* in sole possession of the Liverpool station. Her consort *Blenheim* had already joined the Belfast Steamship Company's vessels in distant waters. Despite this, the charter was not renewed and the company withdrew its service to Liverpool from 16 March 1855. It would be more than six months before it was resumed.

The new screw steamer was named *Semaphore*. Admired for her yacht-like lines, schooner rigged with three masts, she commenced sailings between Belfast and Liverpool on 29 September 1855.

Meanwhile, far away in the Black Sea, the *Telegraph* had been earning a golden reputation for those very qualities which had brought despair to her owners. Her great speed and power made her ideal for the carriage of mail and passengers to Constantinople, the terminus of the cable from London. How appropriate her name had become as she brought despatches telling of the fall of Sevastopol on 9 September 1855, for onward transmission by telegraph. On this voyage she was pressed to the extreme but her hull and machinery bore the strain well even though her passengers never forgot the shaking they experienced. The directors recorded their satisfaction in September 1855 that she was still employed as a despatch vessel and 'were happy for the charter to continue'.

The *Sea Nymph* was caught in 'the most terrific gale ever known in that part of the world' off Eupatoria on 14 November 1854, the same fearful hurricane which sealed the doom of the British Army in the Crimea. Thirty-two transports were reported lost and the *Sea Nymph* herself was said to have foundered with all hands. Fortunately, she survived due to the superb seamanship of her Master in riding out the storm. In recognition of this, the underwriters presented him with a service of plate consisting of a tea and coffee set with a salver inscribed, *Presented to George Harris Tallon by the underwriters of the* Sea Nymph *steamer as a testimony to his seamanship and presence of mind which, under God, preserved her in the hurricane of 14 November 1854, off Eupatoria.*

There is no further record of Captain Tallon in the service of the Belfast Steamship Company. Five years later, the Dundalk Steam Packet Company appointed a Captain Tallon to the command of one of its vessels. The name is a common enough one in County Louth so it cannot be said that it is the same Captain Tallon who served with such distinction in the Black Sea but it is a possibility.

The *Sea Nymph* herself was discharged from government service on 13 April 1855 at Deptford. She was chartered for a further year to the French Government, ending her service with them on 29 May 1856, at Marseilles, and arriving at Liverpool the following 3 July. From 10 July to the following 10 August that year she relieved the ss *Semaphore* which was said to require repairs after a year in service.

The *Telegraph* was discharged from government service at Spithead on 18 February 1856 and sent to London in the hope of either a new charter or disposal. She was laid up until the following November when both she and the *Sea Nymph* were sold to the Chester and Holyhead Railway Company and both vessels were transferred to the Chester Registry on 10 February 1857.

The *Semaphore* was not as fast as the *Telegraph* and needed 12 hours for the passage but, far more important, she had shown a surplus of £1,618.16s, of receipts over expenses for the first half year in 1857. Such was the success of the *Semaphore* that the company was emboldened to purchase the Belfast screw steamer *Excelsior* on 2 July 1857, for £7,200 cash. This vessel was first registered on 8 March 1855 in the names of William Valentine, Robert Lepper, David Grainger and other gentlemen associated with the Belfast Steamship Company. She seems to have been a private venture undertaken with a view to possible subsequent purchase by the company which, in the event, happened.

A monetary crisis occurred at the end of 1857 and caused bank failures, including that of the Liverpool Borough Bank which collapsed in November 1857 with debts of £5,000,000. Not surprisingly, the directors were to report three months later that a monetary crisis had caused a depression in the Belfast/Liverpool trade.

The year 1857 saw a deterioration in relations between the company and its agent and secretary, George McTear. Possibly the transaction relating to the *Excelsior* had something to do with this. By 1859 John McKee, who had replaced McTear as secretary in 1857, was described as agent for the *Excelsior* whilst Mc-Tear retained the *Semaphore*'s agency.

The *Excelsior* cost her owners £3,544 for a new boiler, shaft and propeller in 1859. Not to be outdone, the *Semaphore* also needed a new propeller as well as boiler and engine repairs at a total cost of £2,119. Despite earlier optimism, trade was so depressed in the early part of the year that the *Excelsior* was laid up.

The Belfast Steamship Company made a determined attempt at rationalisation during 1859 in response, no doubt, to poor trading conditions and increased operating expenses. From 15 July, in association with Messrs R & C Langtry, a nightly service from Belfast to Liverpool was offered. Alas, it was clear that this was in excess of requirements and was soon reduced to four or five nights in each direction. It was clear, too, that there was no room for two steam packet companies on the station. Whilst no records survive of Langtrys' financial position at the time, the Belfast Steamship Company was unable to pay dividends and had been compelled to reduce the agents' commission from 7½ to 5 per cent.

To remedy the unsatisfactory and uneconomic state of affairs on the station, the Belfast Steamship Company first proposed close co-ordination of the services with Langtrys, each concern placing one steamer on the route. Langtrys declined the proposal. Next, an amalgamation was proposed but this was also declined by Langtrys who were only interested in a complete sale of their Liverpool trade and the ships engaged on it.

The long Langtry dynasty among Belfast shipowners was coming inexorably to an end.

Richard, the 'R' of R & C Langtry, had been in delicate health for some years and died in 1858. Of his sons, one entered the army, beginning a family tradition, and from him are descended the present day representatives of the family in England. Of the other sons and daughters, nothing is known and they seem to have taken no interest in the business. Charles, the 'C' in R & C Langtry, chose to withdraw in 1859 from the business scene, resigning as a harbour commissioner and retiring to live at Drumadarragh House, Doagh, Co Antrim, where he died, unmarried, three years later.

George Langtry's Fortwilliam estate was inherited by his son, Robert, who sold it to Richard Langtry. Richard's son, Henry, who entered the army, succeeded to the property on his father's death but the estate was advertised for sale the following year. In 1863 it was sold to William Valentine, director and future chairman of the Belfast Steamship Company. Valentine was an early property developer in Belfast and sold off much of the land for a superior housing estate.

George's eldest son, Robert Langtry, had one son, Edward, born in 1847, who achieved an unfortunate notoriety by marrying, as a widower, Emilie Charlotte Le Breton in 1874, otherwise Lillie Langtry. There is no evidence whatsoever that Edward, who was a wastrel, had any association with shipping interests in Belfast. The family business had been disposed of fifteen years before his marriage and this distinguished Belfast merchant family deserves to be remembered for its achievements rather than by the disastrous marriage of a descendant to a courtesan.

The agreement between the Belfast Steamship Company's trustees and Charles Langtry and Elizabeth Langtry (Richard's widow) and Richard Langtry's executors was executed on 1 December 1859. The terms of the sale were that in return for a cash payment of £22,500 and £3,105 in stock, the steamers *Blenheim* and *Waterloo*, including china, glass, beds and bedding on board, Langtrys' premises on Donegall Quay and the lease of Langtry premises at 20 Water Street, Liverpool, would be transferred to the Belfast Steamship Company. There were other shipping and trading interests of the family in

The *Waterloo*. **(National Maritime Museum)**

Belfast and Liverpool and these were not included in the sale.

Changes followed almost at once. The Belfast Steamship Company henceforth conducted its business from the former Langtry offices at 53/55 Donegall Quay. It is possible but not certain that the Belfast Steamship Company's well known red pennant with a white ball came from the Langtry ships. A manager was appointed for the first time. His name was William Langtry and it is believed that he was a cousin of Richard and Charles and had been employed by them. In later years his name appears as a shipping agent in Belfast for he does not seem to have served the company after 1861. In those day, the term 'manager' meant little more than office manager and the company continued to employ agents. George McTear, incidentally, had his agency terminated in 1861. He claimed compensation and was awarded £350 after the matter was referred to arbitration.

In Liverpool, the company's interests continued to be represented by Messrs Grainger, Bristow & Johnston at 4 Chapel Street. In association with the Great Western Railway, a very competitive service was offered to the traveller from Belfast to London (Paddington). Cabin on steamer and first class by rail cost 40/- single and 71/9d return in 1859 with a departure time of 7.15 pm (Irish time) from Belfast and a Paddington arrival at 3.50 pm next day. The equivalent Fleetwood fares were 47/6d single and 74/- return to London (Euston) but admittedly with a much earlier arrival. Certainly by 1861, the practice had arisen of the company carrying all Great Western freight traffic not otherwise specially consigned to and from the north of Ireland via their route and Birkenhead.

In the trading conditions of 1860, four ships were unnecessary and paddle steamers quite uneconomic. Deck passengers were charged 4/- single for travelling in paddle steamers but only 3/- in the screw steamers. The *Waterloo* had to have new boilers and a hull and machinery overhaul during 1860 whilst in the same year the *Blenheim* and *Semaphore* were in collision with each other. In the following year the *Semaphore* needed new boilers, which were supplied by Victor Coates for about £3,000. On the brighter side, the *Waterloo* was time chartered for twelve months from 30 April 1861 to the Midland Railway Company at £80 per month for its service from Morecambe, where it had assisted in the building of a new pier.

The year 1861 brought good tidings for the company as the provisions of the Clearing Act (Ireland) 1860 came into effect. Through booking facilities for passenger and freight traffic to English inland destinations were now conceded by the principal English railway companies, including the L & NWR. However, in return for these concessions wrung out of the railway companies, the company was to come under increasing pressure from them for daily sailings.

The same year, 1861, brought sad tidings too, for Robert Lepper presided for the last time at a shareholder's meeting on 4 March before resigning from the chairmanship due to ill health. A member of Belfast Corporation, Lepper had been a special respondent in protracted litigation in the Chancery Court in Dublin involving members of the corporation who were accused of financial irregularities of which Lepper was personally innocent. Exhausted financially and physically, Lepper died in London, where he had gone for medical treatment, on 14 November 1866, aged fifty-four. His chairmanship had been an eventful one and it was due to his courage, skill and judgement that the Belfast Steamship Company had survived so far the perils that had beset it.

Before Lepper's successor assumed office the company was able to announce the disposal of the *Waterloo* for £9,500 to the General Steam Navigation Company. She was described as no longer suitable for the trade. Less happily the *Semaphore* collided on 10 October 1861 with the Whitehaven brig *Nereid*, laden with iron ore, and sank her. The *Semaphore* was found to blame.

William Valentine. (Northern Bank)

III
Valentine's Reign

William Valentine brought to his chairmanship in 1862 a wealth of experience in linen, banking, shipping and railways. If his quarter century span of office lacked the drama of Robert Lepper's tumultuous decade, it offered scope enough for the wisdom and judgement of the new chairman to apply to the task of consolidating the Belfast Steamship Company as a commercial force to be reckoned with on the Irish Sea. When he took office there were no dividends for shareholders; when he left they were receiving a steady 6 percent.

For commercial success, more investment was needed. To this end, two new steamers were delivered to the company in 1863, designed by Douglas Hebson, built by Tod and McGregor and engined by Victor Coates of Belfast. They were notable for their time in two respects. They were the first of the company's ships to berth the saloon passenger amidships. In a paddle steamer it was natural to place the passenger aft, as far away from the machinery as possible. To continue this tradition in a screw steamer maximised passenger discomfort. They were also the first vessels to introduce the 'ic' termination in the company's fleet, a fashion which was to last for nearly seventy years. Whether this was the conscious intention at the time is uncertain for the theme of communication associated with 'telegraph' and 'semaphore' may have been the inspiration as business became used to the 'magnetic telegraph' and 'electric telegraph' as everyday terms. Whatever the reason, the company anticipated by eight years the well known Belfast built White Star steamers in their style of nomenclature as well as in berthing the saloon passenger amidships.

The *Electric* started early in 1863 and her builders agreed to accept the *Blenheim* in part payment. The latter vessel found her way to the Great Eastern Railway for their Harwich/Rotterdam service and was later sold as a blockade runner in the American Civil War. She met her end in January 1865 at Cape Fear River, South Carolina, when Federal forces captured and destroyed her. The *Magnetic* started in April 1863 and the company was able to pay a modest 4 percent dividend.

The *Semaphore* was not required for the trade but her owners were fortunate in soon fixing a charter for her. Under Captain Robert Crean, a future commodore master, she went out to lay the first Mediterranean telegraph cable. In 1864, however, she was referred to as the 'standby' and it was noted that her charter had ended. In the following year she was referred to as being 'unproductive'. Employment would soon be found for her.

The company was under pressure to introduce daily sailings from the English railway companies in exchange for their recent and reluctant concession of through rates and fares. After hesitation, and no doubt with the idle *Semaphore* in mind, the directors commenced daily sailings in June 1865, expressing the hope that extra traffic would result. Tidal conditions at Belfast and Liverpool made it difficult for a nightly passenger and cargo service to be operated with only three composite steamers. The shareholders were reassured of the 'expediency and propriety' of introducing daily sailings when the directors had to report the purchase of the steamer *Arbutus* for £6,350, a transaction that was soon to be regretted by the company, however necessary at the time. Built in 1854, this vessel had been employed on services from Morecambe, in connection with which her Belfast agent had been the Belfast Steamship Company's former secretary and agent, George McTear.

The directors reached what must have been a most difficult decision when they resolved to purchase, with effect from 1 April 1866, the assets and goodwill of the Londonderry Steam Boat Company for £11,000. Apart from premises in Londonderry and a store and premises at Portrush, the sale included the paddle steamers *William McCormick* and *Enniskillen* engaged on their owners' Londonderry/Liverpool trade. With two-thirds of its capital lost and a resolution on its books to go into liquidation it was scarcely an enticing prospect. The economic hinterland of Londonderry was distinctly unpromising and the sea passage to Liverpool long. The only immediate certainty was that the Derry company was going to bring to its new owners a loss of over £8,300 in the six months after purchase.

All this could not have come at a worse time for, in the following month, the great London financial house of Overend and Gurney crashed, followed by disastrous 'Black Friday' (11 May) on the stock exchange. For three months the bank rate rose to 10 percent and there was widespread unemployment. To add to the misery, the harvest of that summer was ruined by heavy rains.

Why, then, did the Belfast Steamship Company acquire this doubtful asset? It has not escaped the attention of commentators that the Londonderry Steam Boat Company and the Belfast Steamship Company were both represented in Liverpool by Messrs Johnston, Grainger & Co. This firm represented the Belfast Steamship Company in the negotiations and must, of course, have had a powerful motive in trying to ensure that they continued to have the agency for Londonderry traffic in Liverpool. On the other hand, the importance of David Grainger, who came to Liverpool from Belfast in 1835 and was one of those instrumental in establishing the Belfast Steamship Company, becoming a director, cannot be underestimated. At this time, the directors retained the management of the company in their hands and employed John McKee as their agent in Belfast. (By 1866, their first manager, William Langtry, had disappeared from the scene.) David Grainger has been given much of the credit for the successful establishment of the Belfast Steamship Company. His son, also David Grainger, was equally a man of great commercial acumen. The Graingers could probably see that the Derry company could be virtually managed by them from Liverpool and worked at a profit in association with the Belfast Steamship Company.

It is likely that there was an element of defensive strategy in the directors' decision to purchase. If they allowed the Londonderry Steam Boat Company to go into liquidation someone else, less welcome, might come in and establish a near monopoly among the traders of the northwest and might also gain a foothold in Liverpool and have other ideas of expansion into the Irish Sea trade. This understandable attitude was neatly expressed in later years by William Imrie of Ismay, Imrie & Company, managers of the White Star Line, who said, 'Never let a man in the trade in which you are engaged go under; it will make room for a stronger man to replace him and the newcomer might be able to do you down too'.

The company and their Liverpool agents set to work and for the future the voyage accounts were presented under two headings: 'Belfast Line' and 'Londonderry Line'. After the losses of the first six months the directors were able to report that the Derry trade was 'in profit'. This was undoubtedly a tribute to the Graingers' management. In later years the Derry trade was to have varied fortunes but generally 'washed its face'.

Let us look briefly at the antecedents of the Londonderry Steam Boat Company. The first steamship company on the Derry/Liverpool station had been the North West of Ireland Union Steamship Company which commenced its services with the sailing of the paddle steamer *Queen Adelaide* on 27 January 1831. Eighteen months later came the paddle steamer *Robert Napier* which was reputed to take 23 hours on the passage. In 1835 the *Isabella Napier* joined the fleet and the *Queen Adelaide* was disposed of. Then, in 1842, a great improvement in the service was made by the commissioning of the PS *Maiden City*. Built of iron, with engines of 280hp, she reduced the Derry/Liverpool passage to 18 hours. In 1849, the North West Company acquired the screw steamer *Victory* prior to which they had chartered the small screw steamer *John Munn* from their agent who bore that name.

For reasons not entirely clear today, a new company was formed on 3 September 1853 called the Londonderry Steam Boat Company to take over the Union Company services. Mr Munn was given a £200 annuity for loss of office, an obligation which the Belfast Steamship Company assumed in 1866.

Before the new company took over, the *Maiden City* was lost on the night of Wednesday, 6 June 1853, while on passage from Liverpool to Derry after striking the rocks inside Maughold Head near Ramsey, Isle of Man. She had a full general cargo as well as a complement of saloon and steerage passengers. The stranding occurred in thick fog to which that part of the coast is prone. The saloon passengers reached Ramsey before the less fortunate steerage passengers who were not picked up until the Thursday night after they had hailed the iron paddle steamer *Lyra* from their boat. This vessel was on charter to the Union Company at the time and, as we have seen in the previous chapter, was to spend some time on charter to the Belfast Steamship Company in the following year.

Following the loss of the *Maiden City*, the Steam Boat Company acquired the screw steamer *Irishman* built in 1854 and she stayed with them until 1858 when she was bought by Messrs McConnell and Laird for the Glasgow and Londonderry trade. The *Enniskillen* and *William McCormick* were added in 1854 to the Steam Boat Company's fleet. Neither seems to have been an economical vessel and may have contributed to the Steam Boat Company's financial difficulties.

Also in 1854, the Londonderry Steam Boat Company had acquired the Portrush Steam Navigation Company which had been founded in 1835 and had for a time offered a weekly service from Portrush to Liverpool with the steamer *Coleraine*, joined later by the steamer *Mercury*. In common with other steam packets of the time, the Liverpool berth was in Clarence Dock and the agents there were Messrs Forshaw, whilst W H Black was the agent in Coleraine and Portrush. Calls were made off the Giant's Causeway and 'adjacent coast' where passengers were embarked and disembarked from boats. A call was also made at Larne at the timber pier extant there from 1835. By 1845 the paddle steamers *Rover* and *St Columb* were engaged on the service which had been discontinued well before the sale of the Londonderry Steam Boat Company to the Belfast Steamship Company.

One of the two trustees of the Londonderry Steam Boat Company was a George Herdman and it is believed that he was a kinsman of the William Herdman who pioneered steam navigation from Belfast with George Langtry in 1819.

In 1866 a new vessel was ordered by the Belfast Steamship Company, from Scotts of Greenock, to be called the *Galvanic* and despite the losses on the Derry trade they were able to pay a dividend of 5 percent. The directors reporting this good news remarked that the *Galvanic* would be generally similar to the *Electric* and *Magnetic* and would be engined by Messrs McIlwaine & Lewis.

In the same year an extraordinary general meeting was called to amend the company's deed of settlement. Strangely, the company had been tardy in ensuring that they had powers to trade from Liverpool and Londonderry with liberty to call at Portrush. The Isle of Man was added for good measure.

The company remained relatively unscarred by the financial crisis of 1866. Messrs Scott, however, who were building the *Galvanic*, were reported to be in monetary difficulties. Nevertheless, the vessel was delivered in 1867 without serious loss to the company, who were able to dispose of the *Enniskillen* to the *Galvanic*'s builders. Meanwhile, a sister vessel, to be called *Voltaic*, had been ordered from McNab & Company of Greenock, with engines by Victor Coates of Belfast. Expected to be ready at the end of the year, she was the first vessel to be designed by the company's consulting engineer, R M Beath. During the year the *Semaphore* was re-engined so that by the year's end the Belfast Steamship Company's fleet would consist of five screw steamers, two of them built that year. Attention naturally turned to the steamers *William McCormick* and *Arbutus* but efforts to sell them were unsuccessful.

Before we leave 1867, mention must be

made of the Irish and English Traffic Conference established that year in succession to the much more limited Irish Traffic Conference of 1860. The Belfast Steamship Company became a member of the new conference which over the years developed into the Irish and British Traffic Conference. The purpose was to regulate through rates for sea and rail traffic and the railway classification practice was adopted of charging with regard to such factors as value, bulk in proportion to weight, what the traffic will bear, etc. An important proviso in the conference regulations enabled a member to reduce rates below conference level to meet non-conference competition. Conferences in their day got an undeserved bad reputation among certain traders but they served a useful purpose in offering the trader stability and a high level of cross channel service with modern tonnage. At the same time they attempted to prevent the type of cut throat competition among cross channel carriers which would deplete profits and prevent them offering the most modern and efficient facilities. They would be distinctly unfashionable in today's free market climate and the demise of the conference system on the Irish Sea was caused by the development of the ro-ro transport with the consequent decimation of through rail/sea traffic.

The following year, 1868, saw the *Voltaic* in service, the *William McCormick* finally disposed of (the directors 'had despaired of making her working remunerative') and the *Arbutus* chartered, though there were further fruitless efforts to sell her then and in the following year.

The new *Voltaic* was hired by the committee of the Ulster Yacht Club to take members and their friends from Donegall Quay to view the regatta off Bangor on 3 July 1868. The club paid £20 5s 0d but the trip did not receive the appreciation that might have been expected from the trippers. There were complaints that it had not been possible to see the events clearly and that instead of the trip being 'pleasurable' it was a 'tedious inconvenience'. On this not entirely happy cruise the *Voltaic* was commanded by Captain Johnston who may well have been the James Johnston who had been chief mate on the company's pioneer ship *Telegraph* in 1853.

The *Arbutus* was still failing to attract a buyer and instead was refitted prior to being chartered for a yachting cruise in the Mediterranean. She was still unsold and needing repairs after the conclusion of this charter in 1870. The same year found trading on the 'Londonderry Line' depressed and it was felt that this was due to a lack of 'manufacturing or commercial animation'.

Two strokes of bad luck in one month visited the company in the following year, 1871. On 16 June the *Magnetic* ran down the Belfast schooner *Huntress* in the Lagan, causing the sailing vessel to return to port, discharge her cargo and undergo repairs. The *Magnetic* may not have been to blame but the publicity was unhelpful and worse was to follow the next day when the *Semaphore* stranded in dense fog at Burial Island, off Ballyhalbert, Co Down. She was saved with difficulty but such was her damage that she was surrendered to the underwriters, being later bought back from them.

It was as well that economy had been the watchword for that year. Earlier in 1871, with the *Arbutus* still on their hands, the directors had decided to re-engine the *Electric* and *Magnetic* with surface condensing machinery.

In 1872 the company undertook a capital reconstruction, raising £150,000 in £10 shares, £5 paid, augmenting the original capital of £50,000 in £50 shares. At the same time, the opportunity was taken to register the company with limited liability in accordance with the provisions of the Companies Act of 1862. This measure commenced the transformation of what we now call a public company from what was little more than a partnership to the modern plc. New investors were soon amply rewarded by a 10 percent dividend declared in 1874.

As the company grew in stature as a desirable investment, so its relationshp strengthened with the English railway companies, especially the ambitious Midland Railway with whom relations in the nineteenth century were cordial. This was despite the Midland's own services to Belfast via Morecambe and later via Barrow, neither of which appealed to the London passenger who was only prepared to undertake an excessively lengthy rail journey if he had the incentive of

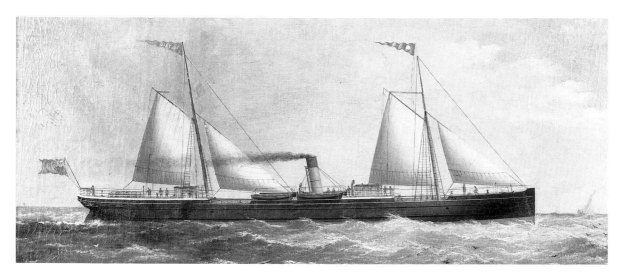

The *Voltaic*. (P&O)

a short sea passage. In 1875, the Midland commenced to serve Liverpool (Central), opened the previous year, with Pullman car expresses to and from London (St Pancras) via Marple and Stockport in connection with the Belfast Steamship Company's sailings. The company in its advertisements drew attention to the Pullman cars offered by the Midland for London passengers. The drawing room cars could be used free of extra charge and each set of cars was advertised as including a saloon, luncheon and dining rooms, smoking rooms, lavatories and ladies' retiring rooms; similar, though not as lavish.

A dark cloud had appeared on the horizon in October of 1874 in the shape of the steamer *Viking* which offered non-conference rates to traders. In reply, the Belfast Steamship Company were able to reduce their rates and records have survived of Johnston, Grainger & Company showing how rates fluctuated with a surprising volatility, eg, '1/- per ton less on the days the *Viking* sails' and even, 'they pay us what freight they consider right'.

The 'battle' continued spasmodically, the *Carrick* succeeding the *Viking* and the torch finally being handed on to the *Torca* which abandoned the contest in December 1877. Johnston and Grainger sent a wire to their principals announcing the good news and received in reply a memo dated 5 December 1877, couched in the following terms, 'Your wire announcing death of *Torca*. Glad tidings

and great joy. Peace on earth, goodwill to all men. Amen'. The *Torca* went to the Antrim Iron Ore Company as the *Glenocum*.

The peace and joy were short lived and a much more determined challenge was mounted in 1878. It is possible that Henry Gowan, who was a former agent for the Donaghadee & Portpatrick Steamers, had been behind the three earlier 'intruders'. He was certainly the guiding spirit in the 'Belfast General Coasting Steamship Company Limited' which proclaimed itself in 1878 as a non-conference line offering additional steam communication between Liverpool and Belfast. The Clyde-built iron steamers *Times* and *Dunvegan Castle*, both chartered, were advertised to sail from Donegall Quay (Dublin Shed) twice weekly.

Fortunately, the Belfast Steamship Company were in a position to meet Henry Gowan's challenge at once. To meet the earlier intermittent opposition they had bought a small steamer, the *Italia*, in 1876. She was the first purely cargo steamer ever to be owned by the company. When the opposition were sailing, she, too, would be on the station. When they were not, she was probably engaged on other channel trades, doubtless under charter. This is the explanation for the statements that have been made stating that this steamer was engaged on 'various channel services' in the period under review. With this steamer on their hands, it was no hard task for the Belfast Steamship Company to form a subsidiary called the Italia

Steamship Company, offering 'cheapest freight and increased accommodation' with sailings twice weekly on the same night as the opposition.

As always, there was a price to be paid for competition, especially at a time of relative trade depression. The dividend fell to 5 percent in 1879 and because the competition intensified the Antrim Iron Ore Company's iron screw steamer *Cargan* had to be chartered to assist in maintaining the Italia Steamship Company sailings. In 1880, even worse, it was found necessary to purchase the Drogheda built, three masted steamer *Glenocum* from the Antrim Iron Ore Company, formerly their old rival *Torca*. The latter company was one of William Valentine's more recent financial interests but doubtless his influence smoothed the way for chartering and purchasing tonnage at short notice to meet the intensifying threat.

The dividend fell to 3 percent in 1880 so the company's shareholders must have been greatly relieved when June 1880 brought news of peace.

Two agreements were signed on 28 June 1880. The first provided for a covenant from the Belfast General Coasting Steamship Company binding them not to compete with the Belfast Steamship Company on the Belfast and Londonderry to Liverpool routes for twenty years. In return they would receive a consolation of £1,000 subject to forfeiture in the event of breach of the agreement. The second agreement was with Henry Gowan personally. For a period of five years, at a salary of £300 per annum, he was to become 'consulting agent' to the Belfast Steamship Company. He was charged with the promotion of the trade and business of the company so far as lay in his power and he was able to pursue his general agency business provided he did not engage in the cross channel trade between Belfast and Londonderry and Liverpool. In fact, he remained as consulting agent until 1887.

Although the opposition had been killed in 1880, the victory had not been bloodless and Henry Gowan, whose name remains to this day part of the Belfast business scene, had come out of it well.

The competition had meant that much

needed modernisation of the fleet could not take place as quickly as the company would have wished. Where the trader may have thought he was gaining, he was, in fact, losing and the traveller, an innocent victim in the freight war, was certainly coming out of it all poorly. The directors were concerned that older, slower steamers, which might have been replaced without the competition, were providing excessively long winter passages and causing diversion of traffic.

To meet the situation, the *Semaphore* was taken in hand at once. In 1880, she was lengthened, reboiled, had her engines compounded and was renamed *Telegraphic*. In June of the same year, the *Glenocum* went to French owners and in March 1882 the *Italia* was sold to N McLeod of Belfast. The company was then able to place an order in the following August with Harland & Wolff at their Queen's Island shipyard for a new express passenger steamer to be called the *Dynamic*.

Larger and faster than her predecessors, the *Dynamic* entered service on 18 December 1883, and was the last of the company's vessels to have an iron hull. She was their first to be built by Harland & Wolff at their Queen's Island shipyard, thus commencing a long tradition of such orders for passenger vessels, which came to an end finally eighty-four years later when the last such vessel to be built for the company came not from Belfast but from Cammell Laird's Birkenhead yard.

The *Dynamic* had barely started when a new threat faced the company, coming surprisingly from the Belfast Central Railway Company. This was a concern of blighted hopes and thwarted ambitions, aspiring to connect by means of junctions the railways serving Belfast and to construct a central station in the town. Chronically short of funds, its aspirations were largely unrealised. By 1884 it had succeeded in reaching Donegall Quay from its junction with the Ulster Railway and now developed maritime ambitions. The Belfast Steamship Company's half yearly meeting in March 1884 was told that the railway company had introduced a bill which would give it powers to run steamers from Belfast to any port. The proposal to start steamer services was hardly a serious one but probably part of the mosaic of contemporary railway politics. The Belfast Central Railway, through a subsidiary undertaking, had proposed a number of impracticable railway extensions from its line to various places, including Holywood, Co Down. This pointed a pistol at the heart of the Belfast, Holywood & Bangor Railway of which William Valentine was a director. The steamship proposals were vigorously and successfully opposed; the competing railway to Holywood was never built and in the following year, 1885, the Belfast Central Railway ended its penurious and frustrated existence when it was amalgamated with the Great Northern Railway and no more was ever heard of cross channel steamship ambitions from Belfast by the Irish owned railway companies serving that port.

Meanwhile, two more express passenger steamers, improved versions of the *Dynamic*, had been ordered from Harland & Wolff despite the fact that traffic was reported to be depressed through 1885. The trade situation, allied with difficulties in operating the *Dynamic* with her older and much slower consorts, was probably the reason for a charter of the *Dynamic* to the Admiralty in May of 1885, on 'very favourable' terms. No details of the charter survive but there would be considerable naval and military activity in the eastern Mediterranean following the nationalist rising in Egypt in 1881, the landing of Wolseley's army there in the following year and the very recent tragic failure to relieve Khartoum in time to save General Gordon. The *Dynamic* must have pleased the Lords Commissioners, probably with her speed, for she was to be fixed again with a charter in 1886 for a voyage to Malta and back.

Meanwhile, the *Caloric* started in December 1885 and the *Optic* in January 1886. They were the first of the company's vessels to have steel hulls, to be lighted by electricity and to be fitted with bilge keels to minimise rolling, a feature of the White Star liners built by Harland & Wolff and a reminder of the heavy weather that could be encountered on this lengthy Irish Sea passage. Their boilers delivered steam at 100lb per sq in, driving their compound machinery at 15 knots. Their owners were not slow to point out that their

The *Dynamic* carrying Belfast Harbour Commissioners on their annual inspection 1896 under the command of Captain J T Ross. (McRoberts Collection)

speed was only equalled on the Irish Sea by the subsidised Holyhead mail packets whilst they could only make their money from what cargo and passenger business they could attract.

Passengers boarding entered a spacious saloon, lit by numerous electric lights, with large ports and heated by a stove. Descending to the main deck, there was a pleasing absence of the sickening odour of oil lamps. Each state room had two beds, one on each side, not one above the other, with brass side rails, and electric lights and bells were a surprisingly modern touch. Hot and cold baths were available and a promenade deck above the midships saloon was provided. On the other hand, passengers still slept on straw mattresses and stewards brought their washing water in brown jugs in the mornings.

On completion of the *Dynamic*'s second charter in 1886, she was given a refit to bring her passenger accommodation up to the same standard as that in the *Caloric* and *Optic*. Electricity was also installed.

The directors reported to the half yearly meeting in 1886 that the new ships had already brought increased patronage and that they proposed to sail at a uniform hour from Belfast now that they had three modern vessels on the route. They could not make this innovation previously as the unequal speeds of the older vessels prior to the commissioning of the *Caloric* and *Optic* had made sailings at a fixed hour impractical from Belfast when tides at Liverpool had to be caught. It would be another eight years before sailings at a fixed hour became possible from the Mersey. Sailings at a uniform hour from Belfast commenced on 1 April 1886. A new pattern was established by which three express steamers, instead of four, could maintain the service and one of these would always lie overnight for most of the year at Liverpool. This pattern was to continue for almost exactly sixty-four years, though three ships would not always be available in emergencies.

At the same meeting, the departure of the *Galvanic* and *Electric* to Harland & Wolff in part payment for the *Caloric* and *Optic* was reported. The *Magnetic* was sold to Messrs R & D Simon of Leith.

Harland & Wolff disposed of the *Electric* to Messrs James Hay & Sons who sold her to Greek owners in their turn. The *Galvanic* went to a Belfast owner with a well known name, W A Grainger. Soon after, the *Galvanic*, still under her original name, was in trouble in the Admiralty Division of the High Court. She was found to blame for a collision between herself and the Danish schooner *Phoenix* in the Thames abreast of the entrance to the Surrey Commercial Docks where she was about to berth. The *Galvanic*, with a cargo of fruit from Valencia, was going too fast as she approached the dock entrance.

The *Voltaic* and the *Telegraphic* now maintained the Liverpool to Londonderry service with four sailings weekly in each direction, described as a very favourite route with passengers in summer from which 'no better view can be obtained of the Giant's Causeway'.

It is time to come ashore and by 1887 it was clearly time for better office accommodation to support the efficient modern fleet. New offices were commenced on Donegall Quay. Designed by Joseph Bell and built by Messrs McLaughlin & Harvey, they were ready for use in 1888.

Stepping back in time a year to 1886, the company had found four sailings per week to and from Londonderry excessive for the traffic offered. They decided to place the *Telegraphic* on a new service from Belfast to Silloth from November 1886. There had been no regular service between the ports since 1865. Silloth was anxious for business since a new dock had been opened there in 1885 following the collapse of the old one in 1879. The North Eastern Railway Company, serving Silloth, was ever anxious to develop trading links with the north of Ireland and the time seemed right for the new venture.

It would seem, however, that the impetus for the new service must have come from Grainger & Company, as the company's Liverpool agents were now styled, for they were also the Liverpool agents for the Silloth Steam Navigation Company. No details of the Silloth side of the operation survive and it was withdrawn after only two months with the results described as 'very discouraging'. There was consolation for this minor reverse in 1887, if prestige rather than profit be consolation. On 6 September the Channel Fleet under the command of Admiral Sir William Hewett called in Belfast Lough. The Mayor of Belfast (it was not yet a city), the chairman of the harbour commissioners and other dignitaries set sail in the *Optic* down the lough to welcome the fleet. Fresh from a complete overhaul, the *Optic* looked almost 'brand new', flying the Union Jack from her main mast, the flag of the harbour commissioners at her fore and the band of the West Surrey Regiment embarked for'ard. Captain Robert Crean, commodore master, was in command.

There had been protests from the Maiden City over the reduction from four sailings to two per week so after the Silloth débâcle the *Telegraphic* was sent back to the Londonderry/Liverpool route. But the financial results from four sailings a week were 'not satisfactory' and by 1888 the directors were reporting the 'Londonderry Line' as uneconomical. Worse was to follow, for in that year the Irish Traders' Co-operative Steamship Company Limited was formed with a proposed capital of £100,000. It had plans to run a non-conference service to Fleetwood and later to a Scottish port. The ex-L & NWR steamer *Stanley* was acquired and the service started. Although the new competitor was 'run off' in 1890, the competition served to call in question the Belfast Steamship Company's policy of using superannuated express steamers for the 'Londonderry Line'.

At the same time as the company's new offices were commenced another development ashore took place. This was the appointment for the first time, since William Langtry, of a manager. He was William Pirrie who held office from 1887 to 1891. He was probably a son of Captain William Pirrie, a native of Fort William who settled in Belfast where he became a merchant and shipowner and later a harbour commissioner. Although William Pirrie replaced an agent in Belfast it is difficult to say whether or not he enjoyed the precise status of the more modern general manager. One achievement stands to his credit for which he deserves notice. It was he who by patient and diplomatic negotiation persuaded the English railways to agree to the interchange of return tickets by their steamships and those of the Belfast Steamship Company . It was a much appreciated facility at the time though less significant as the numbers of through booked rail passengers declined in favour of the accompanied motor car passenger.

On 6 October 1888 an era ended when William Valentine tendered his resignation as chairman. He was also senior director or chairman of the Northern Bank which was his first love in his business life. In 1888, the bank had resolved that directors should devote themselves entirely to the business of the bank and not hold other directorships. He was given an increase in salary by the bank for giving up other positions which he held and it is probable that these included his chairmanship of the Belfast Steamship Company.

We have seen in previous chapters that Valentine must have shared the interest of his fellow directors in the 'short sea passage' to Stranraer or Cairnryan and may possibly have entertained doubts about the length of the passage to Liverpool. In later years he seems to have made efforts to establish the Belfast Steamship Company on the Stranraer/Larne station but there is no hint of this in any book or document still extant of the Belfast Steamship Company.

Research elsewhere shows that in 1870 the *Semaphore* was chartered by James Chaine and his fellow promoters of the Larne and Stran-

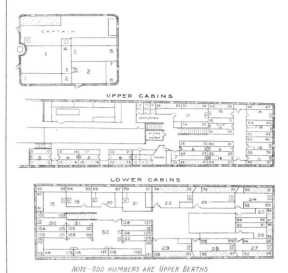

The *Caloric*: passenger accommodation plan. (William Grogan Collection)

raer Steamboat Company for a trip from Larne to Stranraer on 23 August in connection with the promotion of the venture. Valentine was a shareholder and by this time also a director of the Belfast and Northern Counties Railway Company, one of the future partners in the Stranraer and Larne steamers. Valentine proposed that the private shareholders in the Steamboat Company be bought out by the Belfast Steamship Company. This would have resulted in the Belfast Steamship Company becoming a partner in the Stranraer/Larne service as it ultimately developed. The railway companies were not prepared to agree to this. As we shall see, in later years attempts to co-ordinate the short sea passage with the Burns and Laird Lines in the 1930s were to be frustrated by the LMSR and the port of Larne itself was to have no small share in causing the ultimate downfall of the Belfast/Liverpool service when under P&O control. Valentine died five years after resigning his chairmanship of the Belfast Steamship Company which by then was embroiled in a more bitter fight for its traffic than any known in Valentine's day.

IV

Gallaher Takes the Helm

Villiam Valentine's departure left six directors on the Board, William's brother Thomas, Alexander MacLaine, son-in-law of shipbuilder John Ritchie, Thomas Dixon, Joshua Pim, Thomas Gallaher and Samuel Lawther, and of them none felt he had a greater claim to the chairmanship than Samuel Lawther.

Born in 1834 of solid Presbyterian stock from Islandreagh, near Antrim town, Samuel Lawther had entered the shipping business in Belfast as a youth and soon launched out for himself. He owned iron and steel sailing ships, including the *Walter H Wilson* and *W J Pirrie*, built by Harland & Wolff, and by 1888, the year Valentine resigned, was senior partner in the firm of Lawther and Harvey, shipping agents and timber merchants of Corporation Square, Belfast.

Not only were Lawther's qualifications for the chairmanship impeccable but the future success and prosperity of the Belfast Steamship Company seemed to demand his election. 'In general it may be said that no steamship company ever succeeded which did not, either at the start or later in its career, entrust its affairs to men who from small beginnings had literally grown up in the expert business of ships husbandry', proclaimed R H Thornton fifty years later, reiterating the views of Lawther and most of his contemporaries. Of such strength were these opinions that many in Belfast at the time thought the chairmanship had been 'arranged'. Samuel Lawther's name was known far beyond the confines of his own business. He was a scourge of Admiralty and the Lighthouse authorities for their failure, in his eyes, to light and chart the coasts adequately. He was, in later years, to stand as an independent Conservative candidate for the South Antrim seat to draw attention to these inadequacies. If he was unsuccessful here, he has a lasting memorial in the lighthouse at Blackhead, standing sentinel at the entrance to Belfast Lough.

Nor were his good works confined to the seas and coasts. He was passionately devoted to public health and hospitals and was a leading protagonist for the building of Belfast's Purdysburn Mental Hospital. Strangely, his name has survived in Belfast business circles when almost all the others in these pages have long since vanished, for Lawther and Harvey yet survives, though only as a trading division of Northern Ireland Carriers.

Of course, there was a dark side. There were some who remembered too well that Samuel Lawther had only bought BSS shares for the first time in 1880 and continued to buy until the following year when the £10 shares, depressed by Henry Gowan's competition, fell to £4 10s in value and the dividend was a mere 3 per cent. Nor had he endeared himself to his fellow directors for allegations, which he was to repeat in detail more than ten years later, that Thomas Valentine, Alexander MacLaine and Thomas Dixon had each borrowed £10,000 from the company's reserves, and that William Valentine, when chairman, had arranged a loan from those same reserves of £20,000 to the Ballymena, Cushendall and Red Bay Railway Company, of which he was a director and his brother, Thomas, chairman. (None of these transactions at the time was illegal but they had a distinct air of impropriety.)

Lawther's own temperament must have raised some doubts about his fitness to be chairman. He had a love of controversy and an inability to work harmoniously with his peers. He was said to have been 'always happy when counting long odds' and a speaker at a public meeting of merchants remarked that he had known Lawther for twenty years and throughout that period there had never been a time when he 'was not engaged in a battle of either a public or a private nature'.

Colourful, mercurial and volatile, Lawther's great attributes were sadly marred by his inability never to forgive nor forget personal slights, for it was personal spite which was the fuel which drove him to attempt an opposition line of steamers. Far worse, his character defects enabled his Liverpool business cronies, the dour and determined Mack brothers, to establish themselves on the Belfast/Liverpool route and do severe and lasting damage to the Belfast Steamship Company's crucial cargo business.

But let us go back to that fateful meeting of 1889 when Samuel Lawther expected to be elected to the chairmanship on the proposal of fellow director Thomas Gallaher, whom he, Lawther, had been instrumental in bringing on to the Board. Destiny was to decide otherwise. A whimsical account of the proceedings survives. 'Samuel looked across the table enquiringly at Thomas but Thomas only appeared sad, dejected and silent. Suddenly, one of the other directors proposed Mr Thomas Gallaher should be made chairman himself. It was seconded, and although the new nominee modestly protested, he was elected in spite of himself – some say by arrangement also; but you never can tell. Then there was a DECLARATION OF WAR – to the knife between the two men.'

Thomas Gallaher, he of the modest protest, was the archetypal self-made Victorian businessman. Founder of the vast Gallaher Tobacco business in Belfast and of factories and plantations in the United States, he possessed in full all those traits admired in some quarters nowadays. Gallaher was born in 1840 near Londonderry where he began his business life in a room in Sackville Street in that city in 1857, where he ate and slept and hand spun twist tobacco. An unyielding foe of organised labour, a stern critic of government expenditure and an ever reluctant payer of taxes, the picture of Thomas Gallaher is not a pleasing one, but perhaps his shrewdness, ruthlessness and outward façade was what was needed to develop the Belfast Steamship Company not only as a profitable enterprise regardless of competition, but also

as the foremost Irish Sea passenger and cargo carrier. That he was inexperienced in the shipping business was a criticism made by his detractors but would raise no eyebrows today when men who have spent a lifetime in shipping have come to terms with the culture shock of seeing road haulage operators make a success of cross channel freight services.

Samuel Lawther never got over his disappointment, never attended a directors' meeting again and never tendered his resignation. He did, however, dispose of his shares at once. He made handsome profits from the sale of each of his ten £50 shares, receiving £78 10s against an original purchase price of £49 10s each. His 201 £10 (£5 paid) shares, bought for £4 10s each, yielded a sale price of £7 15s. His actions depressed the share price and so did his threat to start an opposition line of steamers. But for 1889 at least, dividends were not affected. Otherwise, for a while, there was an ominous air of calm.

Away from the atmosphere of animosity in the boardroom of the two year old headquarters building on Donegall Quay, 1889 saw the culmination in Liverpool of much work on the part of Grainger & Company to improve the berthing facilities for the company's vessels. South West Clarence Dock was no longer convenient and in July 1889, the Mersey Docks and Harbour Board agreed for a trial period to allocate 800ft of quay at the north end, east side of Prince's Dock, to Grainger & Company, together with sheds and accommodation. The berth was appropriated directly to the Belfast Steamship Company in January 1890.

With a water area of seven acres and entrances 45ft in breadth leading from Prince's Half-Tide Dock to the north (reconstructed from the former Prince's Basin in 1868) and from George's Dock to the south, Prince's Dock in the '1860s' was filled with sailing vessels engaged in the India, South America and West Indies Trade. By 1889 deep sea shipping was moving down river to newer, larger docks and Prince's Dock was about to assume the role for which it was best known in this century, that of a terminal for Irish cross channel traffic. When the Belfast vessels arrived, however, the well-known house flag of Thomas and James Harrison still fluttered over the sheds in Prince's Dock West. The company's Derry steamers did not leave Clarence Dock until 1896. Three years later T & J Harrison departed and the company was able to consolidate its position on the west side although it was not until August 1905 that the berths at Prince's Dock South West were finally secured. These were to be the Liverpool 'home' of the Belfast steamers for more than seventy-six years.

Little more than a year after Samuel Lawther's departure the coming storm rumbled ominously in public for the first time. In May 1890 he had been disqualified from membership of the Board under the company's articles, presumably for non-attendance. In Liverpool on 15 December 1890, the *Journal of Commerce* announced, 'A new steamship line to Belfast'. The paper reported that a new vessel was nearing completion, specially constructed for the cargo traffic between Belfast and Liverpool, and would be on the station in the following February.

The Belfast business community, aware of the animosity between Lawther and Gallaher, learned officially of the new line of steamers a week after the Liverpool announcement in a characteristically flamboyant statement from Samuel Lawther. 'I have the capital, *I* see the opening, *I* am going to take advantage of it, and what is more, *I* mean to make it a success if time, money, the energy, not alone of myself, but of my sons can secure it ...' He went on to speak scathingly of the Belfast Steamship Company and expansively of his own plans. One new ship almost ready, a contract with her builders for another and there was provision for yet another to be started within six months if necessary. Not only Liverpool but Manchester, with its ship canal due to open in three years time, lay within his optimistic sights. Asked if these plans were no more than a 'feeler' to see if he could be bought out, Lawther responded vigorously that as a commercial man he did not invest money for spite or spleen. There was an increasing trade to be tapped out but this could not be done by men 'without experience or knowledge'. Surely there was no spite nor spleen when he added, '... The curse of all limited companies is the introduction to the directorate of men, especially chairmen, who are not practically acquainted with the business of the concern they have to manage ...'

What was wrong with the Belfast Steamship Company's services? Samuel Lawther's criticisms were notably general and unspecific and were answered by Gallaher at the annual general meeting on 13 February 1891. The company's aim, he said, was a first class passenger and cargo service carried on by the express steamers. If there was a special rush of cargo, calls could be made at Belfast by the Derry steamers and this could be done at comparatively little expense. They would soon stop paying dividends if special cargo ships were put on for such occasions. The dilemma was that the passenger trade could not subsist without the cargo and the cargo alone would not support an express service. He gave an undertaking that the opposition would not be bought off; it had come without cause but it 'would have cause for going'. The result of competition could be the loss of an efficient line of steamers for either goods or passengers between Belfast and Liverpool.

The war to the knife which *Nomad's Weekly* had spoken of was about to begin. The forces which Lawther could marshall did not match his boasts. If they had, the Belfast Steamship Company might not have seen the next century. On land, these forces were comprised in the 'Belfast and Mersey Steamship Company' incorporated on 26 January 1891 with a nominal capital of £150,000 divided into £100 shares. In Belfast it would be managed by the firm of S Lawther & Sons, consisting of Samuel Lawther and his two sons. It was quite separate from the firm of Lawther & Harvey although sharing the same address at Corporation Square.

Across the Irish Sea, the Liverpool managers were the firm of J J Mack & Company of Oriel Chambers, Water Street, in that city. The firm had been founded by William D Mack and the business was being carried on at that time by John Mack, Isaac A Mack and James J Mack.

The Macks came from a strongly Methodist and Liberal background and were prominent in local affairs in Bootle. It was not unknown for the brothers to come from a missionary meeting, Bible in hand, to the firm's loading berth where they would lay down their Bibles and lend a hand with trolleys to complete the loading of a ship.

Owning eight vessels, they were in the coastal tramp business and had traded to Belfast since 1877, carrying coal, bulk grain and bagged flour. Lacking return cargoes, they had provided from time to time competition of nuisance value to the Belfast Steamship Company as their agents, Lawther & Harvey, canvassed on their behalf for return traffic to fill their otherwise empty ships. They had never regarded themselves as competitors for the liner trade since much of their outward cargo to Belfast was obtained by overside loading from ocean going steamers lying in the Mersey prior to docking.

An astute, but ethically questionable, stroke of business on Lawther's part was to obtain the services of Thomas Black to manage the affairs of S Lawther & Sons. This gentleman had been agent for the Belfast Steamship Company at Derry until November 1890 when he had left their service to enter the provision trade. He had received a gratuity from the company and in return he had given a covenant neither to oppose nor attempt to injure the company in their business. This he shamelessly broke but it is believed that the company made no attempt to enforce the covenant nor seek damages for its breach.

Perceptive observers in Belfast, who saw the reality of the determination of Messrs J & J Mack to establish themselves in the Belfast/Liverpool liner trade through the extrovert declarations of Lawther, speculated that the new ship would be registered in the name of J & J Mack. In fact, the ss *Manchester*, which was launched on 3 January 1891 from the yard of McIlwaine and McColl of Belfast, was registered in the name of the Belfast and Mersey Steamship Company, to whose memorandum John McIlwaine of the builders had subscribed. The *Manchester*, by her name indicating the ambitions of the opposition, was a well deck, schooner rigged steel steamer with triple expansion machinery. She was lighted by electricity, had large lamps for cargo handling after nightfall and would carry freight at non-conference rates.

The Belfast berth for the *Manchester* was close to the entrance to Clarendon Dock and was known as the Silloth shed. A very convenient berth close to the busy business and commercial centre of Liverpool was allocated on the west side of George's Dock. This lay immediately to the south of Prince's Dock and early in the present century was filled in and its land reclaimed for the construction of the buildings which form Liverpool's magnificent waterfront.

The six months from 1 September 1890 were not happy ones for the Belfast Steamship Company. It opened with the commencement in earnest of the long war of attrition which the port of Larne was to wage with the company and indeed with the cross channel trade of the port of Belfast. The Larne and Stranraer Steamship Joint Committee commenced an accelerated and improved service aided by an annual government subsidy of £13,500 with the object of providing a mail service to all parts of Ireland supplementing the Holyhead route. There was some threat in this to the company's passenger traffic but none to the cargo business; the articulated lorry and its ally the ro-ro ferry were still far away in the future.

At the same meeting in February 1891, at which Gallaher had set out the company's policy, he had to tell the shareholders that there were increases in coal prices to be met, not good news for those operating express steamers. Nor was this all. At both Belfast and Liverpool there were increases in dock dues to be absorbed somehow.

Then there was the opposition steamer. The *Manchester* sailed on her maiden voyage from Belfast on 3 January 1891 under the command of Captain James Barrett, lately an officer in the White Star liner *Germanic*.

Despite the gloomy climate, the Belfast Steamship Company's response was swift and incisive. One hour after the *Manchester* sailed on her maiden voyage, the ss *Dynamic* was despatched from Prince's Dock, Belfast, carrying cargo only. Her speed of 14/15 knots enabled her to overhaul her slightly slower rival and berth in Liverpool at approximately the same time. She carried cargo at cheap rates as her owners were entitled to do under conference regulations when faced with direct non-conference competition.

The *Caloric* and *Optic* maintained the passenger service, probably sailing on most days without cargo. The *Dynamic* sailed twice a week and seems to have been the first example of the Belfast Steamship Company having a vessel on the station purely as a cargo carrier if one excepts the vessels operated by their subsidiary, the Italia Steamship Company, more than ten years previously in response to Henry Gowan's competition.

An early casualty of the competition were the through rates on cargo to English interior destinations offered by the Belfast Steamship Company in association with the English railway companies. The Belfast and Mersey Company had applied for such rates but they had been refused. To the annoyance of the Belfast Steamship Company, the Irish railways quoted through rates from Irish inland stations to Liverpool via the Belfast and Mersey Company. The Belfast and Northern Counties Railway, surprisingly in view of William Valentine's association with it, entered the fray even more enthusiastically. It was to cut its own rates between Derry and Belfast so much that they were lower between the two cities than between Belfast and stations short of Derry. Traders in the latter city saw nothing to complain of in this all-embracing contest but local loyalties were clearly divided when at a later stage the trade of Derry port began to suffer.

A policy of dividend restraint with strict economy in all departments was practised to withstand as far as possible the loss of revenue occasioned by the competition. The dividend declared at the annual general meeting in March 1892 was 5 percent, a reduction of 1 percent on the previous year. It was, in fact, to be alleged some years later that the company's actual profit for 1891 was a mere £525. This was not contradicted.

With little to cheer them from the results of the year's working, the shareholders could not join in the enthusiasm in Belfast for the enterprise of the London & North Western and Lancashire and Yorkshire Railways in commissioning the *Duke of Clarence* for their Fleetwood/Belfast service. She commenced in March 1892 and was larger and faster than any of the other Fleetwood steamers. The company did its best to respond and they let it be known that they were contemplating placing orders for two new steamers for their Liverpool service with Harland & Wolff who would thereby have 'an opportunity of clipping the wings of the new Belfast and Fleetwood boat, *Duke of Clarence*, built by Messrs Laird Brothers of Birkenhead'.

Despite severe financial problems arising from the competition, two twin screw steamers were ordered from Harland & Wolff although only one was an express steamer. There was a loss on the year's working for 1892 and all traffic was being accepted and booked on a port-to-port basis due to the suspension of conference arrangements. The shares had fallen in value but every dark cloud has a silver lining and Thomas Gallaher profited personally by the fall in value in the company's shares. He was now the largest shareholder.

Retracing our steps to 1891 for a moment, Mr Pirrie resigned from the post of manager. No reason emerges from any surviving papers for his departure. He was succeeded by James McDowell who had entered the service of the Belfast and Northern Counties Railway in 1869 in the stores department. He became chief clerk in the goods department and in 1886 became agent in Belfast and the north of Ireland for the Glasgow and South Western Railway Company. His brother, Alexander McDowell, was solicitor to the General Assembly of the Presbyterian Church in Ireland, and sole principal of the rising commercial firm of solicitors, Messrs Carson and McDowell (still extant), and later to be a director of the Belfast Steamship Company. He will appear again in our pages.

Throughout 1892, the company kept the three express steamers on their punishing schedule. Despite what Gallaher had told shareholders about the virtues of operating combined cargo and passenger vessels exclusively, supreme importance was attached to the twice-weekly, cargo only service. It was not allowed to suffer nor deteriorate in quality when the *Dynamic* was off for overhaul or any other reason.

On one such occasion, the *Optic* was maintaining the cargo service and had left Liverpool on Wednesday, 24 February 1892. At about 5 am on the following morning she was inward bound about half way between Greypoint, Co Down, in Belfast Lough and the entrance to the buoyed channel. On her bridge was Captain Dunlop, commodore master for only two days in succession to Captain Robert Crean who had retired after thirty-three years' service. Captain Dunlop could see the masthead light and green navigation light of a steamer apparently opposite the first lighthouse at the entrance to the channel. Then a red light was seen, indicating a change of course. Captain Dunlop ordered the engines to be stopped and a whistle sounded but the approaching vessel took no notice and to avoid what seemed like an inevitable collision, full speed ahead was ordered. The stranger revealed herself as the Belfast steamer *Rathkenny* owned by the Antrim Iron Ore company, with iron ore outward for Dundee. She struck the *Optic* aft of the engine room on the starboard side. The damage sustained was said to be 'trifling' and as she had been about to undergo her annual overhaul she was immediately docked. The *Rathkenny* had to return to port. Captain Dunlop's courageous decision saved serious damage to his ship and cargo at a time of crisis in the company's affairs.

There was no end in sight to the trade war in 1893. The 'Londonderry Line', paradoxically, had shown signs of improvement despite support of the Belfast and Mersey steamer by the Belfast and Northern Counties Railway. More competition was imminent to the Maiden City, however. The Laird Line, in conjunction with the Lancashire and Yorkshire and London & North Western Railways, started a new service from Fleetwood on 5 May 1893. Thomas Gallaher, as a Derry man, was determined not to let the trade from Derry get into other hands provided that the interests of his company did not suffer in the process. The Belfast Steamship Company's ships on the route were far from satisfactory. The venerable *Telegraphic* and slightly younger *Voltaic*, which was absent frequently in 1892 and 1893 relieving the passenger vessels from Belfast to Liverpool in the absence of the *Dynamic*, were no match for any newer vessels which might appear.

It was beyond the resources of the company to build two new express steamers for the

The *Mystic*. (McRoberts/Merseyside Maritime Museum)

Belfast/Liverpool service and build new tonnage for the Derry trade. Instead there had been a masterly compromise. One badly needed express steamer was to be commissioned later in the year. The other twin screw vessel had been specially designed for the Liverpool/Londonderry route. For some reason Gallaher chose to make a mystery of this vessel. No advance announcement had been made of her building and he seemed to take pleasure in the fact that there had been an absence of information on the subject. She was given the name *Mystic*, a very mysterious name as Gallaher told a party of distinguished guests who visited her on her first arrival in Londonderry. Gallaher had a reputation for wit to uphold.

The *Mystic* herself left Liverpool on her maiden voyage, arriving in the Foyle on 28 April 1893. She was much faster than the *Voltaic* and was capable of carrying between 400 and 650 head of cattle in space ventilated by Blackman's steam fans although, for some reason now unknown, on that first trip she only brought in four polo ponies and two terriers by way of livestock. She had the distinction of being the first ship in the fleet to have triple expansion engines and twin screws.

Gallaher left his guests at Derry in no doubt that it was he who had been responsible for bringing a new vessel on to the route and he appealed for support for her, reminding them that he was a Derry man and that Derry men should stand shoulder to shoulder with him. The *Mystic* was but a sample of what Derry men were about to receive but they were asked to remember that the company could not 'live on wind'. That said, they set off for a 'trial spin' down the lough.

The *Mystic* could cater for thirty saloon passengers and had what was described at the time as a charming suite of staterooms amidships on the bridge deck. The saloon itself was decorated in polished hardwoods of teak, satin, walnut and mahogany. The flooring consisted of a parquetry design in oak, walnut and ebony. The passages leading to the saloon were laid in specially designed rubber mats whilst panelling was in maple and walnut with the ceiling finished in gold and white enamel. Elegant upholstery was provided. The berth fittings in the staterooms were entirely of metal with silver-plated hand rails. Wooden frames had gone and were replaced by wire frames. There was a special cabin for cattle dealers and electric lighting from masthead to stokehold. One visitor, inspired by Goldsmith doubtless, summarised his impressions thus, 'Still they gazed and still the wonder stood, that one small boat could carry all she could ...'

A new management approach symbolised by a determination to maximise profits where possible was apparent in the summer of 1893, prior to the advent of the new express steamer. The *Dynamic* was not allowed to rest on Saturdays in between her cargo trips for on Saturdays she offered lough and coast trips for 2/6d saloon and 1/6d steerage. On 1 August for example, the day tripper could sail to Larne and back, going outwards through Donaghadee Sound and round the Copeland Islands. Refreshments of 'first quality' could be had on board at moderate prices whilst the band of the 51st Kings Own Yorkshire Light Infantry, with a pre-advertised programme of music, entertained the passengers. What pleasanter than a sail down the lough in a spanking breeze to the strains of *The Rowdy Dowdy Boys* by Bilton and round the Copelands to the accompaniment of a Grand Selection from '*Boccacio*' by Suppé? For those who found the sea breezes on the outward passage enough, the tickets were inter-

changeable for return by rail from Larne. The *Dynamic* sailed at 3 pm from the Liverpool berth, arriving at Larne three hours later and sailing for Belfast at 7 pm.

There were other trips in the season with minor variations. On at least one occasion the *Optic* was the excursion steamer instead of the *Dynamic*. The military band must have been popular for the Belfast and County Down Railway started to advertise military bands on their excursions the following September.

The new express steamer ran her trials on 10 August 1893 and sailed the following day on her maiden voyage from Belfast. Her building had been a supreme act of faith and it was remarked that her name *Magic* was apt for she would work wonders in the English passenger trade. In reality, the directors had been much less imaginative in their original choice of name for the cost of the new ship had caused a storm in the boardroom and a subsequent resignation, and her name was probably the least of the directors' preoccupations. *Electric* had been decided upon and many of the forgings brought over to Belfast for her construction were so marked. Then it was pointed out to the directors that many might by deterred from travelling in the ship in the belief that she was a veteran of thirty years and not the very latest addition to the fleet. So *Magic* she became.

The influential Alexander MacLaine, an engineer with the invention of a patent piston to his credit, chairman of the Shrigley Mills in County Down and director of the Ulster Marine Insurance Company, left the Board in protest at the expenditure of £65,000, the cost of the *Magic*, at a time when the company was facing serious financial difficulties. Tom Gallaher, ever a pragmatist, bought MacLaine's £10 shares for £6 each, thus strengthening his position in the company still further.

Triple expansion machinery with a nominal horsepower of 493 drove the *Magic*'s twin screws at 19 knots, according to some, perhaps exaggerated, reports. Nevertheless, great store was set by her speed and it was hoped that when the dredging at the Mersey Bar was completed in the following year that the quay to quay passage could be made in a little over 8 hours and Belfast and London brought within 13 or 14 hours of each other.

The *Magic* (William Grogan Collection)

On the other hand, there was a marked disparity with the speeds of the *Optic* and *Caloric* which were only capable of 14½ knots and average passages of 11 hours. This lack of uniformity was probably a contributory reason for the company commencing to state from now on, in their advertisements, which sailings the *Magic* would take.

The saloon was placed for'ard of the machinery space over which ran the bridge or promenade deck some 140ft in length which could be covered with an awning. The saloon deck below had an open deck at the sides and passengers had a total length of 329ft available to them on both sides of the deckhouse and athwart the ship. Passengers embarked and disembarked by way of the open deck and this could lead to congestion when the ship was carrying her full complement of saloon passengers with their attendant luggage.

The saloon itself was handsomely decorated in polished oak with tastefully carved figures costumed after the style of the thirteenth, fourteenth and fifteenth centuries, the deck was laid with parquetry flooring, as in the *Mystic*, and the whole was surmounted by an elegant dome with stained glass. The flooring in the smoking room, which was on the same deck as the saloon, was in rubber tiles as were all the passages on the deck. Easy lounges, chairs and tables furnished the smoking room which was finished in oak and walnut.

The sleeping accommodation was arranged on the saloon, main and lower decks and was for 222 passengers. No stateroom accommodated more than four passengers; all were mechanically ventilated and equipped with electric bells. Transverse passages divided the saloon deck staterooms from the saloon, where sixty-five passengers could dine together, at one end of the deckhouse and from the smoking room at the other.

In the more spartan steerage, separate sleeping accommodation was provided for women. An innovation here was a supplementary charge of one shilling for which a woman could have a berth with a cup of tea or coffee in the morning included. Saloon passengers at this time, of course, did not pay separately for berths.

The *Magic* was specially fitted for the carriage of cattle and horses on two decks. On her first sailing from Liverpool she brought into Belfast the largest cargo that had yet arrived in a cross channel vessel. A large crowd had assembled at Donegall Quay to watch Captain Dunlop swing her at her berth using her twin screws. The next day she was thrown open for the inspection of an admiring public. The company had every reason to feel proud of this graceful, twin-funnelled ship.

As soon as the *Magic* commissioned, the *Caloric* was taken in hand and had her cabin accommodation improved. There is no record of similar improvements in the *Optic*; possibly the company still hoped to order a sister for the *Magic* but this can only be conjecture. In October 1893 the *Telegraphic* was sold. Her new owners used her in various trades, including that between London and the Canary Islands.

The new ship on the express service encouraged the company to develop excursion traffic to cross channel resorts and the summer of 1893 saw through-bookings being offered from Belfast to Bangor, Beaumaris, Llandudno and Menai Bridge, via the steamers of the Liverpool and North Wales Steamship Company.

There was no sign of the Belfast and Mersey Company ending the lone, dogged fight of their *Manchester* against the older company. The *Magic*'s arrival eased the pressure on the express steamers which the maintenance of the twice-weekly express cargo service created. But ahead there loomed a new challenge. The upper portion of the Manchester Ship Canal was to be officially opened on 1 January 1894, in advance of the formal opening by Queen Victoria on the following 21 May. The Macks and Lawther had already threatened to build ships specially adapted to the requirements of the new Manchester trade. Thomas Gallaher and his fellow directors were determined to forestall them despite having had to swallow the bitter pill of a £4,000 loss on working for 1893. Shareholders were consoled, however, by a dividend of 5 percent.

On a happier note, sailings at fixed hours became possible from 1 October 1893, at Liverpool. Dredging work from 1890 resulted in a depth at low water at spring tides of 25ft at least and a channel width of 2,000ft at the Mersey Bar. This had been accomplished by the use of two hopper barges and special dredgers on a plan devised by A G Lyster. Maintaining the channel and the depth at the Bar is a never-ending task.

Cartoon in *Nomads Weekly* after Gallaher's arbitration success. (Arthur Moore)

Nomads Weekly cartoon before Lawther's unexpected final victory in the courts. (Arthur Moore)

V

All at Sea with the Lawyers

The years to the end of the century saw the Belfast Steamship Company constantly trying to improve its services to traders and passengers but continually hampered by the assault on its cargo business from Samuel Lawther and J J Mack under the guise of the Belfast and Mersey Steamship Company. As we shall see, from the summer of 1894 a less serious but none the less irritating attack was mounted from the same quarter on the company's passenger business. At the end of the decade the opposition was to culminate in protracted, expensive and, to the layman, extraordinary litigation.

Let us commence at the old year's end, on 30 December, and sail with the *Dynamic* on a fine Saturday night, almost like summer, on a sea of oily smoothness across the Mersey to arrive in good time to take her place in the procession of ships which would open the new inland port of Manchester to the world's commerce on New Year's Day, 1894. Carrying a large and varied cargo, including 25 tons of Dunville's whiskey, a large number of guests and James McDowell, the manager, the *Dynamic* made a 10 hour run to anchor in the Mersey at 7.30am.

So far so good, but the rest of the trip failed to come up to the expectations of those on board. As the sun rose and the Sabbath forenoon wore on, the tide turned, the *Dynamic* swung round her anchor and her passengers could hear church bells on shore and requested the master, Captain James Brennan, to conduct Divine Service. He declined, saying he was out of practice. Would-be worshippers had to make do with the ship's library and read works 'becoming to the day of rest'.

Eventually, the *Dynamic* weighed anchor and headed upstream for Eastham, entering the vast lock where 'the gates draw together and there you are, a prisoner, awaiting eventualities'. The ship tied up for the night at Weston Point on the lower portion of the canal which had been in use for some time. It was noted that the banks had given way and the navigable width had been reduced. Nor did the country please; it was 'uninteresting' and 'with very little outlay could be converted into a penal settlement'.

On a brighter note, the *Dynamic* was the first Irish vessel to enter the canal and received enthusiastic acclaim from well-wishers on the banks on that account, such as 'Bravo, old Ireland' and 'Success to Belfast'. New Year's morning opened with a keen nor'easterly wind and a hint of frost in the air. The Lord Mayor and Corporation of Manchester and the Mayor and Corporation of Salford headed the procession of ships which moved off but this august vanguard could do nothing to lessen the frustrations caused by the tardy opening of swing bridges *en route* and an inordinate delay at Latchford Locks. The journey's end did not seem worth the two days' sail from Belfast to the passengers. 'The filthy condition of the water of the canal' was noted and it seemed to those on board as though it received all the rubbish of the seven million or so inhabitants of the new seaport and its surrounding cluster of towns.

If the voyage had been a disappointment the commercial results were equally so. Though the company was praised for its enterprise in offering a direct service so promptly to Manchester it was probably premature. There were apparently many initial problems in the canal and it was noticeable that the Belfast and Mersey Company cunningly bided their time despite earlier statements that the *Manchester* was only trading to Liverpool until the canal was open. It seems certain that the 'opposition' succeeded in panicking Gallaher and his colleagues into starting a service before the teething problems of the ship canal had been sorted out. Sailing day was Monday from Belfast (Prince's Dock) and Wednesday from Manchester. Rates were reduced in July but money was lost throughout and the days of the service were clearly numbered had it not ended quite suddenly as the result of a surprise move by the Belfast and Mersey Company.

On 1 August 1894, the ss *Caledonian*, registered at Liverpool in the name of J J Mack & Sons, made her first sailing from Belfast on the Belfast and Mersey Steamship Company's account.

She had been built as far back as 1874 by Messrs Elder on the Clyde for the Ardrossan Shipping Company, had found her way into the fleet of Messrs William Sloan & Company in 1892 and was poised now for a new career.

The *Caledonian* had been re-engined and completely overhauled under the superintendence of Lawther's son, Stanley (who had served his time with Messrs Harland & Wolff). She betrayed her age by her saloon which was situated aft, even though it was tastefully upholstered and decorated and could berth some fifty saloon passengers as well as 200 steerage passengers. She was now equipped throughout with electric light. Apart from competing for passengers, she increased the competition for cargo and could also carry some 300 head of cattle. Such was her schedule, however, Mondays, Wednesdays and Fridays from Belfast and Tuesdays, Thursdays and Saturdays from Liverpool (George's Dock), that her cargo capacity would not be fully utilised. The saloon single fare was 8/-, return 15/-, while the steerage rate was 3/6d single and 5/6d return. Her master was Captain James Barrett, lately of the *Manchester*.

Gallaher's response was swift enough; the *Voltaic* was taken off the 'Londonderry Line' and advertised on the same nights as the *Caledonian*, sailing from Belfast (Prince's Dock). She offered single fares of 3/- saloon and 1/- steerage. She could accommodate forty saloon passengers and it was soon to be suggested by a journal sympathetic to Lawth-

er that the Belfast Steamship Company's steerage trade was now travelling saloon in the *Voltaic*. Very low rates for cargo and livestock were also advertised.

The Belfast and Mersey Company thundered pharisaic denunciations of these competitive rates in subsequent advertisements. 'We feel assured the public will appreciate and support an independent company regardless of the temporary gain advertised by would-be monopolists, absurdly reducing the rates below cost, in their attempt to run off the opposition and return to old or even higher rates, to recoup themselves.'

It was to be 'Farewell Manchester' for the *Dynamic* which was sent to Derry in September to replace the *Voltaic*. The Company would return, however, to the insalubrious waters of the canal in later years.

There would be no return for the firm of Grainger & Company whose agency was terminated in 1894, amid recriminations and allegations of deficiencies by Grainger's clerks. For a while there were rumours of yet another opposition service on the route associated with David Grainger. However, this did not happen and his son was employed as one of the managers in the Belfast Steamship Company's Liverpool office which was divided into two separate departments, one dealing with Belfast trade and passengers and the other with Londonderry.

David Grainger, who had done so much to establish the Belfast Steamship Company on the Irish Sea, lived only two years after his agency was terminated. He died on 10 May 1896, from pneumonia, at his home in Princes Park, Liverpool. He was the son-in-law of William Valentine and there were veiled suggestions of bad feeling before this between Gallaher and the Valentines.

Any dividend which the shareholders received in 1894 and succeeding years came from the meagre profits earned on the Derry service. Working on the 'Belfast Line' lost £6,373 in 1894. The following year, 1895, the loss was £1,705 and there was no dividend. The London and North Western and Lancashire and Yorkshire Railways did nothing to cheer the company's shareholders by adding the *Duke of York* to their Fleetwood/ Belfast route in 1894 and the *Duke of Lancaster* in 1895. They were also able to provide a fine service to London with the London train alongside the steamer at Fleetwood.

Transfer of passengers at Liverpool was to be a continuing problem to the company. In the same year, 1895, that the Fleetwood service had received their latest ship, the Mersey Docks and Harbour Board opened their Riverside Station within a stone's throw of the Landing Stage and Prince's Dock. This was directly connected with the L & NWR mainline via the Waterloo Tunnel and Edge-hill. Riverside Station was well patronised by ocean passengers over the years and the company tried hard but in vain to persuade the L & NWR to provide through facilities in connection with their steamers from River-side. Through-booked passengers then and thereafter had to be conveyed by omnibus to the mainline stations. The history of this part of the company's activities is obscure but there are some grounds for thinking that for a period at least, omnibuses were hired from contractors but when this practice ceased is not known.

In an effort to utilise tonnage to the best advantage, the cruising programme continued and was expanded.

In June 1895, for the first time as far as is known, one of the company's ships undertook a cruising programme around the coast of Ireland. On Friday, 31 May, the *Caloric* under the command of Captain Davidson sailed from Liverpool with a complement of seventy-five saloon passengers in her recently improved accommodation. She called at Dublin on 1 June, and Queenstown (Cobh) on 2 June, where her passengers disembarked for tours to Cork and Blarney. They rejoined the *Caloric* in the Kenmare River and she sailed on to visit the Shannon, Galway, Derry and Belfast before making her way back to Liverpool.

In the next month, the *Caloric* was off again. This time the cruise was from Belfast and was arranged by the Ulster branch of the Royal Society of Antiquaries of Ireland. The destination was Galway where the Society's Connaught province was holding its annual meeting.

There was plenty of variety in the weather which the passengers experienced for the *Caloric* cast off in a thunderstorm on the forenoon of 2 July, and encountered fog at Torr Head which shrouded Rathlin from view. As the fog lifted off the Causeway Headlands the *Caloric* started to roll heavily in a beam sea leaving only the hardiest passengers taking the air on the upper deck and banishing the rest to their staterooms until anchor was dropped thankfully in Loch Swilly that evening.

Mercifully, breakfast was served next morning before the *Caloric* weighed anchor to face white-crested waves rolling in from the western Atlantic. Calling at Tory Island and Arranmore, she alarmed the inhabitants of Inishmurray by sounding her whistle in a futile bid for a pilot before steaming on to spend the night in Sligo harbour.

Off Inishmore, the *Caloric* was visited by some of the inhabitants who entertained the passengers to recitations and songs in Irish. Dancing was commenced on the upper deck as dusk fell under electric lights and the strains of *The Wearing of the Green* and *The Banks of the Lee* wafted, perhaps a little curiously in this sad age, over the waters from this red and black funnelled Belfast visitor.

Next day some of the passengers, a little jaded by archaeology, visited the shop at Kilronan and were pleased to note Marsh's Belfast biscuits on sale.

The coracle men did well from the *Caloric*'s visit and one, who had not drunk wisely, bringing passengers back from the shore tried to grab the ship's accommodation ladder and put his foot heavily on the coracle's gunwale, capsizing it. As a result the Reverend Robert Workman, Presbyterian Minister of Newton-breda, outside Belfast, had an unexpected dip in the strong swell in which the *Caloric* was riding. Miss Workman was rescued by the gallantry of Chief Officer Halsall RNR, who threw off his frock coat and jumped from the *Caloric* into the water at once. Her grateful father later presented him with a silver tea service.

Nor was this the end of presentations. Next day the *Caloric* anchored in Galway harbour without the assistance of a pilot. She had to land the passengers in her own boats with the aid of two local hookers. Before they returned to Belfast by train a silver inscribed cigar case was presented to Captain Davidson by his grateful passengers. While the *Caloric* was away, the *Dynamic* took her place on the express service to help with the July holiday traffic.

Meanwhile, the unrelenting war of rates and fares with the Belfast and Mersey Company continued. The loss for 1895 in working the 'Belfast Line' was £4,100 and the shareholders received nothing by way of a dividend. In April 1896, Lawther and the Macks launched a fresh assault on the company's business. This time Manchester was indeed the target and a new concern was formed called the Belfast and Manchester Steamship Company which commenced a twice weekly cargo service between the two ports. The new entity was never formally incorporated, no vessels were ever registered in its name and it was no more than a partnership between Samuel Lawther and the Macks. For its Manchester service, it chartered the *Manchester* from the Belfast and Mersey Company.

The Belfast Steamship Company decided in 1896 not to continue the cheap passenger steamer in reply to the *Caledonian* and offered the *Voltaic* for sale. She was sold in July of that year for £3,100. The purchasers were Messrs D & C MacIver of Liverpool, who planned to use her in the Dublin trade.

She was chartered almost immediately to the Fishguard and Rosslare Railways and Harbour Company whose extensive works at Fishguard were not yet ready. On 26 August 1896, the *Voltaic*, carrying eleven passengers, thirty pigs and seventy-eight sheep, opened her charterers' service from Rosslare to Bristol. She also sailed to Liverpool, berthing in Clarence Dock, a familiar place to her. She was sold in April 1900 to the Liverpool and Clyde Steam Navigation Company and registered at Liverpool in the name of Alfred Henry Read, a name we shall meet again. She was sold soon afterwards to Russian owners and became a war casualty in 1917.

The *Dynamic* visited less exotic but nevertheless unusual ports in August 1896 when she was chartered by the organisers of the Bangor and Donaghadee Annual Holiday. With Captain James Brennan in command the *Dynamic* left Donegall Quay at 6am. She put in at Bangor, awaited the arrival of the 6.30 train from Belfast, called at Donaghadee and then set sail for the Isle of Man with 800 excursionists and a brass band on board. A very long day ended when the *Dynamic* arrived back at Donegall Quay shortly after midnight.

The wisdom of providing purpose built tonnage for the 'Londonderry Line' had been proved. Although losses had been contained in 1897 with a deficit of only £973 on the 'Belfast Line' and a dividend of 2 percent being paid, the *Comic*, which entered service in January 1897, had to be paid for out of reserves. She was a development of the *Mystic* design, could accommodate forty-four saloon passengers, in addition to the steerage, and came from Harland & Wolff's yard. She was intended for the Derry trade but would come to Belfast occasionally, the shareholders were told at the annual general meeting for 1897.

The *Comic* spent her entire career in the company's service running between Derry and Liverpool. For the greater part of that time she maintained the service on her own, sailing twice weekly in each direction, patiently suffering the name for which Tom Gallaher was doubtless responsible. Her comings and goings were a regular spectacle for children at Moville on Lough Foyle who looked forward to seeing her steam down the lough, loaded with fish for the English markets, the long waves from her bow sweeping gradually ashore and washing over their feet.

Soon after the *Comic* was commissioned, the Derry steamers' berth was moved to Prince's Dock.

Speed brings many problems in its train, among them vibration to which the *Magic* had been excessively prone. Her twin, three bladed propellers were diagnosed as the culprits so in her winter overhaul for 1897 the opportunity was taken to fit four bladed propellers and these reduced the vibration. Passenger comfort ashore was not neglected and in 1897 the Mersey Docks and Harbour Board agreed to make an office and passenger waiting room available for the company at the Landing Stage.

A significant improvement for the company's London passengers came in the following year, which went some distance towards eliminating the handicap which the

The *Logic* sometime between 1906 and 1912 on the express service. (William Grogan Collection)

company suffered in not having trains alongside the steamer at Liverpool. L & NWR at last recognised that the company was not just a competitor whom statute and the conference obliged them to tolerate but was one of its principal 'feeders' of passenger traffic to their up morning and down evening expresses. From 1 October 1898 an up breakfast car express for first, second and third class passengers was put on, leaving Lime Street Station at 8am. Overnight passengers from Belfast via Liverpool could now arrive at London (Euston) at 12.15pm the next day. The *Caloric* inaugurated the new service with her sailing of 30 September.

The *Dynamic*, with her iron hull, was approaching the time when heavy expenditure would be necessary if she was to continue to be available as a relief vessel on the express service as well as carrying cargo at other times. The company had been favourably impressed by the *Mystic* and *Comic*, thus proving, after a fashion, that Samuel Lawther had been right in criticising their policy of building express passenger and cargo steamers only. A replacement for the *Dynamic* was the *Logic* which was launched on 26 October 1897, from the Whiteinch yard of Barclay, Curle & Company by Mrs Gallaher and paid for by her husband. The *Logic* was owned by him and chartered to the company on favour-

The *Logic* as the Laird Line's *Culzean*. (McRoberts/Mersey Maritime Museum)

able terms.

She was of the same dimensions as the *Comic* but they were not sisters. She had more saloon accommodation although the precise number of passengers carried has not been recorded. Larger cylinders provided her triple expansion engines, driving twin screws, with more power. Contemporary reports of the launch describe her as being intended for the company's Belfast to Liverpool cargo and passenger service. She was, in fact, used as a relief steamer when the express vessels were off for overhaul or boiler cleaning in the years before 1912 and was seen less frequently at Derry.

A clause in the *Logic*'s charter provided that Gallaher could call on the company at any time to purchase her at cost price. Whilst still in his ownership she was involved in a collision on 26 June 1902 in Larne Harbour with the steamer *Princess May*, probably whilst engaged on the 'Londonderry Line'. It would be a further two years before the company would be in a financial position to buy her.

The *Logic* started running in January 1898. For a time during this year she was used as a 'Cheap steamer' in opposition to the *Caledonian*. There is no record of her being used in this role after 1898. On 12 July 1898, she was advertised for an afternoon cruise to Fair Head, calling at Larne. Much was made of her 'splendid promenade decks', said to be fully sheltered from the weather, and of the 'refreshments of first quality' to be had on board. On the following Friday and Saturday, 15 and 16 July, the *Logic* offered more select excursions, cruising down the lough to view the races at Bangor Regatta.

Captain William Morgan of Wallasey, a native of Groomsport, Co Down, was appointed master of the *Logic*. He had commanded the *Voltaic* and was to remain in the *Logic* for eleven years until he retired from the service.

A new ship, improved passenger comfort on board their commodore ship and vastly improved railway connections made 1898 a reasonable year for the Belfast Steamship Company and must have made Lawther and the Macks contemplate their own position ruefully. The Belfast and Mersey undertaking was losing money but the Manchester trade was doing better because they had it virtually to themselves. Their twice weekly sailings had been increased to four in each direction from January. To help out with this extra traffic, the three masted, single decked, single screw steamer *Yorkshire* was chartered by J J Mack to the Belfast and Mersey Company. In October, the *Manchester* inward from Belfast collided in the canal with the steamer *Jersey Moor* outward to Venice which got the worst of it with her port bow stoved in. Despite damage to lifeboats and bulwarks, the *Manchester* was able to proceed.

Before looking more closely at how the contestants in the rates and fares war were coping with their financial problems, let us go back to 1897, to pleasanter matters. On 22 June of that year the Diamond Jubilee took place. There was a review of merchant ships in the Mersey in which the *Magic* was included, dressed overall in company with such Atlantic celebrities as the *Germanic* and the *Etruria*. In line ahead from Huskisson Dock up river, all the ships in turn contributed to a grand finale by firing off their night signals at one minute intervals. In that summer the *Caloric* repeated her success of 1895 and sailed out of Galway with another party from the Royal Society of Antiquaries. She sailed southwards to Queenstown (Cobh), calling at the Skellig Islands off the Kerry coast and bringing her passengers to Belfast after a call at Kingstown (Dun Laoghaire).

The Royal Society of Antiquaries of Ireland joined forces with the Cambrian Archaeological Society to charter the *Magic* for a cruise to the Hebrides and Orkney Islands in 1899. The *Magic* sailed from Belfast on 19 June under the command of Captain Dunlop with 140 passengers on board who were reminded that they were being carried 'in a vessel owned by an Irish company and built in Belfast by the firm of Harland & Wolff'.

On the *Magic*'s return in the early hours of 28 June to Belfast, satiated with Celtic culture (only the Bretons had been unrepresented), a presentation was made during breakfast to Captain Dunlop and the first and second officers, Messrs Porter and Dodds.

The *Dynamic* was reported sold at the annual general meeting held on 23 March 1901, so ending an eventful career with the company.

Now we must come ashore and look at the finances of the Belfast Steamship Company which, as the century closed, were not in good heart. The loss on working the 'Belfast Line' in 1898 had been £5,872 and there had been no dividend. The Reserve Fund was said to be gone. Fine ships as the *Optic* and *Caloric* were, they could not stand comparison with the Fleetwood steamers. Even the Barrow Steam Navigation Company with their *Duchess of Devonshire* of 1897 was a reminder that the *Magic* needed consorts.

But Lawther and the Macks were feeling the strain of eight years' competition. No one could go on carrying freight indefinitely at rates 60 percent below conference level between Belfast and Liverpool and the better

The *Logic* as the *Lady Carlow*. (McRoberts/ Mersey Maritime Museum)

fortune, which we have noted, on their Manchester business could not make up the losses which had been incurred. They had received patronage from some notable Belfast firms such as J and T Sinclair, the pork and bacon merchants, who had fallen out with the Belfast Steamship Company. There had been a great deal of extra traffic sent from Belfast to Liverpool by both the Belfast Steamship Company and the Belfast and Mersey Company, mostly diverted from other routes. Such an increase is one of the benefits of competition frequently pointed to by those who believe in a 'free for all', then and now, but such persons are not so ready to admit that no one benefits from the carriage of uneconomic traffic which will surely force all the competing carriers out of business unless some accommodation can be reached. A restoration to the old rates imposed by the conference would simply drive most of the extra traffic back to the routes whence it had come. If the Belfast Steamship Company's fleet was not in the best of order it would be well not to look too hard at the ships which the Belfast and Mersey were using. In a matter of months one of the world's greatest authorities on shipbuilding, W J Pirrie, would report that the Belfast and Mersey's *Manchester* had been worked very hard and was not in first class condition. He would say of J J Mack's *Caledonian* that she was scarcely even saleable other than for breaking up.

Whilst the Macks seemed to have been more phlegmatic in adversity there is some evidence that Samuel Lawther had suffered a severe loss of morale. He had had other tribulations in business which may have lessened his taste for a fight. His beautiful steel hulled barque *Walter H Wilson*, built by Harland & Wolff, had suffered a serious fire in 1899, in her cargo of coal whilst outward bound for America. As she was also carrying dynamite her Master and crew had a hair raising four days extinguishing the fire and bringing her back to Queenstown (Cobh). There she was abandoned to the underwriters and her loss to Lawther was the end of his career as a deep sea shipowner.

Despite Lawther's insistence that rates had been too high before the competition, there was evidence that the Belfast and Mersey Company had made overtures to the Irish and English Traffic Conference. Then an anonymous article appeared in the *Irish Review* for August 1899, suggesting that the time had come for the two competing lines to be brought into closer touch with each other. In the same journal another article emphasised the folly of competition purely for spite and suggested that the Belfast and Mersey Company had come to stay. There was a suggestion that had it not been for the 'chivalrous spirit' of some of the Belfast Steamship Company's directors, the company would have wound up long ago. Some influential merchants in Belfast should try and bring the parties together in the interests of the shareholders of the Belfast Steamship Company and the Belfast and Mersey Company. In commercial circles there was keen speculation over the identity of the anonymous author.

Soon after, Lawther and Gallaher met at Belfast's Commercial News Room. Lawther broached the subject of the competition and suggested that rates could surely be arranged between them so that money could be made. 'Take your steamers off out of that', was Gallaher's response. Lawther was not to be deterred and suggested an arbitration on the lines set out in the *Irish Review*. Gallaher came straight to the point and taxed Lawther with being the author of the articles. 'I think', he said, 'I see the handwriting on the wall'. Lawther denied that he was the author.

From this encounter, by chance or design on Lawther's part, there was an outcome. A meeting took place at the Northern Counties Hotel in York Road. An arbitration was proposed and Lawther seemed so anxious to get the matter under way that he raised no objection to Gallaher's proposal of Alexander McDowell as one of the arbitrators. Coyly, Mr McDowell had appeared reluctant. Was he not a director and shareholder in the Belfast Steamship Company? Was his brother not manager and had he not acted as solicitor for the company? The other arbitrator was W J Pirrie of Harland & Wolff whom Lawther proposed and who was later to attain national stature as Lord Pirrie. After all, Pirrie had built ships for Lawther and Lawther's son, Stanley, had served his time on Queen's Island.

Now that Lawther's spleen had spent itself and he had counted the cost he was only too anxious that there should be no obstacle to a speedy resolution of the conflict. Alexander McDowell must be persuaded at once. Lawther hired a hansom, collected Gallaher at his Greencastle home and together they made all speed for Alexander McDowell's house at Greenisland further down the shore of Belfast Lough. 'Was I not right in taking a hansom so that no one would see us,' Lawther exclaimed on arrival, anxious that no one should see him parleying with the enemy. Alexander McDowell's scruples were all too easily overcome and he agreed to act.

Across the Irish Sea, the Mack brothers were a different and less emotional proposition from their volatile Irish partner. They wanted an agreement on rates. Further, they wanted John Dickinson, partner in the well known Liverpool firm of Hill, Dickinson and Company, Solicitors, specialising in shipping

matters, to be an arbitrator. They wanted the submission confined to rates. Gallaher would not agree to either point. The terms of the submission were, on the contrary, far reaching and comprehensive, dictated by men who sensed victory in their grasp, and were finally agreed to.

Lawther must have had an inkling that the arbitration whose terms he had so readily agreed to without apparently consulting the Mack brothers fully, would spell the end of the Belfast and Mersey Company. Too late, he remembered that his son, Stanley, had thrown his entire resources into the management of the Belfast and Mersey Company. Lawther, with few bargaining counters left, asked Gallaher what they were going to do for his son. 'Every time I meet him I will give him half-a-crown,' Gallaher jauntily replied.

The parties were bidden to attend at 1.30pm on Saturday, 30 December 1899 at the offices of Messrs Carson and McDowell, 51 Royal Avenue, Belfast, for the arbitration. The Mack brothers, for whatever reason, seemed to have been singularly ill-prepared for the serious business with which they were confronted for they came over believing that they were to have a mere preliminary discussion.

The draft of the Award was ready on the following Monday, New Year's Day, 1900. There seemed to have been no 'day of rest' on that Sabbath in Belfast. The terms of the Award were harsh but not necessarily unjust as far as the Liverpool trade was concerned. The arbitrators had formed the view that the Belfast and Mersey Company was hopelessly insolvent. They could do little more than hazard a guess that there was a loss of £30,070 3s 10d in the first eight years of operation as they had no proper balance sheets.

The Award was a disaster for the Mack brothers. By its terms the *Caledonian* and the *Manchester* were ordered to be sold free from encumbrances, together with their boats and stores, to the Belfast Steamship Company. Also included in the forced sale were all machinery, plant and dock offices at Belfast and Manchester belonging to the Belfast and Mersey Steamship Company, the Manchester Steamship Company, S Lawther and Sons and J J Mack & Sons. The Belfast Steamship

Company was only to pay £15,600 to the Belfast and Mersey Steamship Company. They were also to receive covenants from the opposition firms and their individual partners not to trade between Belfast and Liverpool or Manchester nor Londonderry and Liverpool or Manchester on their own account or even as shareholders, partners, agents or employees of any undertaking so engaged for fifteen years.

The 'tramp' business to Belfast carried on by J J Mack & Sons for over twenty years would have to go. They would receive nothing for the loss of their agencies for the Mersey and Manchester Companies in Liverpool and Manchester, nor for the termination of the charter of the *Yorkshire*.

The Macks wasted no time. John and James called on Gallaher on 3 January, and came straight to the point. 'You've got everything your own way,' they said. They claimed that the *Caledonian* had carried 2,441 saloon passengers and 1,450 steerage passengers from April to September 1899. Could they buy her back as well as buying the *Manchester*? Gallaher told them to make an offer. What about their coal trade in their own ships to Belfast carried on for some years for the account of Samuel Lawther's son, Stanley? Gallaher said he would meet them on this. Then came the question which was probably most important to them and the real purpose of their visit: could they have the Manchester agency for the Belfast Steamship Company when they took over the Belfast/Manchester trade? Gallaher would not agree.

In this Gallaher was imprudent and over confident. The Mack brothers had scored a success in the Manchester trade where the Belfast Steamship Company itself had failed ignominiously. It would have been wiser for Gallaher to have given them the agency in Manchester and so detach them from Samuel Lawther and his son, Stanley. Not only would Gallaher's victory have been copper fastened but much expensive litigation would have been avoided.

Lawther was probably relieved that the competition was over though his pride was deeply wounded. But any relief was tempered by the fact that his partnership in Lawther and Harvey was jeopardised since Stanley Lawth-

er, his son, also worked for that firm where, as we have seen, he looked after the Belfast end of J J Mack's coal and cross channel tramping business.

For the Belfast Steamship Company, on the other hand, matters took on a rosier hue at once. On 29 December, their £50 shares stood at a mere £37 10s. On Tuesday, 2 January, with news of the Award in the stock exchange, they rose to £52 10s. The company, with more honesty than tact, gave notice of an immediate increase in cargo rates between Belfast and Liverpool. On 4 January 1900, Alexander McDowell's Dublin agent registered a new company called the 'Merchants' Line Limited' which was a wholly owned subsidiary of the Belfast Steamship Company with a capital of £20,000. It was intended to carry on the Belfast and Mersey business as a separate entity catering for 'rough goods', ie bricks, tiles, cement, hardware, refuse bins, hemps, sisal, etc; in fact, all the cargo which would not normally be carried in the express steamers. The Merchants' Line was destined never to trade.

With nothing to be gained from negotiation, an application was entered in the High Court in Dublin to set aside the Award. The hearing took place in February 1900, in the Queen's Bench Division, before the Lord Chief Justice, Sir Peter O'Brian and three judges. For technical reasons the application was dismissed. Neither party had applied to make the reference to arbitration a Rule of Court so that as a result the court had no jurisdiction to entertain the application. No doubt the failure was due to the haste with which the arbitration was arranged and heard but it was a costly failure for Lawther and the Macks who had to pay all the costs involved in the three day hearing and achieved nothing.

The annual general meeting of the Belfast Steamship Company, held on 13 March 1900, was in confident mood. The directors were warmly congratulated on their conduct of affairs over the past eight years. Their erstwhile, or so it was hoped, opposition had just received a trouncing in the Queen's Bench Division in the previous month and total victory in the rates war was sensed. There had even been trifling reductions in dock dues at

Belfast and, happily, a dividend of 2½ percent was recommended, to be paid out of the underwriting fund.

With no sign of Lawther and the Macks complying with the terms of the Award, May of 1900 found the Belfast Steamship Company back in the High Court in Dublin. This time they were in the vice-chancellor's court seeking specific performance of the Award and an injunction to restrain the defendants from acting inconsistently with it. In the alternative, the company sought damages from the defendants.

Lawther and the Mack brothers had been consulting their legal advisers as well and were determined that the proceedings should not be plain sailing for the plaintiff company. A defence was delivered in June alleging that the Award was invalid on the technical ground that it had not been sealed by either party. A more telling point was that the Award went beyond the powers of the arbitrators; in lawyers' terms, it was alleged to be *ultra vires*. There was a further allegation that the Award was bad because the defendants, apart from the Belfast and Mersey Company, were partnerships and the Award imposed obligations on the partners as individuals and on their business properties.

The proceedings opened on 17 January 1901 before Vice-Chancellor Hedges Chatterton from whom the defendants received curiously short shrift. The learned judge took a dislike to Samuel Lawther, referring to his 'audacious evidence' and castigating him for his 'utter disregard for truth'. So confident was the vice-chancellor of his view of this complex case that he did not even take time to consider his judgment. He ordered a decree of specific performance and refused them a stay of execution pending an appeal.

The vice-chancellor's conduct of the proceedings did not escape criticism and one commentator observed that there was reason for detecting 'a somewhat hasty and petulant tone'.

Leave was obtained on the following day from the Court of Appeal and the appeal to that court was heard in the following April. The result was an astonishing reversal of fortunes. The appeal was allowed. Giving judgment, the Lord Chancellor held that the Award did indeed go beyond the arbitrators' powers and was far too wide in attempting to restrain Samuel Lawther and his partners in the conduct of their own separate businesses. This was the gist of the decision. The court, on the other hand, rejected allegations of misconduct made against the arbitrators personally by the defendants who were consoled by being awarded all their costs save those thrown away in attempting to establish misconduct against the arbitrators.

The Belfast Steamship Company had spent a great deal of money and still had a competitor on their doorstep in Belfast and Liverpool but that competitor would have to engage in more careful housekeeping. The Macks were determined to hold on to the cargo business. The *Caledonian* had been disposed of in 1900 and a new cargo steamer replaced her. She was the three masted, steel well deck steamer *Fleswick* built that year by the Ailsa Shipbuilding Company of Troon. She was registered at Liverpool in the name of the Fleswick Company Limited which was, of course, a subsidiary of J J Mack and Sons.

The *Fleswick* and the *Manchester* would sail on for many years and indeed the *Irish Review* had been correct in prophesying that the Belfast and Mersey Company had come to stay.

Other cross channel lines had wearied of the freight war and would complain formally to that effect to the conference which the Belfast and Mersey Company was still pressing to join. Eventually they would succeed in joining and for the moment they must leave our pages though the Belfast Steamship Company could never forget that cargo traffic to Liverpool and later Manchester had to be fought for and once gained they must fight to retain it.

Samuel Lawther was now a subdued and disappointed man. He withdrew from the Belfast business scene in 1909, leaving his son, Stanley, to carry on S Lawther and Sons. He resigned as a harbour commissioner after twenty-seven years' service. In 1910 he resigned from Belfast Corporation on which he had served for thirty-eight years, never achieving the Lord Mayoralty which he had coveted. He died on 9 June 1913 at Bath House, Tullow, Co Carlow.

VI
Recovery

The new century set the keynote. It was a time for looking forward and forgetting the expensive and disastrous foray into the law courts. An unvanquished foe still sailed the seas between Belfast and Liverpool and Manchester. An early task was to establish a footing again in Manchester.

So another subsidiary company was established. Destined to trade for a time at least, the Belfast and Manchester Steamship Company Limited owned no ships of its own. From 1 May 1902, the *Mystic* was despatched on a twice weekly Belfast/Manchester service. The sailings were on Wednesdays and Saturdays from Belfast (York Dock) and Tuesdays and Fridays from Manchester (Pomona Dock). The *Mystic*'s speed and prompt turnrounds at both ports were essential ingredients for success. No passengers were carried on a regular basis.

The *Mystic*'s new role left the *Comic* to serve Derry alone. She was well able to provide twice weekly sailings in each direction. The saloon passenger business was largely seasonal and could be augmented by the *Logic*, if necessary, at busy times.

The annual general meeting of 19 February 1903 disclosed another threat to their business. This time the year-round passenger trade from Belfast to Liverpool was the target of an attack mounted, from of all places, Samuel Plimsoll's old parliamentary constituency of Derby. Their one time ally, the Midland Railway, with headquarters in that town, was promoting a bill to acquire the Belfast and Northern Counties Railway Company. They were also building a harbour at Heysham near Morecambe and proposing to build steamers for a Heysham/Belfast express passenger and cargo service, charging the same rates and fares as those in force via Barrow.

The Midland had been carrying passengers across to Belfast for many years from Barrow under the guise of the Barrow Steam Navigation Company with Messrs James Little and Company as their Belfast agents. Despite being advertised as the most picturesque route to the north of Ireland, the lengthy railway journey was a deterrent. London passengers left St Pancras at 1.30 pm. The Midland sensibly recognised that Liverpool was more convenient for many of their passengers and a through train left St Pancras at 4.20 pm, at this time, in connection with the company's steamer. The Midland consoled themselves by advertising their Adelphi Hotel in Liverpool in association with their boat trains and offering free transfer of luggage between the hotel and Central Station. The old alliance based on realism between the Belfast Steamship Company and the Midland Railway was threatened by the 'Midland raid on Ireland'. The company resolved to oppose the bill, however; on 23 March 1903, the parties came to terms. The Midland promised to secure to the Belfast Steamship Company equal facilities over its system with its own route to Belfast and, in particular, to safeguard the facilities which they provided for passengers and luggage from Belfast and Liverpool. They also undertook to advertise the Belfast Steamship Company's services properly in their timetables. In return, the company promised not to oppose the Midland's bill in parliament.

Without doubt the company got the better part of this deal. They continued to gain a fair amount of passenger traffic from the Midland system and very little goods traffic went via Heysham in preference to Liverpool. On their side Midland continued to run through carriages unprofitably from their mainline to Liverpool in connection with the company's sailings and so did the LM & SR after 1923, though, one suspects, with increasing reluctance until the outbreak of war in 1939. Well appointed steamers from Heysham caused comparatively little worry to the Belfast Steamship Company, save perhaps in the height of the season. Winter cargo and passenger carryings remained poor from Heysham until the LM & SR withdrew the Fleetwood service in 1928 and concentrated their Belfast traffic on Heysham and Stranraer. Even so, it is doubtful if the Heysham/ Belfast service on its own ever paid its way.

There was pressing need for the company to consider new tonnage for the express service. The Midland challenge and the continuing competition from Fleetwood could not be met by the *Magic*, now ten years of age, and two single-screw steamers nearly double her age. The shareholders were told in 1903 that the reason for the delay in ordering was the recently invented marine turbine and the need for more information on the subject. The turbine was well established on the English Channel by 1903 and the Midland was to introduce the turbine for one of their Heysham vessels.

Speed was important for the London passenger traffic and the turbine could provide this as well as reducing the overall height of the machinery on board, a very important consideration for companies in conditions where shallow draught was crucial. The constraints affecting the company were the Liverpool dock entrances and there was plenty of depth of water for a ship that sat deep in these waters at both Belfast and Liverpool at all states of the tide.

The Mersey Docks and Harbour Board caused further hesitation by introducing a bill in Parliament to alter the method by which dock dues were assessed. Instead of paying on net tonnage, liability would be based on one half of a ship's gross tonnage, thereby penalising the owners of passenger steamers which had a relatively high gross tonnage. The bill was reported withdrawn, then reintroduced and finally defeated before all worries on this score were allayed. At last the stage was set for the order of two express passenger and cargo steamers from Harland & Wolff. After much agonising, turbines lost the day to quadruple expansion machinery on the 'Balanced prin-

ciple' as fitted in the giant White Star liner *Celtic* of 1901 and her three later sisters. This type of machinery was supposed to minimise vibration, a problem which had afflicted the *Magic*.

There was also a financial problem. The dividend had still not advanced beyond 3 per cent for the year 1905 so it is no surprise to find the company issuing £100,000 worth of debenture stock on 23 January 1906, to assist in financing the new ships.

The first of the new vessels, the *Heroic*, entered service on 26 April 1906, and her sister the *Graphic* on the following 26 May. Save for a slight difference in their gross and net tonnages, they were identical. Their engines delivered 6,400 hp to twin screws and it was claimed that they were 'one hour faster' than the *Magic*.

The saloon accommodated 272 passengers, twenty-six of them in single berth cabins and the rest in two and four berth cabins, each of which had mechanical ventilation operated by electric fans which could supply cold air in summer, hot in winter and could be regulated by the passengers themselves. The single berth cabins were fitted in hardwood. The saloons themselves were artistically decorated in Austrian oak in the Jacobean style and in the dining saloon inlaid woods depicted sailing ships from past ages whilst the bar and smoking room aft were decorated in fumigated oak.

For the first time an entrance saloon extended over the full width of the ship with a berthing office situated on the port side, combining the functions of office and cabin for the chief steward. An effort was made soon afterwards to improve the *Magic*'s embarkation arrangements with an office provided for her chief steward on the starboard side of the saloon where passengers could be received instead of at one of the saloon tables as formerly. Arrangements for steerage passengers were still spartan by modern standards but the new ships provided sixteen sofa beds for women passengers travelling steerage.

Both sisters were faster than their predecessors but the *Graphic* gained a reputation which she maintained throughout her career of being slightly the speedier of the two. The

The *Graphic* in her early days. (William Grogan Collection)

company was now able to put the sailing time back one hour so that passengers could leave Donegall Quay at 9 pm (Irish time) instead of 8 pm, with the effect from 31 May 1906. When the *Graphic* started the directors once more expressed the wish that the L & NWR would 'be able to arrange for a special carriage to meet the boat at the Riverside Railway Station, Liverpool, for the convenience of passengers ...'. The L & NWR as usual, were not prepared to oblige. Even so, it was recorded that passengers had left London and reached Belfast by the company's route in just under 12½ hours. Of equal importance to the company's business were the much improved facilities for cargo and livestock as compared with earlier ships.

The express service was now almost the equal of the Fleetwood and Heysham services in quality of tonnage and would soon be superior to them. The *Optic* was withdrawn from the express service with the advent of the *Heroic* and the *Caloric* retired from it the following month. As efforts to dispose of both of them were not successful, employment was found for them on the Liverpool cargo service. The railway companies responded swiftly to the improvement in the company's service by speeding up their con-

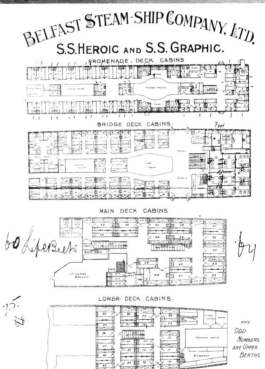

Heroic and *Graphic*: passenger accommodation plan. (William Grogan Collection)

necting rail services. The Midland Railway, for example, advertised that it would convey its passengers from London (St Pancras) to Donegall Quay in 12 hours exactly.

With so much emphasis on speed,

Donaghadee Sound, lying between the main Copeland Island and the coast of Co Down at the mouth of Belfast Lough, presented an irresistible attraction to the masters of ships and their owners anxious to clip 15 to 20 minutes from the passage time between Liverpool and Belfast. Going through the Sound involved an alteration in course in mid-channel and to add to the perils the buoys in the channel were unlit. Captain R Deane, Inspector and Marine Superintendent to the Commissioners of Irish Lights, was not in favour of vessels using the Sound with its tortuous channel after dark considering that the time saved was not commensurate with the risk involved.

On 1 October 1906, James McDowell wrote to the secretary of the Irish Lights Commissioners, using the Belfast Steamship Company's elegant new notepaper with an illustration of the *Heroic* at its head, complaining that the *Magic* had struck 'some substance' on her way through the Sound to Liverpool on the night of 25 September 1906. She had been able to proceed and had apparently sustained no damage when the 'strike' occurred. She had been beyond the Deputy buoy in the Sound with the red of the Donaghadee light showing, was drawing 16ft 7in and expected to be in 26ft to 27ft of water.

The Belfast Steamship Company later revealed that there had been four previous incidents in the Sound. The *Magic* had struck something on another occasion, the *Caloric* had reported a similar incident and the *Optic* two such incidents.

As the result of this complaint the Irish Lights Commissioners referred the matter to the Hydrographer of the Admiralty who carried out an immediate survey. This disclosed previously unsuspected dangers and the rocks which the *Magic* had struck on 25 September first appeared on Admiralty charts in 1908. To this day, they are shown as the *Magic* rocks, ensuring a place for posterity among seafarers for the *Magic*.

In 1911, the Irish Lights Commissioners lit the Deputy, Governor and Foreland buoys. There have been alterations in the characteristics of the buoys since and after a period of closure during the Second World War the channel remains open. Its use for passenger vessels still occasions controversy among mariners.

In 1907, there strode on to the Belfast stage the considerable figure of James Larkin, organiser of the National Union of Dock Labourers. Determined to organise and secure negotiating rights, Larkin seems nevertheless to have been anxious to avoid immediate confrontation with employers. This was forced upon him in May 1907, when two dockers employed on a casual basis at the Belfast Steamship Company's cargo berths in York Dock refused to join the union and the rest of the men declined to work with them. Larkin was already in dispute with Samuel Kelly, the coal importer, following the dismissal of one of his dockers for joining the union.

Gallaher and his fellow directors had anticipated trouble and arranged with the Shipping Federation to bring in non-union men from England and Scotland. Unaware of these clandestine preparations by the employers, Larkin ordered the York Street dockers to go back to work at once. So far from being the press stereotype union leader, Larkin was anxious to avoid trouble and to try and control as far as he could the spontaneous anger of rank and file dockers with what they considered to be unfair conditions of work. He called upon the Belfast Steamship Company with a personal apology. Gallaher's response was characteristic and immediate. The strikers were dismissed on the same day, 8 May. It may be said that in his own factory Gallaher's method in dealing with trade unions had been both ruthless and idiosyncratic. When the Belfast Tobacco Operatives' Society had begun to organise, Gallaher told a deputation that he would recognise the union. As soon as the deputation had gone Gallaher dismissed all known union members in his employment.

The *Caloric* arrived on 8 May from Liverpool carrying fifty non-union men to work on the *Optic* which was lying strike-bound in York Dock. The *Caloric* moored at Donegall Quay outboard of the *Heroic*. It has been said that the company's regular dockers refused to unload the *Heroic* on that day in consequence. Contemporary accounts do not entirely bear this out. Certainly the *Heroic* was able to sail

The *Heroic* in the 1920s fitted with wheelhouse, wing cabs and deck house on the boat deck aft. (PRO (NI)/BSS Co)

as usual that night.

On the following day, 9 May, there was disorder. Those on strike, casually employed in the main, marched to the Liverpool shed on Donegall Quay and stones were thrown at the regularly employed men working on the *Graphic* and the *Mystic*. They were dispersed by the police with a baton charge but not before a constable was struck on the head with a square sett. The company accused the strikers of trying to take the employers unawares and making no representations beforehand. The strikers retorted that this was nothing but a 'lock-out' by the employers.

On 11 May, the situation became even uglier. The *Caloric* had brought in more non-union labour to deal with the *Optic* and the *Mystic* which had also become strikebound. A cadre of dockers loyal to the company was at work on the *Heroic*, guarded by a strong force of police. No attempt was made by the *Caloric* to land her unwelcome passengers; instead she slipped from her berth outboard of the *Heroic* and proceeded down river.

As soon as the strikers saw what was afoot, they ran down the quays ahead of the *Caloric* shouting abuse in an effort to reach York Dock before any attempt was made to land the non-union men there. Though missiles were thrown at the *Caloric* as she came abreast of Harland & Wolff's North Yard and one of her officers received a severe blow on the arm, there was a calm, indeed, before the storm, as the *Caloric* swung into the Spencer Basin. Perhaps the arrival of a dozen police officers had something to do with this initially. However, a crowd soon appeared on the west side of the Milewater Basin, overpowered a member of the harbour police force who offered opposition and commenced a fierce bombardment of the ship with stones and pieces of scrap iron and soon had the non-union men below decks. As she approached her berth in York Dock there was only one man left above decks and this loneliest of men was her master.

At noon some 200 police were on duty at the Liverpool shed and in York Dock. The

Prince's Dock from the Royal Liver Buildings between 1906 and 1912. The *Magic* is berthed for'ard of either the *Graphic* or *Heroic*. The graving dock in the foreground was formed from the passage linking Prince's and George's Docks after the latter was filled in. (William Grogan Collection)

dockers on the *Heroic* worked under police protection while the strikers were reported as waving Union Jacks with the superscription, 'Down with blacklegs'. Understandably, the new arrivals still aboard the *Caloric* were reported as not anxious to start work.

The police were accused by the company of failing to protect the regular dockers trying to work during the strike. The harbour commissioners offered the company 'every facility', doubtless seeing them as carrying the torch for all employers in the face of incipient revolution. The City of Dublin Steam Packet Company unwisely allowed the *Logic* to use their berth immediately down river of the Liverpool berth on Donegall Quay. They had to pay the penalty and their own ship became strike bound.

The dispute dragged on and Gallaher, whose own factory was involved, bitterly

criticised the police for their handling of the situation. He revealed that he was proposing to build two new tobacco factories but these would be in England now rather than in Ireland.

Meanwhile, the striking dockers remained defiant and a meeting in Corporation Square was held on 1 June 1907, under banners which proclaimed, 'Support Larkin and No surrender'. Five years later the last two words of this proclamation would echo and re-echo round a vaster crowd on nearby Donegall Quay who would have all but forgotten the dockers and the tobacco workers in their own absorption in far greater issues.

Eventually, in September 1907, the strike ground to a conclusion and an agreement was reached between the Belfast Steamship Company and the strikers. But would the path of conciliation from the outset not have been less costly to the company which seemed to have been unduly identified with Gallaher's personal stance?

There was one stroke of good fortune for the company to report during the strike. They managed to sell the *Optic* on 15 May 1907, to Barcelona owners. Her compound engines were reported as still capable of driving her at $14\frac{1}{2}$ knots and her sale enabled a mortgage which had been created on her to be discharged. It had probably been raised for the purpose of assisting in the financing of the *Graphic* and *Heroic*.

Moving forward to 1910, a dividend of 4 per cent had been declared for the previous year and the liquidity position was further improved by the sale of the *Mystic* to the City of Dublin Steam Packet Company for their Dublin to Belfast cargo and passenger trade. The minutes state that the sale was arranged 'with a view to replacing her by a more suitable steamer'. This reads strangely as the much older *Caloric*, far from suitable as a purely cargo steamer, was still on the company's hands. The probable explanation is that with the market for secondhand tonnage slack a good offer from a friendly concern for the *Mystic* could not be refused even if it meant keeping less suitable tonnage. An order for a new express steamer was imminent and this would lend urgency to the need for as much liquidity as possible.

The *Patriotic* in her youth. (William Grogan Collection)

The *Patriotic* in the 1920s, probably 1921/22. (William Grogan Collection)

Another step was taken in 1911, which marked the increasing importance of the company as a passenger carrier. Bookings and enquiries had been dealt with hitherto at the head offices on Donegall Quay, not a convenient location for business people and shoppers and not directly served by a tramcar route. In February of that year the Great Western Railway obtained the lease of premises at 7 Donegall Place in the heart of the city. Here they opened an agency and acted as passenger agents for the Belfast Steamship Company at that address until conditions in the impending Great War forced its closure.

The stage was now set for the entry of the company's largest and finest ship, the graceful *Patriotic*. Longer than the *Graphic* and *Heroic*, she had triple expansion machinery rather than quadruple which developed 840 hp and had a speed of 18 knots. Major responsibility rested with the company's engineering consultant, the internationally known naval architect James Maxton of Belfast. Her interior scheme of decoration was, however, said to be 'suggested and approved by Mr Gallaher'.

In her saloon passenger accommodation the *Patriotic* deferred to an increasing and insistent demand from the business community for single berth staterooms. Of these she had no fewer than sixty-two taking up the entire promenade deck and representing 'a heavy item of expense', as Gallaher remarked on the trial trip. In addition she had three special cabins-de-luxe which were finished in Adam style. All the single berth state rooms were decorated in oak, as were the saloons themselves, whilst the smoke room was appropriately finished in fumigated oak. On the bridge, main and lower main decks were distributed forty-seven two berth cabins and thirty-seven four berth cabins. Steerage passengers had improved facilities including a comfortable general sitting room.

The *Patriotic* ran her trials on 28 March 1912, leaving York Dock with the harbour commissioners' tug *Hercules* in charge. As she made her way down York Dock she was saluted by the veteran *Caloric* and in her turn as she passed down the channel she saluted the White Star liner *Titanic* with blasts on her whistle and the discharge of numerous rockets. On board the *Patriotic* as a guest was the White Star Line's marine superintendent, Captain Bartlett.

At a luncheon on board during the trials Gallaher prophesied that the lengthy coal strike which had been afflicting industry and transport that year would mean that in a very short time they would drive their steamers with oil. The prophesy would be fulfilled in little more than a decade. He also hoped that the L & NWR would relent over the problem of Riverside Station. The Mersey Docks and Harbour Board were in favour of through trains in connection with their steamers and the railway company's directors had been approached. This hope, however, was never to be fulfilled.

The *Patriotic* differed from the *Graphic* and *Heroic* externally in having a deeper black top to her funnel and no cowl, also differing from them in having a large deckhouse aft on the boat deck. The two older ships acquired the latter feature as soon as they were taken in hand and fitted with extra single berth cabins.

The *Patriotic* sailed on her maiden voyage from Belfast to Liverpool on 1 April 1912. She was commanded by the company's senior master, Captain John Paisley. The *Titanic*, incidentally, left Belfast on the following day for her 'shake down' cruise to Southampton.

Single berth stateroom in the *Patriotic* (Dr Ernest R Reader)

Some have seen great significance in the name given to the company's new ship. Whatever the political affiliations of the directors, it does not seem that a political stroke was intended at the time. At luncheon on board during the trials, J W Kempster, one of Harland & Wolff's managing directors, proposed what he termed a patriotic toast addressed to the Belfast Steamship Company and in which he made three points about the new ship. One, she was Belfast built. Two, she was Belfast owned. Three, she was to run between Ireland and what the speaker referred to as 'the adjacent island'. No one dissented from this apparent definition of 'patriotic' in the context for the new ship.

Six months later there was to be no doubt about the significance of the new ship's name. On 28 September 1912, the Solemn League and Covenant was signed in Belfast City Hall in an emotionally charged atmosphere following ten days of political meetings throughout Ulster. The covenant was the Ulster Unionist reply to the Home Rule Bill then before Parliament.

Those who signed the covenant pledged themselves to defend their status and use all means which may be found necessary to defeat the 'present conspiracy to set up a Home Rule parliament in Ireland'. Sir Edward Carson was the first to sign and 471,413 followed him, some signing in their own blood. At 8.45 that night Sir Edward left the Ulster Club for Donegall Quay in a decorated brake escorted by a brass band and a guard of honour drawn from the ranks of the Queen's Island Unionist Club.

At Donegall Quay, the *Patriotic* awaited Sir Edward Carson, and Captain Paisley received him on board. From the promenade deck Carson made a short speech ending with the avowal, 'No surrender'.

The *Patriotic* sailed half an hour late to cheers from the shore and salutes from firework displays. She was accompanied down the lough by the Belfast and County Down Railway Company's steamer *Erin's Isle* which was crowded with wellwishers. From Holywood a searchlight directed its beam on to the *Patriotic* and fireworks illuminated the lough shore. Beacon fires burned down the lough to Bangor and beyond and around them supporters of the Ulster Covenant sang, *O God, Our help in Ages Past*, and to each fiery message the *Patriotic* sounded her whistle in response. To watchers on each shore she frequently appeared as a dramatic silhouette against the red glow of bonfires.

Heading out into open waters and a choppy sea, the *Patriotic* had a distinguished passenger list. Apart from Carson, who occupied a state room adorned with Union Jacks, there were the Marquis of Londonderry, Admiral Lord Charles Beresford, F E Smith and may other prominent Unionists and sympathisers.

At last the company's passenger and cargo service from the north of Ireland to the mainland was now second to none. Moreover, it was the only cross-channel service for passengers and cargo owned and operated from Belfast.

The *Magic*, now displaced, retired to spend much of the year laid up in Belfast's Musgrave Channel. Still a fine steamer she was more than adequate as a relief vessel when any of the three express steamers were off the service for any reason. It is known that she

Restaurant in the *Patriotic*. (William Grogan Collection)

Saloon lounge in the *Patriotic*. (Harland and Wolff)

was chartered between 1912 and 1914 on more than one occasion to carry the harbour commissioners on their annual cruise around the harbour and its approaches. The tide had turned for the company but the tides were also carrying the company with the nation unsuspectingly towards world war.

VII
The Great War

War broke out on 3 August 1914 and, unlike other aspects of national life, had an immediate effect on the passenger and cargo services of the Belfast Steamship Company which were suspended two days later. All the company's vessels had been requisitioned and ordered to be at Liverpool on Friday, 7 August. They were to be fully equipped, coaled, victualled for sea and ready to transport troops and stores from Ireland to England. This was a tall order by any standards for it included the *Magic* laid up in Belfast's Musgrave Channel. All seven ships were at Liverpool on the stipulated day.

On Monday, 10 August, cargo services were resumed but it was not until Friday, 21 August, that the *Patriotic* was able to reopen the passenger service with her sailing from Liverpool whilst the *Comic* resumed the Derry sailings. Thereafter life on the Irish Sea seemed to return to normal. The *Magic* laid up once more in the Musgrave Channel and the *Logic* went back to the Manchester trade on which she had been engaged immediately prior to the war.

The outbreak of war had improved prices for secondhand tonnage and yet the acute shortages of ships which were to develop were not yet in prospect. So it was that the *Caloric* was disposed of to Greek owners on 10 October 1914, and renamed *Adriaticos*. Like the *Optic*, a mortgage had been executed on her some years earlier and this was now discharged. She was to have a career of astonishing longevity which only ended in June 1952 when she reached the Italian port of Spezia to be broken up. She was then named *Costas A* and was owned by J G Dayante of Alexandria.

Tranquillity became activity in November when the *Magic* was roused from her slumbers and taken over for service as a naval hospital ship on 16 November 1914. Two days later the *Heroic* was requisitioned as an armed boarding steamer. She was equipped with two 12-pounder guns and on commissioning was given the pendant number M.05 until 1915 when it became M.11. At first she was based at Queenstown (now Cobh) and saw service off the west coast of Ireland.

The *Magic* entered on her new career with her hull painted white and buff funnels. She had a wide green stripe along each side, punctuated amidships with a large red cross, whilst fore and aft two smaller red crosses interrupted the green stripe. As if to leave no doubt, her rails fore and aft carried two further red crosses which were electrically lit, and finally her funnels were emblazoned with red crosses. She was given the pendant number YA.14.

On commissioning, the *Magic* was sent to receive sick and wounded men from the battlecruiser squadron in the Firth of Forth and from the Grand Fleet at Scapa Flow and Invergordon. She carried her complement southwards to channel ports for distribution to hospitals. On one of these voyages she was shadowed by a German aircraft which later showered steel darts at her, a primitive form of air attack apparently practised by both sides in the early stages of the war though mainly directed at land forces.

Meanwhile, back at home cargo and passenger services had to be maintained with a depleted fleet. The *Heroic*'s place on the Belfast/Liverpool service was taken by the *Logic*. Later in the war when submarine activity and travel restrictions reduced the passenger business, the *Logic* reverted to the role of a cargo vessel. More tonnage was needed to cope with the cargo offering. Two vessels were chartered from the Anglesey Shipping Company, both of which were registered at Beaumaris. The newer of the two, the *Linda Blanche*, had been completed as recently as July 1914. Her consort was the *Pennant*, both vessels built by Scott of Bowling.

Transmissions from the German naval wireless station at Neumünde early in January 1915 indicated to British Naval Intelligence that the submarine U21 had set sail for the Irish Sea. Under the command of Kapitan-Leutnant Hersing, U21 was the first German submarine to enter the Irish Sea and the first to venture so far to the west. She was not to spend long there but during her stay she caused havoc and consternation.

On 28 January 1915, reports were received from an armed drifter of two possible enemy submarines off Bardsey Island. On 29 January, an unidentified submarine exchanged shots with batteries ashore on Walney Island, off Barrow. The hostile stranger was the U21 and on the following day she made her presence felt on the Irish Sea when she sank no fewer than six ships and was to cause the closure of the port of Belfast for one day, Liverpool for three days and cause the suspension for even longer of the City of Dublin Steam Packet Company's mail service from Kingstown (now Dun Laoghaire) to Holyhead.

One of the ships which Hersing sank on the thirtieth was the *Linda Blanche* on passage Manchester to Belfast with generals and a crew of ten under the command of Captain Ellis of Bangor, North Wales. The war at sea was still a gentlemanly affair and U21 came alongside her victim at 12.30 pm, hoisting the German flag. The *Linda Blanche*'s boat was directed to the nearby Fleetwood trawler *Niblick* but not before every consideration was shown by the German officers to the crew, including the gift of a box of cigars, and an assurance was asked for and received that the crew had plenty of water. The *Linda Blanche* was despatched by two bombs, one on her bridge and one on her foc's'le.

The *Graphic* had been due to sail for Liverpool on Friday night, 29 January, when Belfast port was closed, probably as the result of the action off Walney Island. After remaining at her berth all night, the *Graphic* sailed at 7.30 am, when the port had reopened. Approaching the Bar, she steamed through

wreckage later identified as coming from Hersing's victims earlier that day. Then a submarine was sighted ahead on the surface.

The *Graphic* was immediately put about and Captain Arthur Porter ran her at speed into the wind. Passengers were ordered to don their lifebelts whilst U21 pursued the *Graphic*. There was a good sea running and the light was fading. The submarine was unable to gain on the *Graphic* which, as she sped towards the Skerries, hoisted signals warning any other vessels that they were standing into danger if they proceeded towards Liverpool. Later, in the comforting blackness of a January night, the *Graphic* resumed her voyage to Liverpool. As soon as the vessel had berthed, the hundred or so very relieved passengers signed a letter of thanks which was presented to Captain Porter. The *Graphic* was only one out of seven ships which U21 intercepted on that day but she was the only one to escape.

U21 returned safely to Germany where all the crew were reported to have received the Iron Cross for their work in the cause of the Fatherland. Her cruise was significant for the German Navy as it suggested endless possibilities for submarines operating overseas far from home bases. It pointed '... to a carefully prepared plan of attack ... to test the possibilities of virtually blockading a great commercial port ...'. The *Graphic* was unable to leave Liverpool again until Wednesday, 3 February, and the *Patriotic* was similarly immured in Belfast.

Hersing later left Wilhelmshaven on 25 April 1915, sailed to the north of the Shetlands into the Atlantic, then southwards to the Straits of Gibraltar. Off the Dardanelles, on 25 and 27 May, Hersing torpedoed and sank the battleships *Triumph* and *Majestic* and also a dummy warship disguised to look like the battlecruiser *Tiger*. After navigating through the minefields of the Dardanelles, Hersing arrived at Constantinople on 5 June 1915, where he was hailed as a hero. It had been no mean feat to escape from him and no small tribute to the *Graphic*'s acknowledged speed and the presence of mind of her master.

Back in the Irish Sea, naval patrols were strengthened as the result of Hersing's cruise. British vessels were instructed to keep a sharp lookout for submarines, display the ensign of a neutral country and show neither house flags nor identification marks. Of more immediate consequence to shippers was the advancing of underwriting risks in the war risk quotations.

On 31 May 1915, HMS *Heroic* sailed from Queenstown (Cobh) for Gibraltar where she arrived on 3 June, proceeding on the seventh for Alexandria. She was to remain in the eastern Mediterranean theatre for the remainder of the war. She soon became involved in the Gallipoli campaign. In August, she was disembarking troops at Suvla Bay when she came under heavy shellfire from Turkish batteries, which was so intense that eventually she had to stand back to sea. The campaign drew to an inevitable but frustrating conclusion. So many lives lost, so much gallantry, so many fine ships lost and yet no tangible result. The final evacuations, however, were achieved under trying conditions and with remarkably few casualties. The *Heroic*'s part in this final phase was to spend thirteen days at the end of December embarking troops off the Anzac beaches and carrying them to Port Mudros on the island of Lemnos which was the British advance naval and military base for the land operations on Gallipoli.

The *Magic* continued to carry sick and wounded from Scapa Flow. She would lie alongside the hospital receiving ships *Garth Castle*, *Agadir* or *Plassy* to receive her complement from them and then set sail for Leith which was as far south as she went now. Sometimes she visited Invergordon and in between her voyages would lie at anchor up the Firth of Forth from Leith, attached to Beatty's battlecruiser squadron upstream of the great railway bridge. An anti-submarine barrier of nets on floats was suspended from the bridge and rose and fell with the tide. To allow transit of vessels through the barrier, a section of it would be towed open by a steam trawler. The battlecruisers lay nearest to the opening section, upstream of them were the light cruisers, then the destroyers, supply ships and finally the *Magic*.

At home, passenger and cargo services continued throughout 1915, unbroken by drama of the type which had opened the year. In the Mersey on 3 December, the *Logic* involved herself in a collision with the steamer *Mourne*, sustaining damage to her stem and plates. Trouble of a different kind was looming on the horizon as sailors and firemen asked for 7/6d extra per week which the company refused following the lead of the Glasgow steamship owners. As a result, in March 1916, all sailings had to be suspended for a few days when the sailors and firemen struck.

On Easter Monday, 24 April 1916, an Irish Republic was proclaimed on the steps of the General Post Office in O'Connell Street. To a nation at war with Germany, this was rebellion and immediate steps were taken to crush it. On 25 April, the *Patriotic* and *Graphic* were chartered to carry troops to Ireland and the passenger service was suspended.

The *Patriotic* made voyages to Dublin and Cork and was released on 28 April. The company received £351 19s 10d for her hire. The *Graphic*'s employment lasted one day longer at a charge of £365 4s 6d on the public purse.

The express service was resumed on 1 May but controls on passenger movements were increased. A perfunctory control had existed since the outbreak of war with oral questioning of passengers; now, however, formal proof of identity was required.

The exceptional difficulties of war conditions did not mean immunity from the ordinary hazards of shipping. Before her brief charter to the government in April 1916, the *Patriotic* was dry docked following damage to one of her propellers caused by fouling a dock gate chain at Liverpool. At the end of July she collided with the South Quay of Prince's Half-Tide Basin whilst manoeuvring. The mishap was 'due to the chief engineer working the starboard engine astern instead of ahead'. In November she was off the service again as a wire rope had been picked up apparently in the Mersey and wound itself round a propeller.

The *Graphic* collided with the sailing ship *Wasdale* in July off the Skulmartin lightship but sustained no damage. She ended 1916 by colliding like the *Patriotic* with the quay wall in the Half-Tide Basin and again the reason was that the engineer put one of his engines astern instead of ahead. The *Comic* opened

HMS *Heroic* in Grand Harbour, Malta. (Imperial War Museum)

1917 by colliding with the dock gates on entering Prince's Dock, denting a plate on her quarter and damaging her belting.

Away in the Mediterranean, HMS *Heroic* continued to patrol throughout 1916, mainly in the Doro Channel operating from Port Mudros but paying frequent visits to Salanis and Malta and visiting Genoa on one occasion for dry docking.

On 21 November 1916, the *Heroic* was one of the ships which picked up survivors from the giant White Star liner *Britannic* which had been sunk four nautical miles west of Port St Nikala in the Aegean as the result of enemy action. As we shall see, there is another almost certain link between the company and this great ship which was never to be seen on the North Atlantic which she had been designed to grace.

Nearer home, a destroyer HMS *Magic* had been launched on 10 September 1915. She soon began to cause problems for the com-

pany's ship of the same name in service with the navy as a hospital ship. During 1916, but precisely when is unrecorded, she became the *Magic II*.

The *Magic* sustained minor damage on 31 October 1916, when she was in collision with the Admiralty collier *Wedgewood*. She was frequently lying in the vast and lonely anchorage of Scapa Flow devoid of any entertainment or social life for crew and medical personnel. No doubt this was the inspiration for a song whose words and music were written and composed by two members of the ship's company. The music was composed by the *Magic*'s chief steward, John Grogan, who had come to the company after being released at Newport News by the American authorities from the Elder-Dempster liner *Appam* which had been captured and taken there as a prize by the German raider *Möwe*. The ship's medical officer, Surgeon Probationer A Lothian Brough, wrote the words and the resulting song was called *Scapa Flow* and achieved success in the fleet when it was performed by the *Magic* concert party. A record was made of it later.

In January 1917, the U-boat campaign against merchant shipping was intensified with Hersing's gentlemanly conduct in 1915 just a memory. In the following May, the *Patriotic, Graphic, Logic* and *Comic* were fitted with wireless by arrangement with the Marconi International Communication Company Limited. This was an overdue step, especially in view of submarine activity two years before, and it is hard to see why the company procrastinated until compelled by government to take action. The Admiralty expressed the view at this time that the company's vessels should be armed, especially those sailing on the exposed route to Derry. The directors agreed to seek Maxton's opinion and there the matter seems to have rested.

There was a need for extra tonnage towards the end of 1917 to cope with the volume of wartime cargo offering. At the same time the *Graphic*'s boilers were reported to be in a very unsatisfactory state and these factors combined were probably the reason for the chartering for the month of December 1917, of the Anglesey Shipping Company's ss *Bangor*. In the same month a prize steamer was allocated to the company by the director of cross channel transportation who was, in fact, Alfred H Read who had recently been appointed to that position by Sir Joseph Maclay, controller of shipping. The prize steamer was not in her first youth, having been built as far back as 1891 at Stockholm as the *Olof Wyk*. She was now renamed *Polwick*.

Industrial trouble was avoided at the end of the year when the company agreed to pay nationally agreed wages following arbitration between owners and unions in London. An able-bodied seaman now received £3 17s 6d per week, as did a fireman, whilst a greaser received £4 and the bo'sun £4 2s 6d. Amid their various tribulations, the directors displayed a softer side to their nature when they recorded the death of Barney, one of the

company's horses in the stables on 3 October.

The *Patriotic* reported a torpedo fired at her which fortunately missed on 27 March 1918. On the twenty-eighth of the following month the *Comic* sighted an enemy submarine on the surface three-quarters of a mile from her and six miles southwest of the Mull of Galloway. The *Comic*'s master, Captain George Reid, altered course and steered for the enemy vessel which immediately submerged. No positive proof exists but it was believed that the *Comic* sank the submarine. Whatever the outcome, Captain Reid was awarded £50 for good seamanship by the Ministry of Shipping. Not everyone would agree that this was good seamanship, or even a wise thing to do. Ramming the enemy has a romantic connotation but recollecting the damage which the *Comic* suffered colliding with dock gates in the previous year, a submarine's hull would be likely to inflict as much damage to the forefoot of a ship like the *Comic* as the submarine could possibly sustain. In the same waters four months later whilst on passage Belfast to Liverpool, the *Patriotic* was struck by the Belfast coaster *Straid* but neither vessel sustained any damage.

There was still confusion between the *Magic II* and the destroyer *Magic*. On at least one occasion the former had returned to Scapa Flow whilst voyaging southwards in response to a wireless message intended for her near namesake. The Admiralty decided to change the name of the *Magic II* to *Magician*. This was to have been accomplished during a refit in Belfast in March 1918. For reasons now unknown, the order was cancelled and she was given the name *Classic* instead on 27 June 1918. The *Classic* spent the last two months of the war as a troop transport in the English Channel and was released to the company on 6 May 1919, when the change of name to *Classic* became official.

The *Heroic* continued to have an eventful time even after the Armistice for she had passed through the Dardanelles and reached Sevastopol on 7 December where she remained for two days. It had been just over sixty-four years since one of the company's ships had been in these far off waters. The precise reason for her visit is not now known but it was possibly in connection with the short-lived Republic of Taurida, which included the Crimea, and had declared its independence from the Bolshevik regime in March 1918.

At the end of 1919, the *Heroic* refitted at Malta and was commanded for a short time by Lieutenant Commander L Ward RD, RNR. He was to become chief marine superintendent of the Cunard Steamship Company in 1926. The *Heroic* herself remained on naval service until July 1920, when she was returned to her owners.

Despite many difficulties, the war had restored a measure of prosperity and at its end a dividend of 5 percent was being paid, plus a bonus of 2½ percent, and a considerable cash surplus had been built up. Nowadays many would see the latter as an attractive incentive to a 'predator'. So perhaps it should be no surprise to find an extraordinary general meeting of the Belfast Steamship Company being called on 14 November 1919. Its purpose was to consider an offer made by Lord Pirrie on behalf of Coast Lines Limited, a company in the Royal Mail Group, to purchase the share capital.

The financial details of the offer were that the original £50 shares were to be purchased for £435 each and the £10 (£5 paid) 'A' shares were to be purchased for £43 10s each. A favourable recommendation from the directors was ensured by the offer of £20,000 each for loss of office. This apparently attractive offer was to be financed by a method characteristic of the acquisitions policy of the Royal Mail Group under Sir Owen Phillips, later Lord Kylsant. The deal was to be financed in part by a loan made by the Belfast Steamship Company from its cash surplus of £549,635 to Coast Lines Limited.

Should this essentially Belfast institution have surrendered its financial independence? It faced an uncertain peace as it had done in the years before 1914. It was the only major passenger and cargo carrier operating between Ireland and England with fast express steamers which did not enjoy the advantage of being part of a large English railway company or having a mail subsidy. Rugged independence is frequently admired but if adopted by choice it can be a very lonely posture. Competition for its staple cargo business had been its lot for much of its career on the Belfast/Liverpool route. There had been little direct passenger competition but a persistent war of attrition had been waged with the Fleetwood and latterly the Heysham routes. In common with all shipping companies, higher fuel charges and increased wages were threatening increased operating costs. In addition, the *Logic* and *Comic* were both approaching obsolescence and another decade would find the *Graphic* and *Heroic* in the same condition. Then there was the additional uncertainty of the political future of Ireland which was wrapped in obscurity.

Other Irish cross channel companies had decided to sell out. For example, in July 1917, Coast Lines had purchased from Furness Withy & Company their substantial shareholding in the old established British and Irish Steam Packet Company of Dublin, together with the balance of the shares of that company. Across in Glasgow the directors of the Laird Line, prominent in the Irish Sea trade, had agreed to accept an offer from Coast Lines and negotiations were in progress with Messrs G and J Burns, whose ships were well known in Belfast.

No one in Belfast would have seen anything amiss in the sale of the Belfast Steamship Company in which their very own Lord Pirrie of Harland & Wolff was so prominently involved. Certainly the company's staff afloat would have had little emotion over the departure of Gallaher who had seen to it that he received an adequate consolation from the company's cash reserves even if it came ostensibly from Coast Lines.

The company had been notable in having only three chairmen to date. All were remarkable men, each one uniquely fitted to guide the company through the particular era of their chairmanship. If Gallaher's character appears unprepossessing, it was his misfortune, perhaps, to be the chairman nearest our day. Men's virtues shine brightly through the mists of time which often shrouds their failings and vices from our day.

So ended the company's financial independence in the sixty-eighth year of its life, a time for a little sadness maybe but not a time for regret for greater days were yet to come.

VIII
Enter Sir Alfred

Alfred Read and the firm of Coast Lines Limited were parvenus on the cross channel scene in 1920. The name Coast Lines had only been in use since 4 April 1917 but, of course, as in all branches of shipping in those days, the origins of the firm were much older. On 30 September 1913, the firm of Powell, Bacon and Hough Lines had been incorporated and held its first meeting at Tower Buildings, Water Street, Liverpool, on the next day, when it was resolved that where necessary the names of their steamers should all be changed so that they should have 'coast' as the last word of their name. This was simply to adopt the practice of one of the constituents of the new firm, F H Powell and Company, who had adopted this distinctive style of ship name early in the present century. Significantly, the directors decided that the company's line be publicly known as the 'Coast Line'.

The firm of F H Powell and Company was clearly the dominant partner in the new enterprise of 1913. Apart from giving the new grouping the style of ship name, they also gave them the black funnel with a white chevron on it which became so well known in practically every port and at every quay where there was water to float a ship around the English coast.

The greatest contribution of F H Powell and Company was their chairman, Alfred Henry Read. This remarkable man, whose name has occurred twice in our story so far, was to dominate the coasting and Irish cross channel trades until the Second World War.

Alfred Read's grandfather, also named Alfred Read, was a master mariner and died, it is said, of fever on a voyage taking stores to the armies at the Crimean War. He was buried at Genoa. Behind him he left one son, again Alfred, and a widow, Mary, whose maiden name was Davey. Now Mary had a

nephew, William Davey, who became a partner of Sir Alfred Jones of the Elder Dempster Line. He had achieved this status by 1879, eleven years after the foundation of the firm, and later became sole partner following the death of Sir Alfred Jones. It was William Davey who introduced his orphaned cousin to the firm of F H Powell and Company in 1869.

Young Alfred Read had business experience in London and was listed at first in the Liverpool directories as an accountant. He is then shown as a cashier with Messrs F H Powell but by 1881 was described as a shipowner, indicating that he had by then become a partner. He married and had two sons and two daughters. The elder son was Alfred Henry Read, born in West Derby, Liverpool, in 1871.

Alfred Read followed commercial tradition and entered his father's firm in which he became a partner in 1893. Before doing so he served a business apprenticeship with the Anchor Line which may have been significant sixty years later in helping to mould a prejudice against a very dangerous rival on the Irish Sea whom we shall meet. And so Alfred Read might have remained like many another well-to-do young man, complacently guiding the destinies of an essentially family shipping business until cautious middle age and harsher times after the First World War might well have encouraged him to dispose of his ships while prices were high and commence a premature but comfortable retirement as a country gentleman.

But Alfred Read was not of the disposition to be ruled by circumstances if he could avoid it. His forceful personality and persuasive manner, with a nature which was restless and impulsive, meant that he towered over coastwise shipowners in Liverpool and F H Powell and Company was unable to provide an

The *Classic*, ex *Magic*, on the express service about 1920. (William Grogan Collection)

adequate outlet for his talents. It was at his instigation that the amalgamations with the Bacon and Hough Lines in 1912 and 1913 were arranged.

A word about the constituents in the 1913 amalgamation. F H Powell and Company had its origin in one of Liverpool's business houses, Messrs Swainson and Cram, who were also shipbuilders. The Swainsons retired from the firm in 1830 and Frederick Powell of Bristol joined them. The firm became Cram, Powell and Company for some twenty years when the Cram interest in its turn retired and it then traded as F H Powell & Company. Their ships sailed regularly to London and Bristol.

The firm of John Bacon Limited traded principally from Liverpool and Preston to Wexford and Bristol Channel ports. Their fleet was notable for including in it at one time the *Montague*, a vessel built with a clipper bow and used for several years as a yacht by the Czar of Russia. It was from the Bacon Line's Wexford service that Alfred Read's first trading connection with Ireland emerged.

John Bacon Limited amalgamated with F H Powell and Company in 1912 and in the following year the firm of Samuel Hough Limited joined them. The Hough steamers traded from Liverpool to London calling at Falmouth, Plymouth, Southampton and Portsmouth. For some years before the amalgamation of 1913 they had worked their services in conjunction with those of F H Powell and Company.

So, in 1913, Alfred Read emerges as a man of commercial stature. Obviously determined to establish a strong coasting liner company on the west coast, he was already a member of the Mersey Docks and Harbour Board and

had been invited to become chairman of the prestigious Liverpool Steamship Owners' Association at the early age of forty-one.

As soon as the amalgamation was completed in 1913, there were significant pointers to the direction in which Alfred Read would steer the new group.

First, Kirk's Cartage Company of Beaumaris Street, Liverpool, was purchased. Not yet mechanised and not seen as a competitor by coastwise shipping, Alfred Read was fully aware of the valuable complementary nature of a cartage company in the continuous commercial fight which they had with the railways. Years later the road haulage interests of Coast Lines would expand far beyond even Alfred Read's dreams.

Secondly, and by way of a contrast, the new company decided in 1914 to apply for membership of the Irish Railway Clearing House. This was an essential move following an agreement with the Dublin and South Eastern Railway by which the railway company took over their coastal trade between Wexford and Enniscorthy. This enabled Powell, Bacon and Hough Lines to withdraw their barge *Enniscorthy* and send her over to Milford Haven where she was sold in 1916 for £625. Agreement with a railway company would not have come easily to a traditional coastal steamship owner. Such was Alfred Read's pragmatism that he was not afraid to innovate. Much better relations with the English and Irish railway companies would be needed when he advanced into the Irish cross channel business. Enmity would have been easy and shortsighted and we shall see that as agreement and good relations with the 'enemy' were essential to the Liverpool/ Wexford trade of 1914, so they would be even more essential in the new 'fields' which Alfred Read was soon to conquer.

Thirdly, the genesis of Alfred Read's Irish interests came just weeks before the outbreak of the Great War in 1914 when 534 shares in the British and Irish Steam Packet Company of Dublin were bought by Powell, Bacon and Hough Lines. This old established Irish company had been in business since 1836, and their principal trade at that time was a coasting liner service between Dublin and London. The Furness–Withy Line of London owned 1,354 of their £50 shares. However, the bond between Powell, Bacon and Hough and the British and Irish Company was strengthened in 1916, when £30,000 was loaned to the Dublin company at 5½ percent per annum.

Fourthly, Alfred Read was no academic but throughout his business career he encouraged the theoretical study of transport and this, incidentally, crystallised in his presidency of the Institute of Transport in 1936. This same interest in theory was demonstrated in the establishment in 1914 of a statistical department to enquire into and report upon the expenditure of any department of the company.

Fifthly, a crucial appointment was made in 1914 when James W Ratledge was appointed secretary to the company. His influence and status as confidante and adviser to Alfred Read cannot be underestimated, nor can his value as counsellor to the whole Group in the trying and dangerous days which lay ahead. Like all great men, Alfred Read had a shrewd ability to select able lieutenants upon whom responsibility could be devolved.

In January 1917, Alfred Read told the Board that he had been approached by Sir Owen Phillips who was interested in purchasing the ordinary shares in Powell, Bacon and Hough Lines. Following negotiations, an offer of £800,000 was accepted from Phillips.

By April of that year Phillips was chairman and Alfred Read, the only survivor from the old board, was still managing director and enjoying a salary of £3,000 per annum. In the same month it was resolved that the name of the company be altered to Coast Lines Li-mited and that future meetings of the Board be held in London. The meetings were held initially at the offices of the Royal Mail Steam Packet Company at 18 Moorgate Street, and then at 1 Seething Lane, until 1919.

The subject of the British and Irish Steam Packet Company was an early item on the agenda of Coast Lines Limited as it now was. Agreement was soon reached with the British and Irish Company for the acquisition of the balance of those shares not held by Furness–Withy. At the same time and, independently, an agreement was reached with Furness–Withy for the purchase of their shareholding in the British and Irish Company. By July 1917, Coast Lines owned all the shares except for one held by 'Mr Barker'.

The move to London had suited Alfred Read personally for early in 1917, Sir Joseph Maclay, the shipping controller, had invited him to become the director of Home Trade Shipping. This important office was to lead to the knighthood conferred upon him in the following year. He had bought an estate in Wiltshire and a town house in Park Lane and was able, in the former, to continue his hobby interest of farming formerly carried on at 'Weatherstones', near Willaston, Wirral, which he had sold.

On the other hand, many management functions were retained and developed at Liverpool. For example, it was decided in 1918 to centralise book-keeping and accounts at the Mersey port, not only of Coast Lines but of the British and Irish Steam Packet Company and all other associated companies.

The Royal Mail Group depended upon a complicated system of cross shareholding from which to some extent Coast Lines and its subsidiaries were excluded. Control was achieved by the Coast Lines share capital being owned by the Royal Mail Steam Packet Company, Elder Dempster, the Union Castle Line, Messrs H & W Nelson, Lamport and Holt and Messrs D MacIver. The rise and fall of the Royal Mail Group has been recently analysed in depth elsewhere but as we shall see later the Coast Lines financial structure was a factor which enabled Sir Alfred Read to maintain a degree of financial independence from the rest of the Royal Mail Group and to save Coast Lines and its subsidiaries from certain sale and possible break-up after the collapse of Royal Mail.

It has been argued that the collapse of the Royal Mail Group was due, in part, to the fact that it '... was a crazy edifice of functionless units, none of which gained anything by association with the rest'. This is an exaggeration in the case of Coast Lines whose ships fitted into the Royal Mail Group's activities admirably with their numerous coasting and cross channel liner services available for the carriage of goods on through bills of lading to and from ports served by the Group's ocean services.

Certainly, as far as Coast Lines was concerned, its operational structure would never be a 'crazy edifice' and the maximum advantage would be gained from the close association and interdependence of the various companies in the Group with each other. Sir Alfred had plans for a new Liverpool/Dublin nightly express service. What more sensible than to establish a marine manager's department in Liverpool comprising marine engineering and catering sections serving the Belfast Steamship Company, the British and Irish Steam Packet Company and Coast Lines vessels?

Full commercial autonomy was retained by the company in Belfast. The trader and passenger would notice little external difference in the company which he had been accustomed to dealing with. On the whole, it was never Coast Lines' policy to obliterate the companies which they acquired. If there were changes tending towards uniformity in group companies they were for a good economic reason and not simply a desire for a corporate identity at all costs. The only loss in autonomy suffered at Donegall Quay at this time was the loss of their own 'shore steward' as the result of the new management structures at Liverpool. Mr Love, their catering superintendent, who had come to the company from the Stranraer/Larne steamers, was 'paid off' with suitable compensation. There had been no full time engineering and marine superintendents.

The Belfast Steamship Company was, however, registered as a private company in 1921. This concept had been introduced by the Companies (Consolidation) Act, 1908,

and its original purpose had been to facilitate the incorporation of family businesses where there was no intention of inviting the public to subscribe to the shares. Private companies were given certain privileges and it was not long before these advantages appealed to large public companies intent on taking over smaller undertakings. The confidential atmosphere intended for a family business was ideal for a subsidiary company whose 'parent' did not wish the outside world to know too much of its financial position. Later legislation has removed these advantages.

Before this change in status the forty-eighth annual general meeting of the company was held, not in Belfast but at 27 Cockspur Street, London SW1, on 15 December 1919, at premises which Coast Lines had leased. This address was close to Harland & Wolff's London office at 1 Cockspur Street.

Sir Owen Phillips succeeded Gallaher as chairman and Sir Alfred Read, Lord Pirrie and J W Ratledge joined the Board. Further use must have been envisaged at the time for the boardroom in Donegall Quay for the lintel of the doorway leading from the general manager's office to the boardroom was raised and a new door fitted. This was done to enable Sir Owen Phillips, inordinately proud of his great height, to enter and leave the boardroom wearing a tall hat.

James McDowell had attained the age of sixty-nine and was likely to remain as general manager as long as he was physically fit in the absence of a superannuation scheme. Nevertheless, his health was failing and the new Board was bound to consider the question of his successor soon. The advice of Sir Samuel Kelly, the prominent coal importer and shipowner, was sought by Sir Alfred. Kelly's suggestion was Samuel Berkeley, superintendent of the Line of the Great Northern Railway (Ireland). This enterprising company was the second largest Irish railway and had a formidable reputation at that time in the facilities provided for passengers. Mr Berkeley was a farmer's son from Gallanagh, near Cookstown, Co Tyrone. Entering the service at the lowest rung on the ladder, he had achieved a position of responsibility and was a prominent figure at the line's Amiens Street terminus. Sir Alfred was not unacquainted with him on his frequent journeys by train from Dublin to Belfast. Samuel Berkeley went to Belfast in 1920, serving initially as manager under Mr McDowell.

So far as the ships were concerned, the last few months of the company's financial independence and the beginning of Coast Lines control saw restricted sailings on the express service as the result of industrial disputes affecting the coal industry and the general atmosphere of unrest in Ireland. At what should have been the height of the passenger season in 1919, there were sailings on Mondays, Wednesdays and Fridays only from Belfast and Liverpool. The fixed sailing hour from Belfast had been temporarily abandoned and sailing times varied from 6 to 9.15 pm. At Liverpool sailings and arrivals were from and to Prince's Dock, avoiding the Landing Stage. The passages were slower and all these measures were intended to conserve coal.

Despite the bad outlook for trade, there was even a threat of competition for the summer passenger trade. This came from Tyneside interests who had bought the wartime shipyard at Warrenpoint. In addition, the optimistic purchasers had announced their intention of building ships to run a passenger service from this pleasant Co Down resort to unspecified English ports in the summer months only under the style of the Liberty Line; no nonsense here about providing a service for the public in the lean and unprofitable months of winter. Fortunately, the Liberty Line sank without further trace.

Meanwhile, the general situation had improved sufficiently to enable nightly sailings at fixed hours to be resumed on 10 May 1920. The service was provided by the *Patriotic*, *Graphic* and *Classic*. The company even issued a sepia postcard of the latter vessel, probably in 1920.

The city passenger agency at 7a Donegall Place conducted by the Great Western Railway had closed during the war. When it reopened on 7 July 1920, it did so without railway involvement but now served Messrs G and J Burns and the Ayr Steamship Company as well as the Belfast Steamship Company. The passenger office moved to 9 Donegall Place in 1925, following the expiry of the lease of 7a. A less welcome change for passengers came in 1920 when they were required, for the first time, to pay berth fees. Until now there had been no additional charge to the saloon fare for a berth and these had been allocated as available.

Strangers now began to appear on the route in the cargo fleet. For example, the Liverpool and Manchester cargo services in 1920 saw the *Hampshire Coast* built in 1911 for F H Powell and Company. She had the doubtful distinction of being one of three total losses suffered by Powell, Bacon and Hough Lines within a two month period when she had stranded at Shoreham on 9 February 1915. Abandoned to the underwriters, she was bought back from them in October 1915, for £24,000, and lived on to serve Coast Lines until 1936, when she was sold to Monroe Brothers of Liverpool.

An interesting bird of passage made at least one trip from Liverpool to Belfast and back in July 1920. She was the cargo and passenger steamer *Killarney* of London, delivered new to the City of Cork Steam Packet Company on 17 July 1919, for an unrecorded sum. She had been built by A and J Inglis who had launched her in that year for G and J Burns as the *Moorfowl*. Due to a dispute they had not taken delivery of her. Now at last on 1 July 1920, on arrival with a general cargo at Belfast, she was transferred to G and J Burns at long last to become the *Moorfowl* for a consideration of £153,745. She became the *Lairdsmoor* on 29 May 1929, and her career came to an end on 7 April 1937 when she was lost in collision with the Shaw Savill liner *Taranaki* off the Mull of Galloway.

The *Heroic* had returned to the service in the summer of 1920. In that same year the Coast Lines Board had taken a two-thirds interest in the Ardrossan Harbour Company. Unfortunately, the unsettled situation in Ireland had probably been the factor which prompted G and J Burns, before joining the Coast Lines Group, to dispose of their Ardrossan/Belfast turbine steamer *Viper* to the Isle of Man Steam Packet Company and abandon the daylight summer service to Belfast at the close of the 1919 season. Here was an investment in a harbour and more settled times suggesting that a daylight service might earn some money in the summer of 1920 and the Belfast Steamship Company now had a spare express steamer. The *Graphic*, with her reputation of being slightly faster than her consorts, was a natural choice for a summer daylight service from the Scottish resort and port. She was able to make a 4½ hour sea passage to and from Belfast (Albert Quay). As she carried mails she was advertised for the first and last time in her career as the RMS *Graphic*. The daylight service was not repeated in the following year. The *Graphic*, essentially a night steamer, could not compare with the *Viper* and could only give Scottish day excursionists 80 minutes in Belfast. The reason for the service lapsing in 1921 may not have been due to any unsuitability on the *Graphic*'s part but to a disastrous three month coal strike which commenced in April 1921.

On the *Graphic*'s return after the summer of 1920, the *Classic* was chartered to the Cork Steam Packet Company for their Liverpool and Fishguard to Cork services. In 1922, civil war raged in the infant Irish Free State severing land communications between Dublin and Cork and enabling the *Classic* to play a part in the dramatic history of the new state. General Michael Collins, Commander of the Irish Army, was murdered on 22 August in an ambush in Co Cork. Due to the disruption of land communications his body was carried in the *Classic* from Cork to Dublin.

The G and J Burns steamer *Spaniel* was transferred on 1 January 1921 to the Belfast Steamship Company for £20,000. Built as far back as 1895 by A and J Inglis, originally with passenger accommodation, since removed, she was renamed *Caloric*.

The Royal Mail Group had bought the Ardrossan Dockyard Company in the previous year. On 1 June 1921, from that yard came the company's first newly-built cargo steamer. A small vessel, costing £35,000, she was named *Optic*.

Also from the Ardrossan Dockyard Company had come two steamers, the *Ardmore* and *Kenmare*, in 1921 for the City of Cork Steam Packet Company. They were to be followed by two fine ships from Ardrossan in 1923/4, the *Lady Louth* and *Lady Limerick*, for the

British and Irish Steam Packet Company's new Dublin/Liverpool express service. Though apparently remote from the day-to-day concerns of the Belfast Steamship Company, all four of these ships had a part to play in boardroom politics in the Coast Lines Group and so affected the company's fortunes. The latter two were to sail briefly on the Belfast/Liverpool service seventeen years later.

To return to Belfast, it was time to say farewell to two stalwarts. On 9 September 1921, the *Logic* and the *Comic* were transferred to the Laird Line for service on the former Ayr Steamship Company routes at a valuation of £15,000 each. The departure of the *Comic* meant the end of passenger facilities on the Londonderry/Liverpool service. Their passenger accommodation was useful in the immediate future on the Ayr/Belfast service where there was still a requirement for saloon and steerage facilities. The *Logic* became the *Culzean* and the *Comic* the *Cairnsmore*. On the cessation of passenger services from Ayr both vessels went to the British and Irish Steam Packet Company on 17 May 1929, when the *Culzean* became the *Lady Carlow* and her near sister the *Lady Kerry*. On this occasion their transfer value was a mere £2,000 each, yet in their old age they carried deck passengers on occasions and retained enough of their good looks to be described as 'little yachts' by a former official of their new owners.

Their story ends when the *Lady Kerry* went to Messrs T W Ward for breaking up in Liverpool on 5 January 1934, for the sum of £1,250. The *Lady Carlow* met the same fate on 28 May 1936, when Smith and Houston of Port Glasgow took her for £2,200 minus £4 10s, for a spare propeller apparently retained by her owners.

Politics are never far away in Ireland and in December 1920, the Government of Ireland Act became law and if it did not satisfy the aspirations of many, it held out at least the hope of an ending of the grave unrest afflicting the country.

A measure of self-government within the United Kingdom was granted to six of the nine counties of the ancient province of Ulster, the six to be known as Northern Ireland. The Act was never applied to the rest of the country which became the Irish Free State and later the Republic of Ireland. The Northern Ireland Parliament was opened in temporary accommodation by George V at the Assembly's College, Belfast, on 22 June 1921.

The company was privileged to play a small but significant part in the opening of the new Parliament. The King and Queen had arrived at Donegall Quay on the twenty-second in the Royal Yacht *Victoria and Albert*. After their brief visit they were to depart on the following morning but there was a problem,. The tide would be too low for the *Victoria and Albert* to berth at Donegall Quay and it was decided that she would sail from Thompson Wharf. Those in authority thought that it was

Their Majesties boarding the *Victoria and Albert* at Thompson Wharf, 23 June 1921, using a Belfast Steamship Company gangway. (William Grogan Collection)

King George V receiving Captain Arthur Porter on board the *Patriotic* at Thompson Wharf, 23 June 1921. (William Grogan Collection)

Special luncheon menu card on the *Patriotic*, 23 June 1921. (William Grogan Collection)

undesirable for the Royal visitors to travel through the shipyard by road to reach Thompson Wharf. The company was asked, accordingly, to make the *Patriotic* available so that the King and Queen might sail downriver from Donegall Quay. The *Patriotic* became the first cross channel steamer on which the King had taken passage and, as far as is known, the first Irish cross channel steamer to carry a reigning monarch.

The company spared no expense in accommodating their distinguished passengers. A suite on the promenade deck was placed at their disposal in which a silver plaque com-

memorating the event was later affixed to the cabin bulkhead. Below, the well-known florists, Messrs Hugh Dickson and Company, transformed the saloon into a 'veritable flower garden'. On the centre table was an ornamental basket adorned with scarlet carnations whilst the other tables were arrayed with carnations, asparagus fern and smilax.

Before the vessel sailed the King received on board deputations from the workforce at the shipyards of Harland & Wolff and Workmen, Clark and Company. As the *Patriotic* moved away from the quay, the King and Queen appeared on deck whilst ashore a Royal salute was fired. On arrival at Thompson Wharf, James McDowell was presented and so was the *Patriotic*'s master, Captain Arthur Porter, whom the King complimented on his ship handling.

Royal duties done, a proud *Patriotic* sailed later that forenoon on a cruise down the lough taking with her to share her pleasure a distinguished company, including the Lord Chancellor of Ireland, Sir James Campbell. They all sat down to a special luncheon on board accompanied by the strains of E Joy Popplewell's orchestra.

Two months later, on 28 August, James McDowell died and Samuel Berkeley succeeded him as general manager. Not for the first time in the company's history when times were difficult the right man was found to match these times. They were to be painful ones for staff and employees. One of Mr Berkeley's first tasks was to implement national agreements which between November 1921 and February 1922 reduced wages and salaries by 10 percent for deck and engineer officers and deck, engine room and catering ratings.

Away from the public eye other crises were unfolding which threatened the stability and even the very existence of the Coast Lines Group. The Belfast Steamship Company, in common with the other cross channel companies, had sought security within the Group in a changing and uncertain world but were they not about to experience a far more perilous insecurity than they could have imagined?

The first and potentially more dangerous crisis arose from a boardroom dispute which had its origins in the vanity and autocracy of Sir Owen Phillips as he then was. It was to lead on to a crisis affecting the whole Royal Mail Group. But before that great storm broke there was to be another crisis, less lethal, but with a potential for serious damage. To take the boardroom crisis first which unfolded towards the end of 1922, Sir Alfred Read had complained of the way in which decisions affecting Coast Lines were taken by Phillips without consulting the Coast Lines Board.

The main bone of contention was the ordering of new tonnage for the Group which Read felt was not all needed and which threatened the Group's viability. He had reason for his concern. Between 25 March 1920 and 11 November 1922, no fewer than ten ships of a total value of over £1,182,000 were delivered to the Group, all paid for initially by long dated bills. All the ships were built at one or other of three yards in the Royal Mail Group, ie Harland & Wolff (Govan), A and J Inglis, or the Ardrossan Dockyard Company. Read was not prepared to sacrifice Coast Lines on the altar of the Royal Mail Group's shipbuilding interests.

A paradox, perhaps, Sir Alfred was expansion minded and certainly was anxious to have three composite cargo/cattle/passenger carriers for the Dublin/Liverpool trade.

Whether he really wanted four such vessels is another matter. It would seem as though he had reservations about such ships as the *Northern Coast*, *Eastern Coast*, *Somerset Coast* and *Ayrshire Coast* turned out from the Royal Mail yards in this period.

In view of the importance of Lord Pirrie on the Royal Mail, Coast Lines and Belfast Steamship Company Boards as well as his position within the Royal Mail Group as head of Harland & Wolff, it is appropriate to refer to recent research which has brought to light intense criticism levelled at Lord Pirrie earlier in the century. It came from the pen of Thomas Hope Robinson, Editor of *Fairplay* at the time when the International Mercantile Marine Corporation was established, and suggested that he lacked sentiment, ie 'Mr Pirrie has about as much sentiment as a Muscovy duck ...'. However, it seems clear that Pirrie's sentiments at all times were directed towards obtaining orders for his yard in Belfast and on the Clyde and for payment as far as possible in cash for the ships which he built. Pirrie was motivated also by the notion, uncommon enough nowadays, that it was the businessman's duty to maximise employment opportunities rather then profits.

In fairness to Lord Pirrie, he sided with Sir Alfred Read in an angry clash at a directors' meeting where fate took a hand. Perhaps he felt that the future of the Coast Lines Group was, after all, being compromised by excess orders for new tonnage. If there was irreparable damage, perhaps its important Belfast Steamship Company subsidiary with its headquarters in Pirrie's own Belfast would face ruin. More cynically, Pirrie may simply have developed an antipathy to Phillips which led him to side with Sir Alfred. Where all this would have led had Pirrie lived longer can only be a matter of speculation.

Apparently in retreat, Phillips sailed the following day to South Africa on a visit which would last through the winter. Retribution swiftly followed his departure. A letter to the Coast Lines Board arrived from the Bank of Liverpool and Martins Bank, as it was then styled, requesting that the large loan be cleared forthwith. Sir Owen was a director of the bank.

Worse was to follow. Coast Lines was indebted to the deep sea companies in the Royal Mail Group for intercompany subventions were a feature of Royal Mail Group internal finances. Demands for the repayment of these loans flooded in following the letter from the bank. 'It looked like ruin'. And so it might have been had it not been for the financial wizardry of J W Ratledge and the sacrificial determination of Sir Alfred Read.

Salvation was possible because much of the Coast Lines capital of £5,000,000 was unissued and these unissued shares were issued at once to the deep sea companies corresponding to the debt owed to them. Sir Owen's absence allowed an artfully drafted letter to be sent to each of them accompanying the new shares and suggesting that this was how Sir Owen wished the matter to be settled. The stratagem worked.

The bank presented a far more serious obstacle. Sir Alfred sold his bloodstock farm in Wiltshire and his London home in Park Lane and he and Lady Read retreated to rented rooms in Kensington. These personal sacrifices were not enough to deflect an unsentimental bank bent on clearing an overdraft. Ratledge's genius came to the rescue again. He pointed out to the bank that their remit had been simply to close the Coast Lines Loan Account. There was nothing to prevent the bank from opening a new account for Coast Lines and making advances on foot of it using the currently buoyant Coast Lines Group's freight earnings as security. At last there was hope and the Group was saved from ruin. But further security was needed and this was achieved by a deposit of shares with the bank. By 1926, Coast Lines was able to create £2,000,000 worth of 5 percent debenture stock with power to create a further half a million, the whole to be secured by a trust deed.

Out of near disaster there had come a measure of financial independence for Coast Lines, even though Sir Alfred's endeavours to raise capital independently for his companies were to cause concern later to the voting trustees of the deeply troubled Royal Mail Group. The strength and prestige which he had gained from this episode undoubtedly enabled him to extricate the Coast Lines Group from the subsequent Royal Mail debacle.

A relief, surely, to turn from City financial turmoil to the delivery of the next cargo vessel to the Belfast Steamship Company. She was the old steamer *Lismore*, formerly the *Broom* and before that the *James Crombie*. She dated from 1904 and the City of Cork Steam Packet Company parted with her on 30 September 1922 for the sum of £4,854 3s 4d. Intended for the Manchester trade, she was named *Dynamic* recalling the famous ship canal pioneer thirty years before. There would be no more new cargo vessels delivered to the company for twenty years.

There had been a proposal for a passenger and cargo steamer to be built at Harland & Wolff's Belfast yard on cost and commission terms. She would have been a repeat of the *Patriotic*. No doubt the financial crisis was the reason for the abandonment of this proposal in November 1923.

We will leave the financial crisis resulting from the Royal Mail collapse until the next chapter. A very serious situation now began to develop in 1923 resulting from the implementation, on 1 January of that year, of the Railways Act of 1921. As far as the Belfast Steamship Company was concerned it meant that the Midland Railway, with which it had enjoyed a reasonable relationship, was amalgamated with the London and North Western Railway which had itself swallowed the Lancashire and Yorkshire Railway in the previous year. Relations with the London and North Western had been correct but frigid and Euston had recently scored a triumph over the only other significant independent company operating express steamers on the Irish Sea when it had finally wrested the Irish Mail contract from the City of Dublin Steam Packet Company with effect from 1921.

Triumphant and jealous of its position at Holyhead, the London, Midland and Scottish Railway was vigilant and suspicious of any development that might remotely threaten its interests. In this tinder dry situation Sir Alfred supplied the spark when he decided to develop the services of the British and Irish Steam Packet Company which had succeeded the now moribund City of Dublin Company on the Dublin/Liverpool trade.

There was plenty of money to be made carrying cattle from Dublin to Liverpool but return cargoes were hard to find so it was a bold stroke to build new composite ships catering for eighty saloon and ninety steerage passengers as well as the cattle trade and sailing at fixed hours instead of with the tide. Such a development, plus shared Liverpool terminal facilities with the Belfast Steamship Company, made sense to Sir Alfred but not to Euston.

The new service from Dublin to Liverpool was at full strength by 1924 when the *Lady Limerick* joined the *Lady Louth* and the former *Ardmore*, transferred from the City of Cork Steam Packet Company, and renamed *Lady Longford* in the previous year. The *Lady Louth* took time off on 14 September 1924 to undertake a twelve day yachting cruise to the 'Scottish Firths and Fjords' on what was termed 'Langland's Service'.

Sir Alfred was determined that his venture should meet with success and there was extensive publicity for it aimed especially at the Irish population in England. The zealous and able Coast Lines publicity manager, Dr Ernest R Reader, sought and obtained the sympathetic ear of no less than the Archbishop of Westminster who expressed his interest in and concern for the large number of Irish children at English convent boarding schools and agreed that it was desirable to make provision for them when travelling with extra stewardesses on cross channel ships. Armed with his blessing, Dr Reader did the rounds of convent schools and publicised directly what he had not done in the Archiepiscopal presence, the new B & I overnight service from Liverpool. Hospitals with Irish nurses also received visits from him. This activity impinged on the Belfast Steamship Company as well as the Dublin company for relations with the LMSR immediately and sharply deteriorated, becoming 'very nasty'.

Sir Alfred had made an appointment as joint general manager of Coast Lines of Percy Wharton who was charged with special responsibility for relations with the railway companies and the LMSR, in particular, as part of his portfolio. He came from a well known railway family associated with the Lancashire and Yorkshire Railway and had latterly been traffic manager with the Great Southern and Western Railway of Ireland at their Kingsbridge, Dublin, headquarters. He proved to be a disappointment, was too deferential to Sir Alfred, indecisive, lacking in stamina and no real match for tough and unyielding English railway officers. He remained as the façade but his letters were often drafted for him by Samuel Berkeley in Belfast who was not deficient in the qualities which Wharton lacked.

Something had to be done to mend the breaches with the LMSR. The latter company was still angry and sensitive about the new Dublin service and as late as the autumn of 1927, was ignoring the existence of the new service from Liverpool to Dublin in its time-tables.

An opportunity arose with the appointment of the formidable Sir Josiah Stamp as President of the LMSR executive from 1 January 1926. Added urgency was given to moves for a rapprochement by disturbing rumours, which soon became fact, emanating from Euston. Sir Josiah was determined to reduce losses on Irish Sea services and was set on a major rationalisation which would close down the old established Fleetwood/Belfast service and concentrate all resources on Heysham from where the mail service to Belfast would operate in future. Three large turbine steamers, coal fired but mechanically stoked, had been ordered from Denny of Dumbarton and would be larger and more luxurious than any ship previously serving Belfast.

In the first place, a meeting was arranged between Sir Alfred and Sir Josiah; the latter not entirely a man for whom Sir Alfred cared. The outcome was an agreement dated 1 July 1928 which established a 'standing committee' consisting of senior LMSR officers and the general managers of the Irish Sea companies in the Coast Lines Group. The LNER was not included in the cabal. This omission was to call for tact and diplomacy from Samuel Berkeley in the future as that railway group comprised companies which had been old allies of the Belfast Steamship Company. Nor was the GWR included. There would be no difficulties here for relations between that

distinguished railway and the company had been reinforced by a new agreement concluded in 1922. All their unconsigned freight for the north of Ireland continued to be carried in the company's vessels via Birkenhead whence it was carried across the Mersey to Prince's Dock on the 'luggage boats' which then plied the Mersey. A GWR agent was given office accommodation in the Donegall Quay head offices which were given as the GWR's address in Belfast. This arrangement continued until the end of 1947 when nationalisation finally swept away 112 years of the GWR.

Meetings of the new standing committee were held regularly at the insistence of Sir Alfred. Success was achieved in improving relations and ironing out some, but not all, of the problems which existed and lay outside the terms of reference of the Irish and British Traffic Conference. We shall return to the committee and the 'tough talking' which sometimes took place, in the next chapter. We shall also consider Sir Alfred's reply to the LMSR plans for Heysham, but first, we must step back to the domestic affairs of the Belfast

Steamship Company: in fact, to a fine, sunny Sunday morning in 1923.

'A sound like thunder' awoke the towns-folk of Holywood, Co Down, on 3 June 1923. Out on the waters of the lough a disaster for the company and its patrons would surely have occurred but for the Grace of God. Shortly before 6.53 am, the *Graphic*, with a strong north-northwest breeze behind her, was inward bound with a general cargo and 170 passengers, making about 14 knots as she was about to enter the Victoria Channel against an ebb tide of about a knot force on a course southwest by west magnetic. A mile ahead of her was the inward bound Fleetwood mail steamer *Duke of Connaught* making about 16 knots. Outward from Belfast, and at the time four miles ahead of the *Graphic*, was the United States Shipping Board's steamer *Balsam* of 392 ft in length and 4,749 gross tons. She was under the charge of a pilot, was bound for Ardrossan for bunkers and was light with a part cargo for Dublin and Cork.

As the *Balsam* and *Graphic* approached each other, Captain Magill ordered half speed on the *Graphic*'s engines and kept her as close as possible to the starboard side of the channel. The *Balsam* kept to her starboard side until she was 300 yards from the *Graphic* when she suddenly sheered to port and blew a number of short blasts on her whistle. Captain Magill ordered the port engine to be put astern and sounded three short blasts on the *Graphic*'s whistle. Although the *Balsam* in her turn sounded three short blasts she did not go astern but contined to sheer and struck the *Graphic* on the port side amidships close to the engine room and just above No 8 buoy in the channel. She tore a gash in the *Graphic*'s side with was later to require a patch 25 ft by 19 ft.

Many sleeping passengers were thrown out of their bunks by the impact that had alarmed the Holywood people and the electric lights failed for a few seconds. The ship took an immediate list to port, settling by the stern. The *Graphic* took but 5 minutes to settle on the bottom of the lough on a sandbank practically on an even keel. Mercifully, the tide had been low and no passengers had been berthed below the main deck.

Passengers were mustered on deck, stewardesses calmed the fears of lady passengers and passengers took to the boats to the accompaniment of popular airs played by the chief steward, John Grogan, composer of *Scapa Flow*, on the concertina. Most passengers were transferred to the *Duchess of Devonshire*, inward from Heysham, which had been astern of the *Graphic*, in the ship's boats whilst one lifeboat landed women and children independently. That there was no loss of life and no panic reflected the greatest credit on Captain Magill and his crew.

The *Graphic* lay on a line between Kinnegar Point on the Co Down shore and Macedon Point on the Antrim side, broadside to the navigable channel which she partially blocked leaving only 50 ft clear for shipping.

As it was Sunday there was no sailing to Liverpool that night but the *Patriotic* was despatched from Liverpool to take up the *Graphic*'s Monday sailing, arriving at noon on the following day. To take the *Graphic*'s place and maintain a three-ship service, the *Classic* which was sailing between Cork and Fishguard at the time was sent north, arriving in Prince's Dock, Liverpool, on 15 June.

The wreck caused much inconvenience and on the following Tuesday the *Culzean* (ex-*Logic*) inward from Ayr grounded in the channel while trying to pass. Whilst astern of her the *Heroic* with 280 passengers from Liverpool had to land them by means of the tug *Hercules*. Later in the day the *Culzean* was refloated and the *Heroic* was able to berth. But

she and all other cross channel steamers were delayed leaving Belfast that night as John Milligan and Company's *Evelyn* had stranded on the ebb tide in trying to pass the sunken *Graphic* and was not refloated until the early hours of Wednesday morning.

Salvage was entrusted to the Belfast Marine Salvage Company under the direction of Captain Horner Adams RN (Rtd), a veteran of the Falkland Islands battle of 1914. Work began two days after the collision but was delayed by strong northerly winds. Eight divers worked in three-hour shifts and after closing portholes on the main deck, their first

The hairdresser's saloon on board the *Patriotic*. (Dr Ernest R Reader)

task was to cut away damaged metal with oxy-acetylene and gelignite. Three steam pumps and a petrol pump were located in numbers 1, 2 and 3 holds and coffer dams were constructed around the hatches to give the pumps an advantage when the decks were awash at high water.

The *Graphic* was raised on Sunday, 24 June, and taken to Clarence Wharf. The tugs *Musgrave* and *Hercules* were on her starboard and port sides respectively, the *Ridgeway* towing ahead and the *Sedgecock* astern for steering. There was a strong north wind blowing at the time.

Proceedings against the *Balsam*'s owners were instituted at once in the High Court in London and came, remarkably quickly, before Mr Justice Hill and an assessor on 5 July 1923, in the Admiralty Division. The *Balsam*, in her defence, blamed the *Graphic* and also joined the *Duke of Connaught* alleging that her speed was such that she created suction in the channel causing the *Balsam* to sheer. The learned judge was advised by his assessor that

Catering staff on the *Patriotic* in the mid-1920s.

this effect was impossible and had no difficulty in finding the *Balsam* entirely to blame.

A rejuvenated *Graphic* celebrated her return to service five months later on 24 November, with a reception on board. She had been reboilered, converted to burn oil, had her single-berth staterooms increased from twenty-six to fifty, was equipped with an electric silver grill and novelty of novelties, was provided with a barber's shop. This feature clearly tickled Sir Alfred's fancy and apart from appearing in the *Graphic*'s two consorts, was repeated at the same time in the new *Lady Louth*.

The *Heroic* and *Patriotic* followed the *Graphic* to Harland & Wolff's for conversion to oil burning, reboilering and improvements to their accommodation. Not only was the nuisance of coaling with all its attendant dirt eliminated but the need to shift berth in Liverpool from Prince's to Bramley Moor Docks became a thing of the past.

The faithful *Classic* which had acted as relief ship from the time of the *Graphic*'s sinking, was also reboilered and converted to oil burning. She was then transferred on 3 July 1924 to the City of Cork Steam Packet Company for a consideration of £40,000 plus £10,000 for 'additions'. Her new owners renamed her *Killarney* and as such she leaves our pages for a while to ply waters with which she had become familiar whilst chartered.

The larger than life figure of Lord Pirrie was removed from the world shipping scene and the boardrooms of Coast Lines and the

Belfast Steamship Company on 7 June 1924 whilst on a trip to South America to study harbour facilities. He died on board the Royal Mail steamer *Ebro*, by an irony of fate one of the few vessels not built for that company by Harland & Wolff but by the rival Belfast firm of Workman Clark. His body was brought across the Atlantic in the *Olympic* destined for interment in Belfast's City Cemetery. It was appropriate that his last journey by sea should be in the *Patriotic*, a ship which he had often referred to as 'my yacht'. She sailed specially from Liverpool on 22 June, berthing at Thompson Wharf, Belfast, with her ensign at half mast whilst her hull bore the blue band traditionally worn by ships in mourning for an owner.

Rationalisation was taking place amid the Coast Lines Group's Scottish companies. The Ayr Steam Shipping Company had been absorbed by the Laird Line in 1921 and in the following year the Coast Lines Board resolved to analgamate G and J Burns and the Laird Line by transferring the latter to the former 'without price or other consideration'. Thus was born Burns and Laird Lines Limited, whose Belfast staff were transferred to the service of the Belfast Steamship Company on 1 January 1924. From that date the company started to act as agents for the Burns and Laird Lines in Belfast who now become part of our story.

In 1926, the company carried mails briefly whilst the Fleetwood mail service and the Heysham steamers were stopped by the General Strike. Thus the *Patriotic* sailed on 6 May, with 250 bags of mail, but two days later the company was forced to announce a reduction to three sailings per week. However, by 13 May normal sailings were resumed. Whilst the Fleetwood mail service was suspended the mails were carried outwards by the company's ships but brought in from Liverpool by H M destroyers *Vidette* and *Westminster* and landed in the Musgrave Channel on 8 and 9 May.

On 9 July 1927, the *Graphic* saluted Royalty with due formality, amidst a curious informality, in the Mersey when King George V and Queen Mary opened the Gladstone Dock. There were only four ships in the river waiting to dock on the afternoon tide. One

A painting by Frank McKelvey of cross-channel steamers at Donegall Quay for the International Tourist Trophy Race, 17 August 1929. The ships are from left: *Woodcock* Burns and Laird Lines from Ardrossan, *Lairdsrock* Burns and Laird Lines from Glasgow, *Duke of Connaught* LMSR from Heysham, *Duke of Rothesay* LMSR from Heysham, *Duke of Lancaster* LMSR from Heysham, *Patriotic* BSS Co from Liverpool, *Heroic* BSS Co from Liverpool and *Eddystone* Clyde Shipping Company from London. (Belfast Harbour Commissioners)

was the *Graphic*, the others consisted of a large cargo vessel and two small coasters. The latter three vessels took only a casual interest when the King and Queen passed downriver in the Dock Board tender the *Galatea*. But as the tender passed the *Graphic* the rails were manned by the ship's company in naval fashion, officers saluted and the ensign lowered. Although the King was not on deck, observers in the *Graphic* saw a messenger despatched and a few minutes later the King appeared from the cabin, approached the side and gave the salute as the *Galatea* passed on her way to the Gladstone Entrance.

The spectre of serious competition from the air for the passenger business was thirty years away in the future, nevertheless, 15 September 1923 marked an opening shot in a contest which shows no sign of ending today. On that date the de Havilland Aircraft Company commenced an experimental air service from Plymouth to Manchester and Belfast (Aldergrove) using DH 9 aircraft and with A J

Patriotic steaming up river from her temporary berth in Huskisson Dock to the landing stage, 1929. (McRoberts Collection)

Cobham as chief pilot. It was intended to carry mail from Atlantic steamers as well as passengers and was of short duration. The spectre of air competition was briefly raised again in 1928 when Imperial Airways began to operate the Shorts Flying Boat G-EBVH *Calcutta* between Liverpool and Belfast on 24 September. The service was discontinued ten days later due to bad weather but the threat was sufficiently serious to prompt conversations between Sir Alfred Read and Sir Josiah Stamp in the following year when air services were discussed.

Launch of the *Ulster Monarch*, 24 January 1929. (PRO (NI)/BSS Co)

A more immediate threat came from the tonnage planned for the new LMSR mail service from Heysham. Sir Alfred was determined that any reply from the Belfast Steamship Company would be a powerful one despite the increasing difficulties of the Royal Mail Group, for if the trumpet gave an uncertain note his own personal financial sacrifices and the inspired genius of Ratledge would have been in vain. Independent financing was essential in addition to the debentures issued in 1926 and Sir Alfred had few scruples over the sensitivities of the Royal Mail directors. Armed with the assurance of loan assistance from the Bank of Ireland, Sir Alfred went to the Queen's Island office of Charles Payne CBE, managing director of Harland & Wolff. There on a piece of blotting paper was roughed the design for the three most revolutionary cross channel ships ever built.

Harry Hudson Rodmell's painting of the *Ulster Monarch*. (Mrs Dorothy T Rodmell)

IX
Jewel in the Crown

For the first time on a cross channel service in the British Isles oil engines were to be used. In contrast the new LMSR steamers demonstrated coal fired conservatism.

Nineteen years had passed since the world's first oil engined ship, the 1,179 ton tanker *Vulcanus*, put to sea powered by a Werkespoor six cylinder diesel engine of 500bhp at 200rpm, and still operating satisfactorily when Sir Alfred visited Charles Payne.

Credit, however, for the development of the modern diesel goes to the great firm of Burmeister and Wain which engined the twin screw motorship *Selandia* in 1912 and made the high powered oil engine a practical proposition. So revolutionary was the *Selandia* that Winston Churchill, then First Lord of the Admiralty, visited the ship and praised Denmark as '...The ancient sea faring nation which had shown us the way and taken the lead in a venture that will form an epoch in the development of shipping..'.

The design called for the first commercial airless injection units to be made in Belfast. The prototype Burmeister and Wain airless injection engined ship was the *C F Tietgen* built for the United Steamship Company's Copehagen/Aarhus service.

Advances had been made in the development of two stroke cycle oil engines but some service problems remained so the new design was to follow the well tried four stroke formula, as did the White Star Line for the *Britannic* and *Georgic* of 1930 and 1932.

The installation for the new ships would consist of two ten cylinder, four stroke cycle, trunk-piston engines of Harland & Wolff, Burmeister and Wain type. The engines were designed to develop 31,000bhp at about 170rpm, with cylinders 630mm in diameter by 930mm stroke, driving twin screws with a maximum speed of about 18 knots.

Special attention was paid to the design of the air compressors and starting reservoirs due to the amount of manoeuvring which the ships would undergo in service, especially entering and leaving Prince's Dock, Liverpool.

Diesel generator sets of 110kW capacity provided for the ship's electrical needs. This would include electric winches and windlass and capstan. But cargo handling gear was less than that in the older ships as Clarke-Chapman electric travelling cranes were to be installed at Donegall Quay and Prince's Dock.

Financial problems, not technological ones, were what exercised the directors when they approved Sir Alfred's proposal to place an order with Harland & Wolff for two passenger and cargo 'steamers'. Five months later the proposal to order a third vessel was approved. The keels were laid on 1 March, 3 March and 22 March 1928 respectively, with delivery on 29 March 1929 for the first vessel and the following 29 May and 29 June for the other two. Yard numbers were 635, 696 and 697. Estimated costs for the three were £261,000 for the first, £259,000 for the second and £255,000 for the third.

Ordering was one thing, paying was another. A personal interview between the Governor of the Bank of Ireland and Sir Alfred Read smoothed the way for the necessary finance. As security the bank was to have eleven debentures, nine of £50,000 and two of £25,000 to be repaid in instalments, the last in 1936, all bearing interest at 6 percent per annum. Further finance was needed to cover the third vessel and this was arranged by means of an overdraft and the issue of further debentures to the bank secured by a floating charge over the company's assets and to carry interest at the maximum rate for overdrawn accounts. One of the members of the bank's

The *Ulster Monarch*'s lounge. (William Grogan Collection)

The *Ulster Monarch*'s restaurant. (William Grogan Collection)

Board at that time, Captain Nutting, was later to succeed Sir Alfred as chairman of Coast Lines and associated companies.

Before the finance had even been secured, Sir Alfred must have given some thought to the names for the new ships. He was undoubtedly influenced by the Nelson Line motor ships building at Harland & Wolff's yard, the first of which, the *Highland Monarch*, had been launched on 3 May 1928. What more natural than *Ulster Monarch*? As early as January 1929 the title 'Ulster Imperial Line' appeared on passenger timetable folders advertising the 'oil burning steamers' *Patriotic*, *Heroic* and *Graphic*. After the new ships were commissioned, stateroom mats and other shipboard furnishings emblazoned with 'UIL' appeared. Ulster names spread to the company's cargo vessels and even to the Clydesdale horses on the quays at Belfast. Perversely, the Ulster travelling and trading public remained unmoved by the regal and imperial overtones of the motor ship age and

stuck to the old familiar name.

The *Ulster Monarch* was launched from Harland & Wolff's South Yard on 24 January 1929, without any ceremony. Samuel Berkeley represented the owners amid rumours that the whole Royal Mail Group might have to be reconstructed and the reality of a collapse of Royal Mail shares on the stock exchange later in the year.

The *Ulster Monarch* was destined to serve her owners for longer than any other ship which they ever possessed despite the lack of warmth at her launch and a cool reception from the technical press where the suggestion was made that the power being installed was very moderate for the class of ship and would result in speed comparing unfavourably with typical cross channel vessels. There was a concession that diesel machinery would result in fuel savings of £20,000 per annum for the company on the express service but, even so, one was given the impression that the contributor still considered turbine machinery as the most suitable for cross channel work. The *Belfast News Letter* did its best by describing the new ship as a 'work of art'. Despite being damned with faint praise she achieved an unassailable position in the affections of the travelling public, had a 'proud and gallant' record in war and was surely one of the few ships to have a rose named after her.

The second of the trio, the *Ulster Queen*, was launched on 28 March 1929 by Mrs Samuel Berkeley, wife of the general manager. The third vessel, the *Ulster Prince*, was launched on the following 25 April by Lady Read in the presence of Sir Alfred. On this same day the *Ulster Monarch* sailed on her trials.

Externally, the three sisters were at first identical. Their hulls were painted a distinctive lavender grey, reminiscent of the Union Castle liners, at that time a familiar sight at Queen's Island. Red boot topping, white superstructure, buff masts and derricks and twin motor ship funnels painted in the company's familiar scarlet and black combined to make a striking modern appearance.

After exhaustive trials, the *Ulster Monarch* was delivered on 10 June, and left Belfast on the following day on her maiden voyage under the command of Captain Arthur Porter. The layout of the passenger accommodation introduced a pattern that was to persist with little modification in succeeding passenger tonnage for the Coast Lines Group until 1957.

Saloon passengers embarked on 'B' deck where a spacious lobby contained the purser's office where passengers were received and met by their bedroom stewards, a shop, baggage room, night steward's station, staircase to decks above and below, and wood and glass screens and doors giving access aft to the spacious dining saloon extending across the whole width of the ship. Furnished in Louis XVI style, panelled in mahogany and softly curtained in pink, tables for two or four with white linen cloths and napkins, monogrammed silver and pink shaded lamps were an irresistible temptation. Aft again of the dining saloon were the galley and pantry and officers' dining room.

A vertical arrangement of saloons at the after end of the midships house was a characteristic of the *Ulster Monarch* and her successors. Above the dining saloon and galley on 'A' deck was the lounge furnished in polished grey wood. Replete with comfortable chairs and settees, writing tables and current periodicals in leather bound covers, this room opened out of the 'A' deck lobby through wood and glass screened doors opposite the staircase. At the head of the next staircase up to the promenade deck hung an oil painting of Langtry & Herdman's PS *Waterloo*. On the promenade deck itself were the smoke room and bar separated from the verandah café by the promenade deck lobby. An attempt was made in these rooms by the use of Tudor style furnishings complete with arched roof, trusses and oak panelled walls, stone mullion windows and antique wall lights to capture the atmosphere of a country inn and so dispel any anxieties felt by drinkers unused to ships. Heaton Tabb were responsible for all interior decor.

The sleeping accommodation comprised four two berth cabins-de-luxe on 'A' deck with showers and toilets en suite. On the same deck were seventy-three single berth cabins. Below on 'B' deck were twenty-eight single and thirty-one two berth cabins. On the main deck, designated 'C', were seventy-

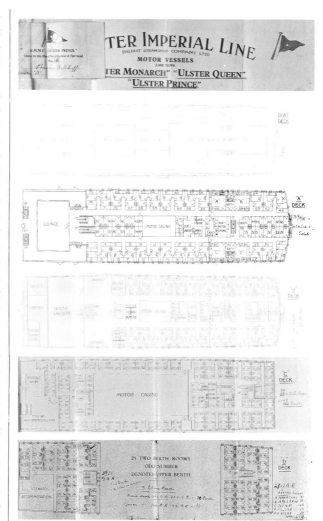

Passenger accommodation plan for *Ulster Monarch* class. (William Grogan Collection)

three two berth cabins. On the lower main deck, designated 'D', were fifty-one two berth cabins.

As far as possible all cabins were arranged on the Bibby Tandem principle so that portholes were available for what would otherwise be inboard cabins. For the first time, hot as well as cold running water was provided and all cabins were mechanically ventilated by the Thermotank system with individual controls. There were reading lamps for each berth and a padded fitting on which a pocket watch could be hung. On winter sailings it was usually possible to cater

The *Ulster Monarch* and *Graphic* berthed at Donegall Quay, 1929. (Harland and Wolff)

for all passengers in the saloon without using 'C' and 'D' decks.

Third class passengers were accommodated aft in the steerage. Some eighty berths were available and a large cafeteria was provided. A criticism that could be levelled was that third class passengers were rather far from the lifeboats on the promenade deck amidships.

The *Ulster Queen* was not delivered until 11 February 1930 and the *Ulster Prince* on the following 3 March. Part of the delay was due to a strike of joiners but there was another reason. Experience with the *Ulster Monarch* had suggested a need for a slight increase in the scantlings of the other two ships. This resulted in their light ship weights being greater than that of the *Ulster Monarch* whose scantlings remained unaltered. As the load displacement for all three remained the same, the *Ulster Monarch* had a slightly greater deadweight capacity and thus could carry more cargo than her two sisters. As this was an important consideration in the 1930s, it is probably the reason why the *Ulster Monarch* was not despatched on weekend cruises from 1933 onwards.

The three ships carried a fair amount of top weight and were, accordingly, on the tender side. For example, the *Ulster Monarch*'s metacentric (gm) average was about 1.5. In postwar years, when the amount of cargo carried per voyage was reduced due to the shorter dock working hours, her handling required care and, as we shall see, alterations were made to reduce her top weight.

Before the new ships could enter service, alterations had to be made to the Prince's Dock entrance and installation work was also necessary for the new transporter cranes. During 1929, the berths were moved temporarily from Prince's Dock South West to Huskisson Dock.

The advent of the three new ships brought a coveted prize. For the first time the company's passenger ships were able to fly the Royal Mail pennant and describe themselves as Royal Mail ships.

Hot water in the cabins was probably the reason for the absence of a barber's saloon. But the new ships each sported a 'policeman' who was in each case an ex-Liverpool City police constable and a purser was borne in addition to a chief steward. By 1931, glass and wood screens were fitted at the fore end of the promenade deck enabling passengers to enjoy a view for'ard in sheltered conditions. But the hulls soon became black as the earlier shade was found to be unserviceable in Irish Sea conditions.

What of the old faithfuls now displaced by the newcomers? Part of the strategy for building the new ships had depended on the success of the Dublin to Liverpool overnight express service introduced by the B & ISP Company. Patronage had been such that vessels with more saloon accommodation and a little more speed were now needed. Unusually for shipowners, even for those days, Sir Alfred Read had a love for ships and an especial fondness for the *Patriotic* and her two older consorts. Here was a chance to give them a new lease of life in developing further the potential of the Dublin service. The *Patriotic* was transferred to the B & ISP Company for her book value of £35,000 and the *Graphic* and *Heroic* for £25,000 each. The *Graphic* was transferred first on 10 June 1929 and was renamed *Lady Munster*. The *Heroic* followed her on 5 March of the following year, becoming the *Lady Connaught*, whilst the *Patriotic* went on 22 March to become the *Lady Leinster*. No internal changes were made but the hulls were painted silver grey and the poop decks were extended right aft. The most

The *Ulster Prince*, outward bound, manoeuvres in Prince's Half-Tide Dock, probably about 1931. (R A Feilden)

striking change was the replacement of the tall graceful single funnels by twin funnels. The after funnel was a dummy. It has been suggested that aesthetic considerations were secondary to a practical proposal to place additional water tanks in the dummy funnel. If this is so, and there is no evidence now extant, it is possible that there was an intention to install hot water in the saloon passenger cabins. It is believed that the plan was dropped as stability would have been affected.

These fine steamers with their graceful lines and grass green and black topped funnels and black painted hulls, which had soon replaced the silver grey, made a splendid foil for their successors with which they so frequently shared Liverpool's famous Landing Stage.

No sooner had the new ships started when dark financial clouds bore down again upon the company as the parent Royal Mail Group's finances took a sharp turn for the worse. On 13 November 1930 the Court of the Royal Mail Steam Packet Company had appointed a committee to consider the economies that could be achieved and wherever possible put them into effect. The Group's

The *Ulster Monarch*, assisted by tugs, berthing in Huskisson Dock, in 1929. (McRoberts)

creditors were safeguarded by the appointment of voting trustees with control over the finance and management of the Group companies, each of which would be asked not to enter into capital commitment, declare dividends, nor lend nor borrow without the trustees' permission. Coast Lines and the Belfast Steamship Company duly gave such undertakings.

The chairman of Coast Lines and the Belfast Steamship Company, Lord Kylsant (the former Sir Owen Phillips), was given 'leave of absence' on 16 June 1931 at his own request and tendered his resignation in the following October which was accepted 'with

The *Ulster Queen* in Prince's Dock about 1931. (R A Feildon)

A later view of the *Ulster Queen* at anchor in the Mersey. (R A Feildon)

very deep regret'. Sir Alfred Read now became chairman, in addition to his office of managing director, of Coast Lines and associated companies in December of that year.

Meanwhile, in July 1931, Lord Kylsant was convicted at the Old Bailey on a charge of making false statements in a prospectus inviting subscriptions to a new share issue in the Royal Mail Steam Packet Company and sentenced to twelve months' imprisonment. The statements were false in the sense that an impression was given that trading profits had been made in the years 1921-27. Though dividends had been paid in those years, the prospectus omitted to state that, in fact, substantial losses had been incurred. Some considered his sentence to be savage, others have considered it to be merited. His cavalier and callous attitude to the Coast Lines Group ten years before for no other apparent reason than spite might be said to disqualify him from sympathy in Belfast.

Operating economies at Liverpool at this difficult period were compounded by a policy of bulk purchasing of such items as silverware, crockery and linen for all the Coast Lines companies. The only gesture to a 'corporate identity' was an attractive emblem comprising *inter alia* an anchor, rose, shamrock and thistle which appeared on crockery and silverware and other places including the purple lapels of stewards' mess jackets.

Group advertising and publicity under the charge of Dr Ernest R Reader in London involved the engagement of an ex-art editor of the *Observer*, Ronald Massey, to look after artwork for the Group. It was he who engaged the well-known marine artist Harry Hudson Rodmell whose fine painting of the *Ulster Monarch* was extensively used by the Company. It appeared in railway enquiry offices, travel agencies and on postcards in which guise it was used for many years as an attractive and original way of confirming postal applications for sleeping berths.

Retrenchment, doubtless in obedience to the economy measures throughout the Royal Mail Group, saw the closure of the passenger agency in downtown Liverpool at 21 Castle Street and was pursued so vigorously that a 10/- debit from the LMSR towards publicity material relating to sleeping berths was brusquely refused by the Belfast Steamship Company.

A pleasant honour came the company's way at the end of 1932, in the midst of financial turmoil. The Northern Ireland Parliament buildings at Stormont were to be opened by HRH The Prince of Wales on 17 November 1932. A special charter of the *Ulster Prince* was appropriately arranged to carry the Prince across the sea from Liverpool.

On the sixteenth, the Prince had a busy schedule in London concluding with a broadcast to mark the tenth anniversary of broadcasting. He left Euston at 9.15 that night in the Royal saloon which was attached to the rear of the Glasgow sleeping car express. At Crewe the saloon was detached and worked forward to Liverpool (Riverside) as a Royal special. Accompanied by Admiral Sir Lionel Halsey, Sir John Gilmour, Home Secretary, and an equerry, an informally dressed Prince boarded the *Ulster Prince* at the Landing Stage.

On board, Samuel Berkeley received His Royal Highness on behalf of the company. A full dinner had been prepared but sandwiches were all that the Royal passenger wanted. These had been prepared, just in case, and were eaten in the restaurant. At 2.35am the *Ulster Prince* sailed under the command of Captain Arthur Porter, senior master, who had been specially transferred to her for the occasion. She was escorted by the cruisers *Dorsetshire* (wearing the flag of Vice-Admiral Ashley-Rushton) and *Exeter*. At the mouth of Belfast Lough the *Ulster Prince* was met by six aircraft of the Ulster Bombing Squadron based at Aldergrove. 'Making a brave show against the dark grey of the distant hills', the *Ulster Prince* with the Royal Standard fluttering from her foremast made her way up the channel, peaceably followed by a flock of gulls. The Prince had indicated that no money should be spent in elaborate decorations in Belfast; despite this every crane in the harbour was decorated. Informality had characterised the Royal progress throughout the voyage, so much so that even a steward on duty outside the Royal suite was surprised by the clearly heard Royal reaction to the temperature of the water in the shower.

The Prince returned via Larne and Stranraer. The *Ulster Prince* carried a plaque in the cabin-de-luxe which had been the Royal suite for the rest of her career whilst on her foremast she proudly carried a replica of the Prince of Wales' feathers. Early in her career the *Ulster Queen* had acquired a weather vane on her foremast and only the *Ulster Monarch* remained innocent of any masthead adornment. As a consequence, it became possible from the general manager's office to tell at a glance which of the passenger ships was lying alongside from the masts rising over the sheds.

The *Ulster Monarch* herself had a special charter 'within the family' earlier in the year. She was chartered by the British and Irish Steam Packet Company for a single voyage to Dublin and back carrying the Roman Catholic Archbishop of Liverpool, Dr Downey, and his entourage to the Eucharistic Congress being held in Dublin.

In the early 1930s, cruising was appealing to a new middle class market. The depression

Sir Alfred Read. (D P Neill)

years had meant that many passenger liners, unable to earn an adequate living otherwise, were more profitably employed in offering cruises. Some of the deep sea companies were already complaining by 1933 that the 'competition was too intense.' For those who could not afford to cruise further afield or did not choose to do so, Coast Lines decided to develop the 'yachting cruises' to the Scottish Highlands and Islands that had been resumed after the war by the old G and J Burns steamer *Tiger* sailing from Liverpool. The cruises had a much longer pedigree, being a feature of the services offered by Messrs Langlands prior to 1914 and to their absorption by Coast Lines in 1919.

The *Killarney* was transferred from the ownership of the City of Cork Steam Packet Company to Coast Lines on 31 December 1931 at her book value of £7,000. In 1932 she commenced cruising from Liverpool sporting yellow funnels and a grey hull, at first, and soon became popular with a wide clientele and created the atmosphere in which the Belfast Steamship Company re-entered the cruising market in 1933. Much faith was needed to take this step for even the mini cruise market seemed close to saturation. In 1932 the LNER had dispatched their Harwich/Hook of Holland steamer *Vienna* on weekend cruises and the Southern Railway had likewise sent their *St Briac* cruising. Yet Sir Alfred was conscious that three vessels maintaining the passenger service meant that

The *Ulster Monarch* leaving Donegall Quay late on Saturday night, 18 July 1931. (William Grogan Collection)

a lot of time was being spent alongside the quay which might be more profitably employed. There was the example of the MV *Innisfallen* built at Belfast to the same design as the *Ulster Monarch* and her sisters, but without passenger accommodation on the main and lower main decks, for the City of Cork Steam Packet Company. She had left Belfast in June 1930 to take up service on her owner's Cork/Fishguard run and was at sea six nights a week, often exposed to the full fury of Atlantic gales. Even so, it was found possible to fit in cruises on a Sunday from Cork, thus keeping this slightly smaller *Ulster Monarch* continuously employed in the summer season. From these stern economic considerations was born the Belfast Steamship Company's weekend cruises to the Highlands and Islands. All the cruises departed from Liverpool on a Saturday, most arrived back on a Monday, but occasionally were extended to Tuesdays. Inclusive fares ranged from 50/- to 60/-. The amount of planning and organisation demanded from the ship's company was enormous. A morning arrival at the Landing Stage after an overnight crossing

from Belfast, followed by the normal cleaning of the ship and then preparation for embarkation and an early afternoon sailing on a totally different routine, catering for different and more varied meals and the storing necessary as well as arrangements for fresh milk and supplies at ports of call, were problems never suspected by the eager passengers who patronised these popular cruises. Overnight from and to Belfast passengers ate and slept; cruising to Scotland meant that they ate, slept and had to be entertained. After arrival back in Liverpool the ship had to be cleaned out again and stored to sail on her normal liner run that night to Belfast.

Outward the cruise was to the east of the Isle of Man passing the Mull of Kintyre, through the Sound of Islay to Iona and Staffa and thence to Tobermory. Fort William and Oban were visited, where on one celebrated occasion a dairyman, to whom a message had been sent requesting milk supplies, waited on the quay with a single pint bottle. The homeward passage was through the Sound of Jura to the Mull of Kintyre and so south through the Irish Sea to the Bar.

The number of passengers on each cruise was limited to ensure comfort. Even so, the restaurant could not accommodate all and the overflow was conducted aft to the third class cafeteria which was equipped as a restaurant.

As on the *Dynamic*'s day cruises of forty years before, music was not overlooked and was provided by the now well-known Liverpool pianist, Ronald Settle, and the violinist Eric Roberts. When the cruises ended and the peak summer season commenced these artistes could be found on one or other of the express steamers playing in the restaurant.

Although all the ships were advertised initially in connection with the cruises, it is doubtful if the *Ulster Monarch* ever sailed on them as her greater cargo capacity was too valuable on the express service. In fact, after 1934 the *Ulster Prince* seems to have been used exclusively. It was this vessel that was so beautifully depicted in a model that graced the Coast Lines Passenger Department in the Royal Liver Building for so many years. In 1946 it was renamed *Ulster Monarch*. Nowadays intensive utilisation of tonnage has banished forever the weekend cruise and we are only left with the passenger lists that were issued for each of them and left to conjure with names of the great and the good or the fascinating such as Countess Melikoff, a personal friend of Sir Alfred and Lady Read's.

By now the company could hold its head high to the outside world. It had three fine vessels of strikingly modern design, a mail contract for the first time in its life and the recent distinction of carrying the heir to the throne to Northern Ireland. It seemed only too fitting that in 1933 the BBC's Northern Ireland Region should feature a sailing from Belfast by the *Ulster Queen* in a series called 'Dips in the Broadcast Bran Tub'. Listeners were given a sound picture of the scene in the entrance saloon and Captain Paisley forecast the weather for the passage. The company was approaching the zenith of its fortunes. No wonder that Sir Alfred, looking at his group of companies, described it as 'the jewel in the crown'.

A position of such apparent prestige could only be maintained by much patient hard work and by assiduous but often frustrating efforts to co-operate fruitfully with the LMSR in the joint committee. But above all more finance was needed to maintain and expand services despite the improvements in freight and passenger earnings brought about by the new motor ships.

To take finance first, an agreement was hammered out with Martins Bank whose head office was in Liverpool. In exchange for first statutory mortgages on the *Ulster Monarch* and her two sisters and the deposit of £500,000 5 percent first debenture stock, the bank agreed to advance £500,000, the debentures to be security for any further advances. The directors thought the terms were stiff and after representations the required deposit of debentures was reduced to £200,000.

Provided earnings continued to rise, a secure foundation for the flotation of Coast Lines Limited as an independent financial entity, free from the entanglements of the Royal Mail collapse, had been secured. The testing time was to come three years later. Despite financial worries, Sir Alfred remained optimistic and even sought further outlets for his own restless energies. The directors of Coast Lines might have been surprised to hear that conversations had taken place with the chairman of Union Castle to discuss a possible involvement in the Southampton/Continental trade. This imaginative but surprising initiative, almost at the time when Sir Alfred was pleading with Martins Bank for easier terms, was probably unwise and nothing further was heard of this proposal.

The unspectacular but important work of the Joint Committee since 1929 did not seem to live up to the promise engendered by the aura of efficiency and economy created by Lord Stamp, as he later became. The LMSR simply seemed to be the obdurate old L & NWR in a larger and more menacing guise. In vain did the Belfast Steamship Company raise again the subject of Riverside Station at Liverpool. Ashton Davies, chief general superintendent for the LMSR at Derby and an old LYR officer, cited 'serious working difficulties' which would prevent through trains. Never one to take no for an answer, Samuel Berkeley discussed the matter informally with some railway officers and thought that maybe working in Riverside might be given a trial but J Ballantyne squashed this officially by claiming that freight traffic was too heavy and that transatlantic boat trains were only run in pursuance of 'old agreements'.

There was no joy from a proposal by the company that the 5.55pm Liverpool down express be renamed the *Merseyside, Belfast and Dublin Express*. There was a firm negative from Euston to a suggestion that the company's vessels might be allowed to berth at Holyhead when fog closed the Mersey, a not infrequent occurrence in those pre-radar days.

There were grudging minor concessions. The company's buses and vans at Liverpool could use Platform 6 at Lime Street Station and could also use Platform 1 at the Cheshire Lines Committee's Central Station. Not a great deal is known, incidentally, about the company's omnibus arrangements in earlier years. There is evidence that motor buses were in use about 1910, although the registration mark of one such vehicle has led to a suggestion that it may have been as early as 1906. The minutes of the Belfast Steamship Company suggest that towards the end of its financial independence it was relying on contractors, latterly Messrs Morton, to provide the link between ship and train in Liverpool. A possible explanation is that an illustration showing a bus labelled 'Belfast SS Co Ltd' depicts a vehicle of earlier vintage than 1910 but owned by a contractor and hired out to the company. However, by the period with which we are dealing, the company had its own single deck Maudslay buses with Park Royal coachwork painted red and white and red luggage vans lettered 'Ulster Imperial Line'. The Dublin vessels were also served by these vehicles and at peak times Liverpool Corporation Passenger Transport buses were hired. Their 1928 single deck Karrier three axled buses often undertook this task.

These meagre concessions from the LMSR at Lime Street and Central Stations were won at the price of hard hitting attacks from the redoubtable Mr Ballantyne on the cross channel steamship companies. With understandable logic, he saw Coast Lines and themselves as a single entity. Now Sir Alfred had recently proposed, as a consolidation and economy measure, to amalgamate the Coast Lines' road haulage and cartage interests and it was this which had raised the ire of the LMSR. It was inconceivable that Coast Lines should develop their road activities whilst seeking to retain a friendly business association with the LMSR, was the message from Euston and it was understood clearly that the Coast Lines subsidiary Thomas Allen and Company gave special offence to railway interests.

Thomas Allen had founded a cartage business at what is now known as Hermitage Wall, Wapping, in 1854. His landlord was James Hartley & Company, Wharfingers, who were agents for the British and Irish Steam Packet Company and the City of Cork Steam Packet Company as well as being London managers for the well-known Dublin brewing firm of Guinness, for whom Thomas Allen handled deliveries in the London area. Coast Lines bought the company on 1 January 1920, and developed a large bulk haulage fleet with an extensive depot at Stanford-le-Hope, opened in 1922.

To all this, the representatives of the steamship companies could only respond that the answer might be for the LMSR to interest itself in road haulage. This only made matters worse and was seen by Ballantyne as further evidence of Coast Lines wanting to 'run with the hare and hunt with the hounds'.

There was something positive from the Joint Committee in the sense that the LMSR and the Belfast Steamship Company might have seen warning signs from the activities of Messrs Craig's Belfast and Preston Transport Company, a non-conference firm. They were undercutting rates and forwarding cargo from Preston to inland destinations exclusively by road and would not reach any agreement with the conference companies. This time it was the LMSR who were all for vigorous action by means of rate cutting. The positive action only extended as far as concern by all the committee members and no action was taken.

Embarrassment for the company came from the LNER which included the Great Central and Great Northern (of England) Railways, old allies of very long standing. Why, wrote their advertising manager, were their trains from Rugby, Leicester, Nottingham and Bradford not shown on the company's folder whilst LMSR ones were? Samuel Berkeley did not relish the idea of the LNER knowing that they had to get permission from the LMSR under the 1928 Agreement to advertise LNER services. From Derby, Ashton Davies was adamant and the best that could be suggested to the now probably suspicious LNER was that they issue a folder of their own.

Sir Alfred was not short of further imaginative ideas in the interests of economy. He never allowed Sir Josiah Stamp to forget the letter of 3 June 1927, which he had written to Sir Alfred prior to the establishment of the Joint Committee, in which he had expressed his concern about uneconomic and competitive routes. Why not pool weekend resources from Belfast by operating one sailing only to Heysham or Liverpool on Saturday and Sunday nights? The Heysham passenger steamers sailed seven night a week and the Belfast Steamship Company six (Sundays excepted). The LMSR had agreed that they could save £8,000 a year by cutting out one round trip from Heysham. The proposal was that the Heysham steamer would sail on Saturday but not on Sunday. The Liverpool vessel would load on Saturday but not sail until Sunday, cutting out the late 11pm sailing on Saturday nights traditionally used by returning theatrical parties and their 'props'. Ashton Davies, as usual, was the stumbling block and seemed suspicious, citing newspaper contracts as a reason for maintaining seven sailings per week.

In 1934, Sir Alfred returned to the attack. This time the target was the short sea routes from Scotland to Northern Ireland. He had concentrated the mind of the LMSR here by reviving from 1933 the traditional summer Ardrossan/Belfast daylight passenger service. The Belfast Steamship Company's interest, of course, was as agent for the various Burns and Laird services. The turbine steamer *Riviera* dating from 1911 had been purchased for £4,100 from the Southern Railway on 18 November 1932, and entered service the following year as the *Laird's Isle*, a useful complement to the Coast Line's financial interests at Ardrossan.

Now why not concentrate the Ayr, Ardrossan and Stranraer services on Ayr and work them all to Belfast? Burns and Laird still operated their night service from Ardrossan for passengers and the recent investment in the *Laird's Isle* would suggest a substantial concession to the LMSR if a move was made to Ayr.

The LMSR seem to have done some work on the idea. A quay to quay schedule of 4 hours 15 minutes was suggested if turbine steamers similar to those on the Stranraer/Larne route were used. They did point out that it would mean a deceleration of the night mail service from Euston and a longer sea passage. Once again, it was the LMSR which appeared unwilling to face the implications of the Stamp/Read agreement of 1927 and the Ayr concentration scheme was not heard of again.

The railway company was on the defensive when the company accused them in 1934 of running the *Duke of Abercorn*, formerly the Holyhead/Greenore *Curraghmore*, as a relief vessel from Heysham from June to September as a one class ship with steerage passengers having full use of the saloon. The LMSR admitted the impeachment pleading in

The *Heroic* in her new guise as the *Lady Connaught*. (McRoberts/Mersey Maritime Museum)

The *Graphic* as the *Lady Munster*. (McRoberts/Mersey Maritime Museum)

mitigation that she was 'old' and 'very inferior' to the Belfast Steamship Company's vessels. Nor had Euston any answer to charges of issuing cheap return fares at less than single fare for Association Football matches in England. They pleaded lamely that revenue had been produced for them in England by these fares. The company followed suit reluctantly but pointed out that they were suffering a serious loss of revenue without any other benefits such as the railway company was enjoying. It was agreed that there would be no further such fares without the personal sanction of Ashton Davies.

No quarter was asked and none was given at the meetings in this period. Why had the LMSR advertised day excursions to Blackpool from Irish stations in association with the GWR and the Great Southern of Ireland, showing railway steamship services and never once mentioning the independent steamship companies? Then the LMSR accused the

William Grogan, Purser, and S M Pritchard, Chief Steward, on board the *Ulster Prince* at the landing stage. A Dublin vessel lies astern, some time in the early 1930s. (William Grogan Collection)

Belfast Steamship Company of providing free meals for passengers on occasions. The response was vigorous and to the point. There were free meals when the vessels had not reached port within 15 hours of sailing. Anyway, the LMSR services were not so liable to disruption on account of fog. (And they were not prepared to help the company with facilities at Holyhead.)

A particularly evil report concerning the associated B & ISP Company had reached the ears of outraged railway company's officers. Was it or was it not true that on a Saturday before Christmas 1933, every child passenger had been given a box of chocolates?

Advertising by the railway companies and the quality of service offered by connecting boat trains exercised Samuel Berkeley who arranged for Ernest R Reader in London to carry out a clandestine survey of stations and trains. The 1927 Stamp/Read accord had provided for equal advertising of cross channel services on LMSR stations and an agreed annual sum was being paid by the company for the facility. But were there cases where Heysham posters were being displayed without Belfast Steamship Company ones? Dr Reader used a car to visit forty to sixty stations

per month and evidence of breaches of the accord was assembled for use by Samuel Berkeley at the next Joint Committee meeting. Surprisingly, the LMSR had not envisaged the car being used as a means for covering so many widely scattered locations and believed that the company had a team of up to fifteen inspectors travelling by train to report on advertisements. The accord had provided for some 1,000 Liverpool/Belfast posters to be displayed for about six weeks each per annum on the LMSR.

At Euston, Reader posed as a railway enthusiast. Armed with platform tickets he inspected the quality of the rolling stock and dining cars provided and attempted to assess the comparative adequacy of the accommodation for steamer passengers on the 5.55 pm *London–Merseyside Express* (as it was then called) and the 6.10 pm *Ulster Express* (Heysham).

Following the failure of the Ayr concentration scheme to take off, Sir Alfred decided to re-equip the Burns and Laird Glasgow/Belfast overnight service with a view to discontinuing the Ardrossan/Belfast overnight service. For the first time the Northern Ireland Government appeared on the scene. An agreement was entered into in 1935 between the Ministry of Finance for Northern Ireland and Burns and Laird Lines for a loan of £146,000 from the Midland Bank to be guaranteed by the Ministry. This would provide for 75 percent of the construction cost of a twin screw motor ship for passengers, cargo and cattle to be built by Harland & Wolff at Belfast. A second vessel of the same type was contracted for two months later on the same terms.

These ships were, of course, the *Royal Ulsterman* and *Royal Scotsman* which commenced service between Glasgow and Belfast on 15 June 1936. A little smaller than the *Ulster Monarch* and her sisters, they had a more elegant profile, lacking the stiff and uncompromising lines of the earlier ships. A raked stem and a single pear shaped funnel made their appearance and 225 saloon passengers could be carried on three decks in the midships house whilst third class passengers had two berth cabins with hot and cold running water.

A change in the Burns and Laird funnel colours occurred with the commissioning of their motor ships. After some experimentation with other colours, a narrow saxe blue stripe was inserted between the main colour of crimson and the black top. It was widely believed that Lady Elena Read, a widow whom Sir Alfred had married in 1920 soon after the tragic death of his second wife, bore the main responsibility. She influenced her husband strongly on matters of decor and the stripe soon became irreverently known as '*Lady Read blue*'.

These fine ships were limited in their potential versatility in the Coast Lines Group by their inability to enter Prince's Dock, Liverpool. For some design reason now unknown, their twin screws were so arranged that each propeller projected outside the half beam of the vessel. If supplementary tonnage was needed by the Belfast Steamship Company, these two ships were of little value for they had to lie at the Landing Stage at Liverpool and could not dock, for example, when chartered for the Ulster TT Races in late summer.

The Silver Jubilee of King George V in 1935 was made the occasion for a special cruise from Liverpool by the Royal Mail MV *Ulster Prince* as the company proudly advertised her. She sailed on 13 July from Liverpool for Spithead under the command of the company's senior master, Captain W J Paisley, nephew of a former senior master. On 16 July, the King in the *Victoria and Albert* reviewed the Home, Mediterranean and Re-

The *Royal Scotsman* Burns and Laird Lines 1936. (BSS Co)

The *Killarney*, now a Coast Lines 'yacht', and the former *Magic*, in the Mersey. (McRoberts/ Merseyside Maritime Museum)

The *Killarney* laid up off season in Liverpool. (McRoberts/Merseyside Maritime Museum)

serve Fleets, after which the *Ulster Prince*, in common with other passenger carrying vessels, passed up and down the lines of anchored warships.

Once more in our story, the public face of Coast Lines and its subsidiaries appeared serene whilst behind the scenes anxious

negotiations were trying to ensure the future continuance of the Group. It would be necessary to escape from the maw of the stricken Royal Mail undertaking. That Coast Lines was able to do this was due to its excellent earnings. In 1934 it had earned profits of £359,644, the highest figure since 1921. In 1935, the Coast Lines board decided to pay arrears of dividend on preferential stocks from the earnings of Burns and Laird and the Belfast Steamship Company. They would then seek a stock exchange quotation for the Group's two million ordinary shares.

Hambros Bank handled the issue and two conditions were imposed. First, the Group's debenture stock must be redeemed and a draft Debenture Stock Redemption and Conversion Scheme was prepared and approved by Sir William McClintock, a Royal Mail Voting Trustee and Coast Lines director. The second condition was that Sir William McClintock would ask the government of the Irish Free State to take a controlling interest in the British and Irish Steam Packet Company, City of Cork Steam Packet Company, Dundalk and Newry Steam Packet Company and Michael Murphy Limited.

Negotiations proceeded with the Ministry of Industry and Commerce in the Irish Free State in 1936 and a new subsidiary company was formed to hold the Group's interests in the State, British and Irish Steam Packet Company (1936) Limited. There is evidence that the services it operated were to be marketed as 'Irish Free State Lines' in expectation of the government's forthcoming controlling interest and Bradshaw's guide carried an advertisement to that effect in 1937.

No reason is now apparent why the negotiations ultimately failed but by April 1936 the directors were imposing conditions. They stipulated that Coast Lines must retain a controlling interest in the British and Irish Steam Packet Company and that any sale of shares must be on a strictly commercial basis and subject to the shareholders' approval. It may well be that the unexpectedly good financial position of the Group, to which the Belfast Steamship Company made no small contribution, was responsible for the Coast Lines Board's more independent attitude. The sale of the British and Irish Steam Packet

Company remained on the agenda on a recurring basis until it was eventually accomplished almost thirty years later.

The committee of the London Stock Exchange gave permission for dealings in the two million Coast Lines ordinary shares on 12 December 1935. The Belfast Steamship Company's own debt to Martins Bank was cleared on 6 February 1936 and the mortgages on the three passenger vessels discharged six days later.

A far-sighted decision was made in 1936 to take a financial interest in Railway Air Services Limited. Postwar politics, unfortunately, deprived the company of reaping any benefit from its investment. An old ally, the Great Western Railway, obtained powers to operate air services in 1929, though it did not exercise them until 1933. The four main line railway companies and Imperial Airways formed Railway Air Services Limited in 1934. The Belfast Steamship Company and Burns and Laird Lines took an interest, comprising 400 shares, in the services from Belfast to Liverpool, Glasgow, London and Stoke-on-Trent for which they paid £17,847. Flights were in de Havilland Rapide aircraft and special motor cars conveyed passengers to Newtownards Aerodrome whence they could fly to Liverpool in 80 minutes at a return fare of £4 10s. Inter-availability of air with sea tickets was offered and air passengers could send their luggage in advance by sea and rail.

Sir Alfred was determined to pursue economies in operation and running the Belfast/ Liverpool service with two ships instead of three was a priority. As far back as 1934 he had requested the Mersey Docks and Harbour Board to consider the provision of a deep water lock entrance in the vicinity of Prince's Dock, allowing vessels of medium size to dock and undock at all times. At last, in 1936, a deputation from the Liverpool Steamship Owners' Association (Coastwise and Short Sea Section) was informed of a scheme for a new deep water entrance to Prince's Dock.

The Board also had plans for a new Canada Dock entrance and for deepening the Sandon entrance and there was a feeling in its Docks and Quays Committee that the works in the North Docks might obviate the need for a new coastwise entrance. The Board's Pilotage

Committee had some slight reservations about leaving such an entrance on a strong flood tide. However, the Board's Finance Committee recommended that the new entrance for Prince's Dock be undertaken provided that outward coastwise town dues waived in 1929 be reimposed on completion of the work.

The Coast Lines marine superintendent saw no problems from a navigational point of view and anticipated no trouble arising whatsoever in docking or undocking, perhaps an unduly optimistic appraisal. In 1937, the Dock Board's engineer was authorised to construct the lock. The war was to delay its completion until 1950. 1936 was a momentous year for the Coast Lines Group in many ways. A minor development in itself but significant if future trends are considered was the provision of hot and cold running water in the third class cabins of the Belfast Steamship Company's vessels, following the example of the new Burns and Laird motor ships. But in the same year came a development which was to affect the company in years to come when an order was placed with Harland & Wolff, Belfast, for two new passenger and cargo motor ships for the Dublin/Liverpool service of the British and Irish Steam Packet Company.

One of these new vessels was destined to spend the greater part of her career in the Belfast Steamship Company's ownership whilst the other would end her short career on charter to the company on the Belfast/Liverpool run. Once again, the Midland Bank provided the finance; £380,000 by way of loan guaranteed by the Ministry for Finance in Northern Ireland, and estimated to be two-thirds of the construction costs. As negotiations were still proceeding about the future of the Dublin company with the Ministry of Industry and Commerce in the Irish Free State, the Northern Ireland Ministry for Finance imposed a condition that the ships were not to be transferred to the ownership of the British and Irish Steam Packet Company until the loans had been repaid.

With 1936 astern, the *Ulster Prince* was off cruising again to Spithead. This time it was for the Royal Naval Review in May 1937, following the coronation of King George VI.

Her passenger complement of 131 comprised a diplomatic selection of notable residents of Belfast and Liverpool and all were guests of Sir Alfred and Lady Read. The Belfast Steamship Company was paid £750 by Coast Lines for the charter of the *Ulster Prince* and it was doubtless for this occasion that a new pianoforte was supplied to the vessel early in 1937 at a cost of £34 15s.

The first of the new Dublin vessels, the *Leinster*, sailed on her maiden voyage on 4 November 1937 from Belfast for Liverpool on charter to the Belfast Steamship Company and under the command of Captain Paisley. Her sister, the *Munster*, had gone down the ways on the previous day.

The reason for the charter was twofold. First of all, new accommodation for the sisters at North Wall, Dublin, was not quite ready. Secondly, but of equal importance, was the decision to send the *Ulster Monarch* to Harland & Wolff for an extensive overhaul. She had arrived in Belfast, without cargo, on the morning of the day that the *Leinster* sailed. An effort was to be made to reduce the vibration level which was the only blemish on passenger comfort in this otherwise splendid ship and her sisters. The treatment included fitting new propellers and encasing the main bearings in rubber. It is possible, incidentally, that the peculiar arrangement of the Burns and Laird passenger motor ships' propellers was prompted by a desire to reduce vibration.

The *Leinster* herself was a much larger version of the *Royal Ulsterman*, was the largest vessel to date in the Coast Lines Group and was a magnificent looking ship despite the startling, almost raffish, external colour scheme adopted. Indeed, she and her sister must surely rank as the finest traditional passenger vessels ever to sail on the Irish Sea. Her well raked stem, stepped bridge front and single pear shaped funnel were complemented by a longer poop than on the *Ulster Monarch* and her consequently slightly shorter after well deck meant that the main mast was stepped on the poop itself.

She could berth 425 saloon and 120 steerage passengers, accommodation that proved to be much in excess of requirements in the winter months on the Dublin service where the passenger business was even more markedly seasonal than on the Belfast run. In service the *Leinster* had the reputation of being slightly slower than the *Ulster Monarch*. She cost £293,693.

The *Leinster*'s entrance saloon was lined with polished hard woods of various textures and grainings, the main note of colour being set by mahogany veneers. The purser's office had a deeper tone of mahogany whilst this was set off by a wide surround of olive ash round the enquiry windows. The restaurant was furnished with bleached and limed oak relieved with contrasting walnut and syca-more. Mirrors and marquetry work decorated the after bulkhead whilst blue curtains, blue leather chairs and gaily patterned flooring completed a room whose main colour scheme otherwise was warm grey.

On 'A' deck above, golden damask curtains set off the theme of pine and painted walls in the lounge. The main staircase to the boat deck emerged not in a lobby but in a generally enlarged smoke room and bar from which a recessed glass screen with doors at the after end gave access to the deck. On the smoke room walls were portraits of the Irish-bred Grand National winners, *Royal Mail* and *Reynoldstown*.

Soon after the ships took up sailings from and to Dublin, woodworm was discovered in the woodwork of some of their cabins. The problem was only cured after a workman was employed for many months boring holes in the woodwork and injecting fumigating che-micals each day that the ships were in Liver-pool.

The *Leinster* and her sister had buff hulls with green boot topping and white upper-works. While the *Leinster* was chartered to the Belfast Steamship Company she flew their flag and wore their funnel colours. In doing so, she introduced a change. Scarlet gave way to crimson and 'Lady Read blue' appeared between the crimson and the black top. This style was to be adopted by the company's motor ships as they underwent their over-hauls early in 1938. It did not become them. Ship lovers can at least be grateful that a favourite colour of Lady Read's, 'dusty pink', did not appear in passenger cabins as mooted. Her parallel fondness for green was the presumed inspiration for cabins being painted in this colour in immediate postwar years, despite green being traditionally a colour of ill omen among seafarers.

The *Leinster* and *Munster* were launched with *Liverpool* on their sterns. Neither, in fact, was ever owned by the B & ISP Company to whom they were both chartered by Coast Lines. Presumably the Ministry for Finance, Northern Ireland, relaxed their conditions to some extent for the *Leinster* changed her port of registry to Dublin in 1938 and the *Munster* was registered in Dublin before entering service.

The *Ulster Monarch* was back on station in February 1938. During her overhaul, the opportunity was taken to combine her smoke room, verandah café and boat deck lobby into one large room on which the staircase from below emerged so that she was practically compatible with the *Leinster* with whom she was to share the Belfast/Liverpool express service in postwar years. The new arrange-ment at least had the merit of allowing the lobby, which was a space measured for tonnage purposes, to be put to revenue earning use. Curiously, her two sisters were never altered and retained the more genteel arrangements.

Rationalisation was still in the air in 1937 when the *Leinster* started. Sir Alfred proposed to amalgamate the Belfast Steamship Com-pany and Burns and Laird Lines and it is possible that the adoption of the saxe blue stripe on the funnels of both companies was connected with this plan. No details of how the amalgamation would have been carried out survive and the next Coast Lines Board meeting was told that the matter had been deferred. No more was heard of it.

Throughout the 1930s the *Lady Leinster*, *Lady Connaught* and *Lady Munster* reappeared from time to time in their birthplace when they were chartered at peak periods for single voyages between Liverpool and Belfast. Usually their regular B&I master was accom-panied by a BSS mate holding the requisite Belfast pilot's licence. Thus on 9 July 1937, the *Lady Munster* arrived at Belfast and sailed again for Liverpool with passengers and motor cars under the command of Captain W J Hughes with J B Wright (a later senior master of the BSS) holding the Belfast pilot-

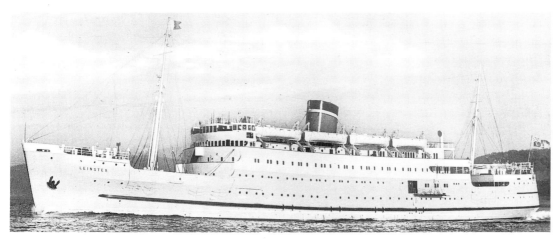

The magnificent *Leinster*, later the *Ulster Prince*, of 1937. (BSS Co)

age certificate.

When the *Leinster* and *Munster* took up duty on the Dublin service the *Lady Munster* and *Lady Connaught* were immediately displaced. Within the higher echelons of Coast Lines, voices were raised urging that they be sold even if only for scrap. Sir Alfred refused to countenance this. Apart from his known regard for both vessels, he felt that war was looming and they would both be needed. His wisdom was more than justified by the sterling work both ships put in during the war years and after.

The *Lady Connaught* became the *Longford* in March 1938 and was laid up in the West Float at Birkenhead. The *Lady Munster* became the *Louth* at the same time and put in some useful work before the outbreak of war. With her funnels painted yellow she made some sailings from Liverpool to Greenock in connection with the Glasgow Empire Exhibition in 1938. In the following year she made one trip at least from Liverpool to Belfast with passengers under the command of Captain J McGugan, of Burns and Laird Lines, arriving on 6 July. She sailed for Glasgow on the following day and during the same month made a number of sailings between Ardrossan and Belfast nineteen years after her last visit to the Ayrshire port.

The *Lady Leinster* was required as the third ship on the Dublin run until the new entrance lock was ready. She was renamed *Lady Connaught* on 4 April 1938. By coincidence she was back in Belfast on the same day as the *Louth*, 6 July 1939, when she came in from Liverpool with passengers and cars under the

command of Captain John Hawthorn, of the B & ISP Company. Sir Alfred put a proposal before the Coast Line's Board in 1938 to acquire the *Lady Connaught* from B & I and convert her into a cruising vessel at a cost of £50,000. Although the proposal was authorised, one suspects this may have been a ploy by the chairman to convince the Board that the *Louth* and *Longford* must be retained, for two months later he had had second thoughts about the conversion as the 'time was not yet opportune'. The *Munster* was back in Belfast later in July in less happy circumstances. On 19 July she had been struck on her starboard side abaft the bridge off the Skerries by the American steamer *West Cohas* belonging to Lykes Brothers. Some eighteen state rooms were wrecked and one passenger, a Franciscan friar, injured. The Moelfre lifeboat was on the scene almost at once but was not needed. Weather conditions were poor with a thick fog and heavy swell but despite this the *Ulster Queen* on her way to Belfast was soon standing by, later joined by the *Ulster Prince* bound for Liverpool. The latter escorted the stricken *Munster* back to the Mersey.

How had the company's cargo fleet fared while their more glamorous consorts caught the limelight of the 1930s? The *Optic* left the company's fleet on 1 February 1929, when she went to A F Henry and McGregor Limited of Leith for £7,702 net of commission. On 16 January 1932, the elderly *Caloric* went to Clayton and Davie, Dunstan-on-Tyne, realising £1,000 minus commission.

The *Dorset Coast* built by James Towers and Company of Bristol in 1924 was transferred to the company on 8 June 1929 from Coast Lines for a price of £12,000. She was renamed *Logic* and became the *Ulster Hero* in August 1935. A larger vessel, the *Lady Kildare*, dating from 1920 when she had been built by Beardmores, was transferred to the company on 31 October 1931 from the B & ISP Company for a consideration of £25,000. She was renamed *Ulster Castle* and spent much of her career on the Derry trade.

Cattle from Belfast had always provided a problem for the company, which the Lawther and Mack interests started to exploit about this time. No cattle could be carried on the passenger vessels because the length of the passage precluded calls at Woodside Stage before disembarking passengers and entering dock. Ingenious scheduling of the cargo vessels was resorted to. The Liverpool/Derry cargo steamer would sail from Liverpool for example on a Monday with general cargo for Belfast and return with cattle on a Tuesday. She would then sail for Derry on the Thursday.

At the end of 1937 the steamer *Scottish Coast* was transferred from Coast Lines for £26,290 becoming the *Ulster Coast*. She had been built by A and J Inglis in 1922 as the *Lurcher* for G and J Burns before transferring to Coast Lines ownership on 1 January 1925. She had made some sailings on the company's account before becoming the *Ulster Coast*.

But other vessels in the Group appeared on the company's cargo berth from time to time. Thus the *Denbigh Coast* of 1937 fitted in sailings between Belfast and Liverpool in the course of her regular Belfast/Manchester and Glasgow triangular sailings. Occasional calls at Belfast on the company's account were made by the *Lairdsdale* (former Sligo Steam Navigation Company's *Sligo*) in the course of her long Liverpool/Sligo voyages. Even the B & I veteran steamer *Wicklow* appeared in 1939, as did the *Glamorgan Coast*, better known until 1 January 1939 as Michael Murphy's *Finola*.

Near disaster was narrowly averted on the *Ulster Prince*'s last 50/- cruise in 1939. Homeward bound on a Sunday evening in early June she approached the high cliffs of Rathlin, off the north coast of Antrim, sounding her whistle so that passengers could see the thousands of sea birds who roosted on Rathlin taking wing. The coastguards shared the birds' alarm and waved energetic warnings to the *Ulster Prince* to keep off. The waves, misunderstood, were enthusiastically returned by passengers including important guests on the bridge until the apparently unheeding *Ulster Prince* struck a rock, listed and slipped off into deeper water. She had to make all speed for Liverpool and supplies of fresh water were restricted for the rest of the cruise. Ten days were spent in Langton No 2 Graving Dock where damage to her plating and fresh water tanks was estimated at £6,000. Her unfortunate, but much respected, master, over anxious to please his passengers, spent some months ashore as a result.

As the decade neared its troubled end, the company was indeed at its high noon of success with ships whose names were household words on both sides of the Irish Sea and which provided accommodation and service second to none afloat in the narrow seas. The express captains were celebrated ashore and afloat, perhaps too much at times ...'which way are we going, steward?'... was the invariable question from one well-known skipper when his morning tea appeared in his cabin. 'You should know, Sir', the braver spirits replied. Perhaps the 1930s were a time of self deception but where else and when could a passenger be carried in palatial comfort, enjoy a single berth state room for 5/-, have a breakfast of porridge, toast, a pot of tea and a pot of jam on white linen with a pink shaded lamp and pink curtains as a background for 1/6d? What matter, either, if one clergyman ate the whole pot of jam for his eighteen pence? Indeed, if you crossed by Heysham first class you were a first class passenger but if you crossed by Liverpool you were *somebody*.

X

To War Again

Days before the British ultimatum to Germany expired on 3 September 1939, the *Ulster Monarch* and her sisters sailed with closed scuttles and saloon windows blacked. Spaces giving access to open decks were bathed in a sinister blue light as if the long shadows of war had already snuffed out all that had been bright and hopeful in the decade that was dying.

Soon to be in action in far off seas, victims of all out war in home waters and under pressure from the insatiable demands of hostilities on every square inch of shipping space in the Irish Sea, some at least of the Belfast Steamship Company's ships emerged, battered but ready, in 1945 to serve their owner's patrons once again. The war did bring, however, a small but important peace of a different kind; the end of the commercial rivalry between the successors of Samuel Lawther and the Mack Brothers and the company. So let us travel through the six long, dark years from 1939, seeing first how the company's ships fared in going about their lawful business in face, at different times, of mine, bullet and bomb. Then let us voyage out into unfamiliar waters with the company's ships on active service, though these two strands from the tangled web of wartime events may coalesce. Finally, we shall see peace achieved with the Mack family, represented in the Belfast, Mersey and Manchester Steamship Company. Or was it?

Maintaining the Service

On the very day that the war commenced, the Donaldson Atlantic liner *Athenia*, outward bound for Montreal having made a call in Belfast Lough, was torpedoed 250 miles to the nor'west of Ireland with the loss of 112 lives by U30 which had mistaken her for an armed merchant cruiser. The war at sea had become an instant reality. Twenty-four hours after the *Athenia* had been sunk, the *Ulster Prince* under the command of Captain W J Arbuckle left Belfast for the last time on Monday, 4 September. She had a full complement of reservists. Deck lights were extinguished and smoking on deck was forbidden. Arriving at Liverpool, the reservists were disembarked and the ship was requisitioned. Some of the older hands were paid off and the *Ulster Prince* set sail that afternoon for Newport, Monmouthshire.

For the next few weeks the express service was maintained by the *Ulster Monarch* and *Ulster Queen* with the *Prince*'s place being taken by the *Louth* which had been running with Burns and Laird in the summer of 1939. She was commanded initially by Captain J Wilson. In the first week of the war Sir Alfred's determination to retain the *Louth* had been vindicated.

The war brought an end to the company's coveted mail contract. It was never to be regained. Working expenses were soon to increase due to an alteration in the course followed in the Irish Sea. Passenger and cargo vessels had been accustomed in peacetime to keep to the east side of the Isle of Man on occasions to avoid an excessive battering from westerly gales. Throughout the war this was to be the normal course with a further diversion which brought the ships down almost to the Skerries, off Anglesey, before turning to head for the Bar. This would lead to an additional 2 hours on the passage time. Immigration control was introduced at the outbreak of war though the issue of travel permits was initially unrestricted.

The *Ulster Monarch* departed finally in early December with Captain Wilson in command. Her replacement was the *Munster* which had spent just over two months laid up in Barrow.

The two handsome Dublin sisters had been

The unlucky *Munster*. (BSS Co)

the subject of a dispute between crews and owners. Prior to the war Irish registered ships had worn the Red Ensign. After the outbreak of war Irish registered merchant vessels flew the tricolour as the Irish Free State was neutral. Crews objected to sailing neutral ships through belligerent waters without protection and demanded danger money. As a result crews went on strike and the *Leinster* arrived at Barrow from Liverpool on the afternoon tide on 4 October, her sister following her three days later. Agreement was reached with the crews and the *Munster* left Barrow on the morning tide of 11 December 1939. She sailed on charter to the Belfast Steamship Company on 15 December from Liverpool. Captain W J Paisley, the company's senior master, was in command and it was he who had, of course, taken her sister ship out on her maiden voyage just over two years before.

When she commenced her charter, the *Munster*'s buff hull had become black and the Irish Tricolour was painted on each side. She was not destined to serve her charterers for long.

On 6 February 1940, the *Munster* sailed from Belfast with 180 passengers on board. At about 6 am the following day, some twenty miles from the Bar Light vessel in a position 53°36′ N by 3°24′ W, there was an explosion which seemed to come from under the port side of the bridge. The fore part of the vessel was lifted into the air and fell back on the water with a thud. Such was the force of the explosion that the compass was thrown out of the binnacle on the bridge, the upper deck hatches fell down below and the radio equipment was destroyed, preventing the transmission of distress calls.

In the accommodation, lights went out and the galley collapsed. In many of the saloon cabins the washbasin, mirror and splash panel were blown off the cabin bulkhead by the force of the explosion. The *Munster* had become the victim of a magnetic mine and sustained a mortal wound in her auxiliary pump room.

Captain Paisley suffered a broken arm and dislocated shoulder and had to be persuaded to leave his ship by Mr Wrigley, the chief officer. Though a sea was running and the *Munster* had taken a list to port and was going down by the head, passengers were got away in the boats safely with surprisingly few injuries reported. Flares burned on the *Munster* were sighted by the collier *Ringwall* at about 7 am, and she picked up the *Munster*'s passengers and crew landing them some five hours later at the Landing Stage.

The unlucky *Munster* took about an hour and a half to sink and she died with dignity within six weeks of her second birthday. There was almost an atmosphere of informality about the way in which the passengers left her. One woman carried a sleeping baby in her arms into a lifeboat and it was still sleeping when she brought it ashore. Another passenger had taken his place in one of the lifeboats when he remembered that he had left a sum of money in his cabin. He boarded the *Munster* again, recovered his money and returned to his lifeboat.

Though no member of the crew lost his or

her life, Captain Paisley, approaching retirement, never really recovered from his injuries or the experience. He did not return to duty and died within a year of the loss of his ship. Mr Wrigley was awarded the OBE for his gallantry.

The *Munster* was the first Irish registered vessel to be sunk in the war but De Valera's government made no protest to the German government. The diplomatic view at the time appears to have been that the *Munster*'s employment between two belligerent ports rendered any diplomatic protest inappropriate.

The company's passenger service went through a bleak period in the winter of 1940. The *Munster* lost and the *Louth* off to join the *Ulster Monarch* carrying troops to France, left the *Ulster Queen* carrying the burden alone and, hazards of war apart, the age-old perils of the sea had still to be reckoned with.

The *Ulster Queen* left Liverpool for Belfast on 27 February with ninety-three passengers and 370 tons of general cargo aboard. She was commanded by Captain W J Arbuckle, who only a few days before had relieved the B & ISP Company's well known master, Captain John Hawthorn. It was a voyage that was to be her last on her owner's account.

On a foggy morning at 2.35 the *Ulster Queen* grounded at Maughold Head, 1.8 miles from Ramsey, Isle of Man, with her bows tight into a sandy bank on the headland between Stack Mooar and Cor Stack. Fortunately, the weather was fair though deteriorating.

Help was at hand in the shape of the LMSR turbine steamer *Duke of Lancaster* on passage from Heysham to Belfast. Could ships but speak, the *Duke* must have sympathised for she herself had grounded on the Manx coast in thick fog near Jurby Head the previous year.

Flares were burned on the *Ulster Queen* to guide the *Duke of Lancaster*'s approach to a position about a mile from her stricken competitor. Passengers had gone to their emergency stations and then been taken across in the ship's lifeboats, which were towed two at a time by the Ramsey lifeboat, to the *Duke of Lancaster*. With one of the *Ulster Queen*'s officers aboard carrying the ship's

The *Ulster Queen*'s crew abandoning ship by breeches buoy, 28 February 1940. (Alfred Dennis)

papers, the Heysham packet proceeded at 8 am for Belfast.

That day, 28 February, a tug arrived from Liverpool and a potentially disastrous attempt was made to tow the *Ulster Queen* off in the teeth of a strong east–nor'east gale swinging the luckless motor ship broadside on to the beach. This time the crew had to abandon ship and were taken off safely by breeches buoy although some had unpleasant immersions in the icy waters as the vessel listed.

Salvage promised to be a difficult and protracted operation as Commander G H Smith of the Liverpool and Glasgow Salvage Association discovered when he arrived on the scene by air soon after the crew had been taken off. Some wondered if she would ever be refloated. Before returning to Liverpool, her purser stood on the cliffs and saw her visibly shake as she was pounded by the merciless seas as if appealing to the watchers, 'Can't you do something to get me off here?'

Only four days before the *Ulster Queen* had stranded, the ss *Lairdscastle*, the former *Lady Limerick* of 1924, had arrived in Belfast from Liverpool under the command of Captain J McGugan at the conclusion of her first voyage from Liverpool. She had been chartered from the associated Burns and Laird Lines to support the *Ulster Queen* on the passenger and cargo service following the loss

The *Ulster Queen* broadside on to the beach between Stack Mooar and Cor Stack, Isle of Man. (Alfred Dennis)

of the *Munster*, now that the *Lairdscastle* herself was on her own. Her sister, the *Lairdsburn*, captained by D McCallum, sailed from Liverpool on 4 March for Belfast. The two sisters were to spend some eight weeks on the Belfast/Liverpool service.

In the meantime, following the loss of the *Munster*, the *Longford* had been brought out of lay-up in Birkenhead and her port of registry changed from Dublin to Liverpool. She sailed on 1 March from Liverpool with Captain J Hawthorn in command and Mr Wrigley, holding a pilot's licence for Belfast, as chief officer. The *Louth* returned from trooping duties and sailed from Liverpool on 5 May. Her master was Captain C G Colebrooke of the Belfast Steamship Company. Finally, on 6 June the *Lady Connaught* sailed from Liverpool for Belfast under the command of Captain R J Gray. The old *Patriotic* had been maintaining the B & ISP Company's Dublin/Liverpool passenger and cargo service in company with the *Innisfallen*, after the departure of the *Leinster* and *Munster* for Barrow. Providence had been on her side on the morning of 7 February 1940, when on her way to Liverpool she had passed over the same position where an hour later the *Munster* had been mined. In the following April on passage to Dublin she had struck a submerged

object with some force in Liverpool Bay and passengers went to emergency stations. The *Lady Connaught* appeared to be undamaged and resumed her voyage but what she had struck remained a mystery to her master, Captain Peter Mullan.

For the moment, though, let us return to the *Ulster Queen*, driven so far up the beach under Maughold Head that high water around her reached a mean height of only 11ft 2in whilst her mean free floating draught was 15ft. At low water she was high and dry and was entirely unsupported for a distance of 180ft from the stem. From the foremost point of support she was resting on an uneven spur of rock and boulders for about 120ft whilst the remaining 46ft of her afterbody was again unsupported. In addition, she had a list to port, her seaward side, of 12 degrees. Abaft the for'ard funnel, her starboard side was impaled on a spur of rock running seawards from the foot of the cliffs and this had caused indentations of the ship's side and the bottom for several feet under the bilge which had been badly buckled with many rivets sheared. However, she had made no water except into Number 4 tank, where there was a visible fracture, and the for'ard tunnel compartment. Following the east-nor'east gale a rough sea was running which was striking her on the port bow causing the serious vibration problems that those ashore had noticed and raising the fear that she would break.

The Liverpool and Glasgow Salvage Association's vessel *Ranger* was soon in attendance and it was clear that much delicate blasting would have to be undertaken of the cliff against which the starboard side of the vessel was bearing and of the spur of rock which was causing the 12 degree list to port. The plan was to take advantage of the maximum spring tides due towards the end of March and, with the aid of the *Ranger* and the tug *Maycock*, heave the *Ulster Queen*'s bows to seawards and then lift the stern by flooding the forepeak and Numbers 1, 2 and 3 double bottom tanks. Blasting of the rocks to seaward of the vessel was also necessary so that a path could be cleared for her as she was 'heaved' into deep water. But first of all she had to be lightened. Her 370 tons of general cargo was offloaded into a shallow draught coaster which could

come alongside at high water. Portable equipment such as the eight lifeboats, anchor cables, buoyant apparatus, wartime bridge protection material and stores as well as fresh water ballast were taken off. Then much anxious thought had to be given to her stability, in view of her metacentric height, following the lightening which had taken place.

Events were reaching a crisis by 25 March when the spring tides would pass their peak. Some movement of the stern to seawards had been achieved but progress, on the whole, had been disappointing. On that day more blasting was undertaken under the starboard bilges, around the stern and under the port quarter. In an ultimate effort to lighten the ship, a search was made in the engine room for any spares or parts which could be dismantled. Heaving was resumed at noon and the forepeak and chain locker were pumped out to correct any tendency of the bow to pin the stern as it was hove seawards.

At 1pm on the twenty-fifth, the *Ulster Queen* floated free to the cheers of the crowd on shore and was taken in tow by the *Ranger* towards Ramsey Bay where at 4pm she was anchored one and a half miles off the North Breakwater lighthouse. Her perishable cargo had been sold on the island but the rest was loaded again on board and she was made fit for the passage to Belfast.

At 5pm on 27 March, the *Ulster Queen* arrived in Belfast a month to the day after leaving Liverpool. Captain John Hawthorn was in command of her once more. There had been no fatalities directly resulting from the stranding though her cook, R Dixon, never recovered from the ordeal and died some months later. The company hoped to have the *Ulster Queen* repaired and back in

service, but it was not to be. Soon after her arrival at Harland & Wolff's yard, she was requisitioned by the Admiralty for conversion into an auxiliary anti-aircraft cruiser.

Without any of their motor ships, the company was able to offer a nightly cargo and passenger service with the *Lady Connaught* (ex-*Patriotic*), *Longford* (ex-*Heroic*) and *Louth* (ex-*Graphic*). Back to old times indeed. The *Lairdsburn* and *Lairdscastle* had been returned to their owners, fine ships but, as with the Dublin service, a little on the slow side for the company's needs. Unfortunately, the *Lairdscastle* was to be lost as the result of a collision between Glasgow and Belfast on the following 4 September.

Early in December 1940, the B & ISP Company's Captain Peter Mullan resumed command of the *Lady Connaught* still on charter to the Belfast Steamship Company. It was to be an eventful month for master and ship.

On 20 December 1940, the *Lady Connaught* was at Prince's Landing Stage with 550 passengers embarked and a general cargo for Belfast. As she was about to cast off, an air raid warning was sounded, all lights were extinguished and Captain Mullan decided to remain alongside. Hundreds of incendiary bombs suddenly fell on the stage and its sheds and a fire started close by the ship which had five or six near misses within an hour, one bomb falling a mere 100ft ahead. It was almost certain that the *Lady Connaught* could now be seen by the enemy so she left the stage and anchored opposite Canning Dock. Her

The *Ulster Queen*, probably soon after commission, 26 July 1941, but prior to the installation of additional armament, searchlights and radar antennæ on the foremast. (Imperial War Museum)

The *Ulster Monarch* photographed after August 1942, when she was converted to a landing ship (infantry). (Merseyside Maritime Museum)

passengers had a trying time, remaining below decks whilst the hull reverberated to the explosions of bombs landing in the river.

After sheds containing cotton at Brunswick Dock had been set on fire, their roofs caved in and the river and the vessels at anchor on it were illuminated by the flames. Captain Mullan accordingly decided that the safest course was to take his ship outside the Bar lightship, a passage fraught with drama and incident. On her way downriver she passed the *Innisfallen*, also outward bound and under the command of the B & ISP Company's commodore master, Captain G C Firth. Soon after she passed, the *Innisfallen* prepared to follow her to sea but was blown up by a mine with the loss of two lives as soon as she started her engines. Passing the Rock lighthouse, the *Lady Connaught* had to sail through a low anti-aircraft barrage and as she reached the Crosby lightship the third officer reported aircraft close by. The *Lady Connaught* was armed with one 4.7in, one Hotchkiss gun and

one Lewis gun and opened fire with the machine guns as two enemy aircraft closed in on either bow at bridge level. One of the aircraft dropped a bomb which exploded close to her quarter. The remainder of the voyage was uneventful.

The *Lady Connaught*'s luck finally ran out a week later when she had sailed from Liverpool for Belfast at 9.30 pm on 26 December, with passengers and 136 tons of general cargo. She passed the Bar light vessel at 11.15 pm. Soon after, Captain Mullan left the bridge and had just sat down for a cup of tea in the saloon when at about midnight in a position 53°37'N by 3°43'W an explosion occurred, apparently amidships under the engine room. The ship lifted, was shaken from stem to stern and there was an immediate smell of explosive.

Mr Watterson, the second officer, on watch at the time reported that there was no flame nor was any water thrown up. Everything on the bridge was enveloped in steam and the ship started to list to starboard and settle by the stern. The chief engineer, Alexander McKay, despite the absence of light in the engine room which was full of steam, made his way to the main starboard discharge valve and shut it off. Had he not done so, the ship could not have been saved. Even so, he had to report 8ft of water in Number 3 hold and 5ft in the engine room and tunnels but thought that the vessel would last a few hours longer. The two dynamos were cracked, all the bearings on the propeller shafts were blown completely off and practically all the connections in the engine room were fractured.

In view of the damage, Captain Mullan decided to abandon ship and the passengers, who had remained calm throughout, and part of the crew, were put into the boats under the supervision of Mr Watterson. An SOS message was sent out and tugs were requested.

Within 20 minutes, the Belfast, Mersey and Manchester Steamship Company's ss *Greypoint*, Captain Charles Peacock, master, arrived on the scene and took on board those in boats. The *Lady Connaught* requested a tow to Liverpool from the *Greypoint* which was inward bound. The *Lady Connaught* was drifting with a 20 degree list to starboard and her degaussing gear out of action. Whilst it was probably an acoustic mine which had maimed her, there were probably plenty of magnetic mines still in the area to which she was now vulnerable.

The *Greypoint* started to tow at 3 am on 27 December but could only manage a speed of one knot. At 5 am the tug *Crosby* arrived and took over the tow which now proceeded at a speed of three knots. Even this tow was not achieved without incident for near the Bar light ship the *Lady Connaught* lost two of her starboard lifeboats in a collision with one of HM trawlers. At 10 am the tug *Vigilant* met her and a salvage pump was put aboard on Number 3 hatch which kept the water in the hold in check but could not prevent it entering the engine room. At 1.30 pm the *Lady Connaught* anchored off Canada Dock. The then 'National Fire Service' put another pump on board and the engine room was cleared of water.

On the following day, Saturday 28 December, the *Lady Connaught*'s stern had been raised enough to enable her to enter Langton Dry Dock where she was safely docked at 2 pm. Her only casualty had been slight injury to one member of her crew but her own miseries were not over for on the following day a fire broke out in the stokehold where Harland & Wolff's men were working with acetylene lamps, but was soon brought under control.

Nothing more was attempted than to make the *Lady Connaught*'s hull watertight. When this was done she was brought round to Prince's Dock. There she lay for many months in a sorry state with her teak deck planking displaced by the force of the explosion. Not surprisingly, she was abandoned to the underwriters as a constructive total loss and her future looked bleak.

The burden of maintaining the express service, such as it was, fell now solely on the *Longford* and *Louth* who could between them offer four sailings per week in each direction.

The eight consecutive nights of aerial bombardment which Liverpool endured in May 1941, gave the long-lived *Louth* a second opportunity to fight off an enemy attack made upon her while on passage from Belfast to Liverpool. This time the foe came from the skies and had none of the chivalrous instincts of Kapitan-Leutnant Hersing a quarter of a century before.

It was on 3 May 1941 that the *Louth* inward bound for Liverpool with Captain D F Owens in command had to drop anchor at the Bar and spend the day there waiting for the channel to be swept before she could move up river to dock. As darkness fell German aircraft flew low over her masts dropping flares. The *Louth* replied energetically with her machine guns trying to bring down aircraft or, at least, extinguish the flares. Though she claimed no hits, she beat off her attackers. Later that night she docked downriver from her usual berth, not far from Huskisson No 2 Branch Dock where the Brocklebank liner *Malakand* was lying half laden with a cargo of explosives consisting of 500lb and 250lb bombs. The port was under intense attack by German bombers and the crew of the *Malakand* had already put out one fire on board caused by incendiary bombs.

The *Louth* had a narrow escape when a bomb struck the shed alongside her which then collapsed on top of her. At 7.30 am on 4 May, the *Malakand* blew up after fire which had spread to her from the dockside sheds finally defeated her crew, none of whom had suffered any casualties. Platings and castings from the *Malakand* were scattered far and wide and one heavy piece of metal made a great rent in the *Louth*'s for'ard funnel. She was able to shift berth to Prince's Dock but on the following night was once more covered with debris when the shed alongside her was struck by a bomb.

On 5 January 1944, the *Louth* commenced sailing from Heysham to Belfast in company with the LMSR steamer *Cambria* from Holyhead, replacing the *Duke of Lancaster* and *Duke of Rothesay* which had been requisitioned for the forthcoming invasion of Europe. The company's vessels, in common with all others in the Group, had been subject to the Liner (Coasting and Short Sea) Requisition Scheme and the *Louth* was loaned to the LMSR under this scheme. The company's own service to Liverpool for passengers was now maintained twice weekly by the *Longford*. The *Louth* sailed for the LMSR until 21 April 1944 when she, too, was called away in preparation for D-Day. She resumed service from Heysham to Belfast on 18 December 1944, and was still so engaged when the war in Europe ended on 9 May 1945 and that in the far East on 14 August 1945.

The *Longford* was taken up for trooping immediately after D-Day and arrived off the beaches for the first time on 15 June 1944. For over a year there was no passenger service to Liverpool; the first time for over ninety years that there had been such a long lapse.

Meanwhile, the *Lady Connaught* continued to lie in Liverpool through the air raids. Despite her abandonment to the underwriters it was unthinkable that any tonnage for which a use could be found should be scrapped or remain idle. Later in 1941, she was taken to Belfast and dry docked. On 12 January 1942, the hulk was bought from the underwriters for £8,500. She was sent to the Liffey Dockyard in Dublin where most of the work was carried out to convert her into a cattle carrier. She then went to Belfast and was placed on risk, after reconstruction, at midnight on 31 May 1943. The total cost for her return to service had been £93,687. Under the command of Captain Mullan she commenced to sail regularly between Belfast and Liverpool. Sailing from Prince's Dock on a Monday, her routine was arduous. After discharging cargo on a Tuesday in Belfast she would load cattle and sail for Birkenhead (Woodside Lairage) where she would arrive between 5 am and 6 am on Wednesday. She would discharge cattle in about 2 hours, return to Belfast, load cattle again and sail on the Wednesday night, repeating this on Thursdays and Fridays. On a Saturday she would go into Prince's Dock and lie until Monday. When the cattle 'season' was over, she would carry cargo only and make two to three trips per week. In January 1944, she went to Barclay, Curle's Yard in Glasgow for conversion into a hospital ship and there we shall leave her for the present.

If final vindication was needed for Sir Alfred Read's decision to retain the *Louth* and *Longford*, it came on 22 July 1945 when war with Japan still raged and the LMSR steamer *Hibernia* sprang a leak at Holyhead and had to be withdrawn from the Dun Laoghaire mail service at once. Her sister, the *Cambria* was despatched from Heysham to take her place, leaving the *Louth* to maintain the Heysham/Belfast mail service alone. She and the *Longford* sailed with grey painted hulls in deference to the state of war which existed although their funnels were painted crimson, blue and black as both were still chartered to the Belfast Steamship Company whose flag they wore. Indeed, the *Longford* retained her war ballast and could carry no cargo, which made her more buoyant in rough seas than the passengers who thronged her decks appreciated. For a period of three months these veterans were the sole direct link between Northern Ireland and England and this at a time when air services as understood nowadays simply did not exist.

So far we have considered only the services offered by composite passenger and cargo ships. The volume of pure cargo business undertaken during the war years was enormous and brought at different times a variety of tonnage on the Belfast/Liverpool route. From 19 August 1940, coastal and short sea liners were requisitioned. The nucleus of the control machinery had been established in 1938 in the principal ports including Belfast where the Belfast Steamship Company's office had been designated as the local control headquarters. From December 1939 there had been a form of voyage licensing but licenses had been issued as a pure formality. In May 1940, there had been sharp increases of freight rates on the Irish Sea of 65 percent. These were to cover such items as War Risk Insurance, higher wages and longer voyages. When tonnage was requisitioned in August it had the effect of transferring the heavy war risk costs for the future to the government.

The *Ulster Hero* left the company's fleet on 23 October 1941, when she was transferred to J and A Gardner of Liverpool for £12,500 minus a commission of £312 10s. Nine months later the company received their first new cargo vessel for twenty-one years when the motor ship *Ulster Duke* was delivered from the Ardrossan Dockyard Company on 8 July 1942. She had one continuous deck and a shelter deck and her diesel engine was placed aft. She cost £60,634.

Ships from other companies in the Group appeared frequently. From Coast Lines itself, the *Hampshire Coast* and the *Carrick Coast* were regular visitors. The *Southern Coast*, which was delivered in June 1943 by the Ardrossan Dockyard Company, spent her early years in company service and was still so engaged for some months after the war's end. Another Coast Lines vessel which spent some time in the company's service was the *Monmouth Coast*. She dated from 1924 when she had been built at Irvine as the *Grania* for Michael Murphy of Dublin and had been transferred to Coast Lines in 1933. On leaving the company's service she was to be the tragic last victim of enemy action suffered by the Group's fleet. She was lost off Sligo on 2 April 1945. Of her ship's company of sixteen only one survived.

An interesting steamer which spent much of the war years between Belfast and Liverpool was the *Western Coast*. She had been built in 1919 by the Caledon Shipbuilding and Engineering Company, Dundee, as the *War Leven*. As her name implies she was a standard ship and was bought by James Moss & Company of Liverpool, in 1919, to become the *Limoges*. Coast Lines bought her on 16 February 1922, for £85,000 when she became the *Western Coast*. She had two decks and a shelter deck and had accommodation provided for a few passengers on the Liverpool/

Well known in Belfast during the war as the *Western Coast*, the *Meath* continued to serve the Belfast Steamship Company for some months after the war. (McRoberts/Merseyside Maritime Museum)

London trade on which she was employed. On 31 March 1941, she was transferred to Burns and Laird Lines without change of name and retaining Liverpool as her port of registry. The intention was to use her on the cattle trade to either Glasgow or Liverpool. In fact, she traded mainly to the latter port with Captain John Hawthorne as her master. In 1945 she became the *Meath*, still owned by Burns and Laird Lines and registered in Liverpool. Her crisis of identity, one of the problems of belonging to an extended family, finally ended when she was transferred on 1 January 1948 to the B & ISP Company, at a valuation of £50,000.

There were other ships 'not of this fold' which sailed for the company during the war years. These included the Southern Railway Company's *Maidstone* and *Whitstable* and the larger *Sheringham* owned by the London and North Eastern Railway.

The *Leeuwarden*, a steamer with a cruiser stern, owned by the General Steam Navigation Company, part of the P&O Group, sailed for the company regularly in the latter years of the war. As she remained on the service for several months after the war she was painted in the company's colours. Perhaps this was a case of coming events casting their shadow.

The *Leeuwarden* returned to her owners and to more familiar waters at the end of 1945. On 25 February 1946, eighteen miles north of Dieppe while on passage to that port from London with a cargo of potatoes, she had the misfortune to be lost by a mine, fortunately without loss of life.

The former Dublin/London liner *Wicklow* sailed frequently on the Belfast/Liverpool service during the war and later ended her days on it. (McRoberts/Merseyside Maritime Museum)

A fast wartime visitor, the *Whitstable*. (The World Ship Society)

As far as is known the first vessel with a welded hull to serve the company was the *Kutno*, built by the Ingalls Shipbuilding Corporation of Pascagoula, Mississippi, in 1944. She was one of five Baltic-type coasters allotted to the Polish flag whilst on time charter to the United States Maritime Administration and transferred by them for use in the United Kingdom in October 1944.

A brief and rare visitor early in 1943 on the company's cargo service was the American-owned *Naushon*, built in 1929 by the Beth-lehem Shipbuilding Corporation and owned by the New England Steamship Company of New Bedford, Massachusetts. There can never have been a stranger ship on the Belfast/Liverpool station. Lacking double bottom ballast tanks, with fine lines, channel bar framing, light scantlings and a high superstructure built of wood from the main deck upwards, she was completely unsuitable for Irish Sea service or for any sea conditions which would subject her to heavy rolling. She and seven similar vessels, all built for trading on the great rivers, estuaries and sounds of the American eastern seaboard, were requisitioned by the United States government ostensibly for use in the European Invasion and, assembled in a convoy dubbed convoy 'Maniac', were brought across the Atlantic in September 1942 by 550 brave volunteer officers and men drawn from the Coast Lines Group. Three of this intrepid but foolhardy armada were sunk by enemy action but the *Naushon*, captained by J J Murray, reached Londonderry safely. The real purpose of the convoy may have been to decoy enemy U-boats from another great munition and troop convoy which set out from the American seaboard at the same time as convoy 'Maniac' left St John's, New Brunswick.

For the record, after serving as a hospital ship under Coast Lines management, the *Naushon* survived the war and returned to American waters to become the *John A Messeck*, registered in New York, in 1947.

Ashore, significant changes were set in train during the war years in the company's stevedoring operations. As far back as 1938, Coast Lines Limited invited the long-established firm of Scruttons Limited to undertake their stevedoring in London. Scruttons were pioneers in the use of mechanical appliances in dock work. Clearly they had impressed Sir Alfred Read, tireless in his search for operating economies. They assumed responsibility for stevedoring facilities for the Coast Lines Group in Liverpool in February 1941, their biggest contract to date. They extended their activities to Belfast in 1944.

The company's livestock business was greatly increased in the war years. Carrying capacity was augmented throughout these years from time to time by the fine modern motor ships *Kilkenny* and *Dundalk* from the B & ISP Company.

Far Away on Active Service

When the *Ulster Prince* arrived at Newport, Monmouthshire, the crew were put on foreign articles. Some 1,500 army personnel were embarked, army stores were loaded and she set sail for Nantes and St Nazaire in company with other vessels and escorted by two destroyers. She returned to Newport alone and unescorted, where she lay for some days before taking her place on cross channel trooping duties.

The German invasion of Norway in April 1940 brought the *Ulster Prince* to more perilous 'fjords' than those to which she carried weekend cruise passengers in prewar years. In company with the *Ulster Monarch* she carried troops, stores, ammunition and petrol. With the *Ulster Monarch*, she evacuated British forces from Narvik early in the month of June. She also carried an army detachment to Thorshaven in the Faroes where the Royal Marines had already landed after the Danish surrender.

After this the *Ulster Prince* had crossed the Bay of Biscay to bring home 250 grateful British nationals who had escaped from France and made their way to Lisbon. She was to win a thankful place soon after this in the hearts of many hundreds of servicemen who had endured the misery and fatigue of the evacuation from St Nazaire to achieve a short-lived security on board the troopship *Lancastria*. On 17 June 1940, the *Lancastria*, laden with 6,000 troops, was bombed and sunk off St Nazaire. Many of the survivors were picked up by the *Ulster Prince* which sailed, packed to the gunwales with nearly 3,000 servicemen, from the 'hell of St Nazaire to the quietness and safety of Falmouth'. Captain J Wilson was her master on this epic occasion.

British forces had occupied Iceland in 1940 and until substantially relieved by the United States in 1941, there was much need for troop and supply vessels to make regular voyages to these inhospitable waters. The *Ulster Prince* which had been commissioned under the White Ensign on 29 August 1940 as a stores carrier, then put in some trips between Iceland and the Clyde, in this period.

From November 1940, the *Ulster Prince* was in the eastern Mediterranean carrying stores between Port Suez, Suda Bay, Piraeus, Alexandria, Sollum and Tobruk. She continued this mission later carrying some of the 35,000 British troops sent from Alexandria to Greece in a brave but futile attempt to stem the German advance into Greece. By mid-April 1941, it became obvious that the troops would have to be evacuated and men were sent from port to port hoping to find ships to take them off. One of these ships was the *Ulster Prince* which had been sent to the port of Argos. Troops hoping to board her at that port had their hopes cruelly dashed for the *Ulster Prince* was at nearby Nauplia where a local pilot had run her ashore during darkness. Her naval captain had refloated her at high water and under the guidance of the pilot made another attempt to come alongside the mole at Nauplia. This time the pilot put her on the rocks. Efforts were made to refloat her again but she was too firmly wedged between two rocks. The captain and crew abandoned her in the ship's pinnace while it was still dark. At dawn the next day, 25 April 1941, the *Ulster Prince* was bombed by Stuka dive bombers who left her a blazing wreck. Several days later one of her would-be passengers passing through the area again saw the *Ulster Prince* burning, with ammunition still exploding inside her hull which now glowed red.

Her crew spent two hazardous days ashore in a bleak and inhospitable countryside, sheltering where possible from the attentions of low-flying German aircraft and their machine guns. They were rescued by a British cruiser and taken to Crete. Her engineer officer, Arthur Luke of Belfast, received the DSC for his gallantry. Chief petty officer, Arthur Cross of Liverpool, her writer in prewar days, received the DSM.

The *Ulster Monarch* carried troops across the channel in the winter of 1940 and went to the Norwegian theatre with the *Ulster Prince* in April 1940. She played a prominent part in the final days of the evacuation. A decision had been taken to capture Narvik from German forces so that the power station, railway and iron ore loading plant could be destroyed. After completion of this operation, stores and troops were embarked at Harstad, north of Narvik in Vaagsfjord. The *Ulster Monarch* was the last merchant ship to leave, which she did on 7 June. On board were some of the survivors of the veteran cruiser *Effingham* and the anti-aircraft cruiser *Curlew* which had both been lost by shipwreck on the Norwegian coast.

Eventually, the *Ulster Monarch* reached the Clyde where she underwent repairs. Fit for service again, she was soon on her way to the western seaboard of France to embark as many men as possible of the BEF, who had made their way there in the wake of the Dunkirk evacuation. From mid-June she was engaged in bringing home troops from Brest.

An embarrassing but necessary task was to repatriate those French troops who had given their allegiance to the Vichy regime in 1940. They were taken to Casablanca where the *Ulster Monarch* was far from popular as feelings ran high after the Oran incident in which an attempt had been made by British forces to immobilise units of the French Navy to prevent them from falling into German hands. No serious incident occurred and after disembarking those who had opted out of the war, the *Ulster Monarch* sailed for Gibraltar to continue her part in winning the war. Next stop was Madeira where she landed civilian evacuees from Gibraltar, the rest of whom were brought home to the United Kingdom. She took part in the occupation of Iceland and the Faroe Islands and was soon landing troops in narrow and inhospitable Icelandic fjords.

In October 1940, the MV *Ulster Monarch* became HMS *Ulster Monarch* when she hoisted the white ensign. Designated as a special duty vessel, she joined the Combined Operations Fleet under the command of Admiral Sir Roger Keyes. At this stage of the war minor landing craft were not available and there was a need for ships which could berth alongside an enemy quay and disembark troops. She so impressed Sir Roger Keyes by her manoeuvrability and accommodation and by the ease with which she could disembark troops as though they were her peacetime passengers that she was followed into his command by other vessels of similar type such as her 'cousin', the Burns and Laird *Royal Scotsman*.

Much rapid and intensive training with the newly formed Commando squadrons took place. Recent research has shown that the Admiralty had the *Ulster Monarch* and similar ships in mind for an operation which fortunately was never needed. This would have involved the occupation of the Spanish Canary Islands to secure the harbour of Puerto de la Luz should Gibraltar be lost. Diplomacy throughout 1941 prevented Gibraltar from falling into enemy hands.

In March 1942, HMS *Ulster Monarch* was allocated to Western Approaches Command and spent some time trooping to Iceland. Next she was back in Gibraltar carrying Hausa troops of the West African Frontier Force to such ports as Bathurst, Freetown, Takoradi and Lagos. Finally, she left Freetown for the Azores where she took on fuel and fresh water. It was nature and not the enemy which made this a voyage never to be forgotten. A terrific Atlantic storm had her rolling to 45 degrees, submerging her bulwark rails, smashing two ports on 'C' deck, far too close to the waterline for comfort and setting twenty large drums of oil adrift on deck. Worse was to come. Water entered the oil fuel and the engines stopped. Those on board believed she was finished. Miraculously, it seemed, she came round into the wind, a characteristic of the *Monarch* and her sisters, and hove to until her engines were restarted.

Reaching Liverpool safely, the *Ulster Monarch* underwent repairs and modifications, being designated an LSI(H) from August 1942.

With assault craft in place of her lifeboats, she commenced amphibious manoeuvres with British Commandos and their American counterpart, the Rangers. With the latter embarked, she sailed in convoy from the Clyde in September 1942, for the North African landings. She was the first ship to land much needed supplies at Arzeu.

On the day after the landing, the Canadian Pacific liner *Duchess of Bedford* (renamed *Empress of France* after the war) ran ashore in an increasingly heavy swell and her position soon became perilous. She was brought to safety by the combined efforts of the *Ulster Monarch* and the *Royal Scotsman* who acted as powerful tugs.

Her next mission took the *Ulster Monarch* to Oran where she picked up survivors from HMS *Walmer* and HMS *Hartland*. These ships had crashed the boom guarding the harbour under point-blank fire and had been sunk with heavy loss of life. The survivors from this operation, to deny the enemy the use of French naval units, had been badly treated by the French who had taken them prisoner. They were taken to Gibraltar.

The *Ulster Monarch* left Gibraltar on 14 November 1942, bound for the Clyde in convoy and destined for an adventurous passage. In the early hours of the fifteenth she made an emergency turn to starboard which put the aircraft carrier *Avenger* directly ahead of her. A torpedo struck the *Avenger* in her petrol storage tanks and she sank in a sheet of flame with the loss of 613 officers and ratings. The *Ulster Monarch* stopped engines but went over the wreck of the *Avenger* as damage was discovered to her bottom plates. Heart-breakingly, she had to ignore cries for help from survivors in the water and sail on. Later on the same day the 11,000 ton P&O managed transport *Ettrick* was also torpedoed close to the *Ulster Monarch* and later sank.

January 1943 found the *Ulster Monarch* in 'Force W' for combined operations. After a visit from Lord Louis Mountbatten, as he then was, she set off on a voyage which would have astonished her designers. Calling at Gibraltar and Freetown, Cape Town, Durban, Mombasa and Aden, she eventually reached Suez. There she embarked the First Special Air Service Regiment under the command of the well known, but controversial, Ulsterman, Colonel Paddy Mayne DSO and Bars. They trained with her and landed on one occasion in the gulf of Aquaba in the shadow of Mount Sinai.

Back to Suez she came, to prepare for the invasion of Sicily in July 1943. Before the canal transit General Montgomery visited the ship to address the SAS troops on board and the ship's company. He described her as the 'spearhead', and so she was. Despite the bad weather, she put her troops ashore off Syracuse and closed the beach to act as control, receiving on board the dead and wounded, and subjected throughout to heavy air attack.

Meanwhile, the enemy had retaken the port and town of Augusta, to the north of Syracuse, and a seaward assault to drive them out again was put in train. The *Ulster Monarch* re-embarked her SAS troops and steamed north. Under covering fire from her light armament, her craft were lowered and the enemy vanquished. Allied HQ sent her a signal which was received with pride, 'Augusta taken by troops from *Ulster Monarch*'.

Her career almost came to a fiery end when she was carrying troops and supplies on the triangular Sicily, Malta and North African ports run. Returning from Bone to Tripoli, the *Ulster Monarch* was attacked by aircraft off Cape Bon on the night of 18 August 1943. One bomb penetrated her poop where there was a gun platform and ammunition and the ship's magazine just a thin steel deck away. Four hundred gallons of petrol were set ablaze and ammunition began to explode and fly in all directions as heroic efforts were made to put the fire out. These were successful but not before two ratings were killed, the first lieutenant, later Captain T F Wrigley OBE, was seriously injured and three other ratings were wounded.

The fire put the *Ulster Monarch*'s steering gear out of action, but using her engines to steer with she was able to proceed at 15 knots. An examination of the steam-filled magazine showed that three thermometers had burst with the heat. How near calamity had been! Repairs at Tripoli took a fortnight and the *Monarch* was fighting fit once more in early September 1943 to land the first assault wave at Salerno in the Allied invasion of Italy. Some more trooping was accomplished and it was time to return to the United Kingdom for a thorough refit.

The *Ulster Monarch* steamed more than 100,000 miles on war service and carried over 200,000 men. Almost to the end of hostilities, she was in the fray. On 6 June 1944, she was off Courseulles with the first D-Day assault courses. Her landing craft loaded with troops reached the beaches safely save for two, one of which was lost and one badly damaged by a mine. She ended her active service on the cross channel trooping shuttle from Tilbury to Ostend.

The only survivor of the prewar trio, the

Ulster Monarch returned to Belfast on 10 September 1945, minus her main mast, battered, but still recognisable as the pioneer celebrity of sixteen years before. It was to be eleven months before she would leave Belfast again to earn money for her owners.

We had left the *Ulster Queen* under requisition in Belfast at the end of March 1940. Turning her into a cruiser involved drastic alterations, including the removal of her boat deck, one funnel and the fitting of armour plating over her hull.

By the summer of 1941, her transformation was complete. Bristling with six 4in guns, arranged in three twin turrets, two for'ard and one aft, two four-barrelled pom-poms, two quadruple 0.5in machine guns and four single Oerlikons, her crew considered her to be one of the best fighting ships afloat. In addition, she was fitted with torpedo tubes on each side and a depth charge chute aft.

She was commissioned on 26 July 1941 at Belfast. Her first commanding officer was Captain Donal Scott McGrath RN, whose desire to meet and engage the enemy was such that he was nicknamed 'Dangerous Dan' by the ship's company. It was he who designed the crest for the ship, consisting of a regal lady surmounting an Irish harp with the side wood divided into sections depicting the ship's armament. Unfortunately, this was an 'unofficial' crest and it was not taken ashore and placed in store when the *Ulster Queen* finally paid off.

She ran her sea trails in the Clyde and guns were tested off Ailsa Craig. Some indication of her likely theatre of operations was given to the ship's company when they were kitted out with 'Arctic gear', duffle coats, woollen head coverings, wellingtons, etc.

The *Ulster Queen* was regarded as a very successful conversion. With so much top hamper removed, she had no stability problem and was a good sea boat with that same manoeuvrability which had so impressed Admiral Sir Roger Keyes in the *Ulster Monarch*. Armament apart, she was also equipped with twin directors, plus long-range air warning radar and gunnery ranging radar. Her immediate past gave her a great advantage for her holds could be used for magazines and it was this great capacity which made her such a valuable unit in the Russian convoys in which she was so soon to play a dramatic part.

If she had a fault, it was in the positioning of the Asdic dome which tended to rip off in heavy seas or when she carried out depth charge attacks. She went through three in her first commission. In any event, the Lords Commissioners were sufficiently pleased with what her builders had done to her that they purchased her outright from the company on 20 September 1941.

She was soon to see action for, in November 1941, she escorted two convoys and was attacked by enemy aircraft on both occasions. In the following December she escorted out into the Atlantic the last convoy to sail for Singapore before it succumbed to Japanese forces.

In a series of dramas played out in Arctic waters through 1942, the *Ulster Queen* had adventures no less stirring than those of the *Ulster Monarch*. She sailed in April as part of a convoy escort, arriving at Murmansk in May without damage. On the voyage she experienced repeated attacks from submarines and aircraft. The northern Russian ports were the only channels of supply to Russia, with the limited exception of Vladivostok which was closed as soon as Japan entered the war. Neither Murmansk nor Archangel were properly equipped to receive military cargo. However, before she sailed for home the *Ulster Queen* distinguished herself by shooting down a German aircraft. She made a safe landfall at Belfast, where she was based, to receive much needed maintenance from her builders.

Captain McGrath was relieved by Captain Charles Keith Adam RN, and under his command the *Ulster Queen* set off once more for Russia as one of the escorts of Convoy PQ 18. The convoy sailed on 2 September 1942 from Lock Ewe, making first for the Denmark Strait and then for Archangel. The German Army had got uncomfortably close to Murmansk and the Russians could no longer use it. On the voyage submarines attacked on 13 September and the onslaught continued when a force of forty bombers attacked immediately afterwards. The two starboard columns of the convoy were wiped out and eight ships sunk. After the bombers came torpedo-carrying aircraft which were driven off by intense fire from the escorts. For two days there were repeated air attacks with bomb and torpedo on the hapless merchant ships and the *Ulster Queen* had some near misses. At last the battle-weary ships entered the port of Archangel on 21 September save for three which had run aground outside the harbour. These had to be defended by the *Ulster Queen* from repeated attacks by German aircraft which were successfully beaten off. The ships were safely refloated and the *Ulster Queen* was able to berth. She was there until November and during her stay there was no rest from air attack and her guns joined in the anti-aircraft barrage. A band had been formed from the ship's company and whilst in Archangel they frequently played ashore. Before she left Archangel on 17 November, the ice had closed in sufficiently for people to walk around the ship and when she steamed out eventually, she was clearing a passage through the ice, not only for herself but for following merchantmen. She returned to Belfast after a voyage characterised by severe Arctic weather. On arrival she paid off and went into dockyard hands. She had come back full of honours, credited with the destruction of six Ju 88 aircraft and six Heinkel 111s, whilst twenty-seven out of forty merchant ships that sailed in PQ 18 had reached their destination. She could be proud. She had received an illuminated address from the Russian authorities at Archangel in token of the efforts which her band had made to entertain those ashore. Her captain received a DSO, but sadly had to leave her on the grounds of ill health. Engineer Commander M W Mann RNR of Belfast, her peacetime chief engineer, was awarded the Russian Medal of Valour.

Some thought seems to have been given to improving her Arctic capabilities for the intense cold had caused great hardship to her crew in the midst of perils from the enemy. Even in the engine room duffle coats had been worn. Instead there was a change of plan. A need had been identified for radar-fitted escort vessels to call fighters up and direct them on to their targets, ie attacking enemy aircraft. At first RAF Fighter Command had considered the idea impracticable but by June 1941, agreement had been reached on the principles involved in co-ordinating the anti-aircraft activities of the two services. The *Ulster Queen* was chosen for conversion to a fighter direction ship and in June 1943 was commissioned for service in the Mediterranean. In the following July she took part in the Sicilian landings. On 29 August, whilst voyaging from Gibraltar to Oran, she had the unpleasant distinction of being the first vessel to be attacked by a rocket projectile whose approach was detected neither visually, nor on radar. The explosion, some 10 ft from her starboard side, temporarily disabled her but there were no casualties and she was able to restart her engines and reach Gibraltar safely.

From September 1943 to January 1944, the *Ulster Queen* was present at the Salerno and Anzio landings and claimed ten enemy aircraft. She had a brief refit in the United Kingdom and was in the Mediterranean by July of 1944 to take part in the invasion of southern France in the following month.

From September to October a sophisticated offensive role in fighter direction using night Beaufighters, was played out in the Aegean. Enemy transport aircraft flying between Crete and Athens were her targets and the fighter aircraft under her control destroyed nineteen enemy aircraft.

Almost on the eve of VE Day, after a refit at Cardiff the *Ulster Queen* sailed out to the Far East where she served again as a fighter direction ship. She made her way to Colombo and embarked at Trincomalee the Commander-in-Chief, East Indies, Admiral Sir Arthur J Power KCB, CVO and his staff. Wearing an Admiral's flag, she was the first British ship to sail into Rangoon after the Japanese left. Her career as a flagship ended after fourteen days. Next she visited Madras and from there sailed to Port Swettenham where she acted as naval control ship. She left Bombay for home on 1 October 1945, and paid off at Devonport from which port she had been manned throughout her service. She had steamed an estimated 177,000 miles in just over four years.

It would have been a happy climax to her amazing career as warship if she could have returned to her native waters. Unfortunately, this was not to be. Quite apart from the drastic alterations which had been made, the 4in armour plating which covered her sides had set up an electrolytic action which corroded her plates, making them wafer thin in places and rendering her useless for peacetime service. Her doom was quickly sealed for she was paid off into reserve and disposed of on 1 April 1946, nine days after her return from the Far East, to the General Steam Navigation Company. The latter arranged for her ultimate disposal to Belgian shipbreakers two years later.

Throughout the winter of 1940 the fine motor ship *Leinster*, still owned by Coast Lines Limited, on bare boat charter to the B & ISP Company and registered in Dublin, had languished in Barrow where she had been since 4 October 1939. She slipped out of that port on the morning tide of 3 April 1940. She was re-registered in Liverpool and underwent conversion to a hospital ship. Later in the year she sailed from Liverpool with Captain J Wilson, late of the *Ulster Prince*, in command. He was to walk her bridge for over thirteen years in war and peace. Her destination was Iceland and she was based for over six months at Akureyri in the north of the island.

For part of her time in the Icelandic winter she was frozen in and her ship's company was relieved to return to Liverpool where she was refitted as a troop transport even though this meant visiting Iceland again. In July 1941, she was included in 'Operation Substance', a hazardous mission to supply Malta, then under virtual siege from the west. She sailed on 11 July from the Clyde in a convoy under the command of Vice-Admiral Sir James Somerville. On board were 1,000 troops including vital maintenance crews for the RAF squadrons based in Malta. The convoy spent two days in Gibraltar and sailed on 21 July, but the *Leinster* was not destined to reach the beleagured island for soon after sailing she ran ashore sustaining damage which put her into dock in Gibraltar.

In November of the following year, 1942, she was part of a north bound convoy from Gibraltar in company with the Union Castle liner *Warwick Castle* when the latter was torpedoed and sunk by a German submarine.

For four hours the *Leinster* stood by picking up survivors in perilous waters through which the *Ulster Monarch* also sailed one day later when the *Avenger* was sunk ahead of her.

In May 1943 the *Leinster* underwent yet another conversion, this time into a hospital carrier. She sailed for the Mediterranean to take part in the North African and Italian campaigns. She was on hand at Salerno to pick up survivors from the hospital ship *Newfoundland* and was attacked by German aircraft off Anzio when the former GWR steamer *St David* was bombed and sunk. On that occasion she again picked up survivors. She was at Bari when an ammunition store exploded and once more was to the fore succouring the wounded.

The rest of the *Leinster*'s 'war' was spent in Adriatic waters. Before she came home, Captain Wilson was the proud recipient of a message from Field Marshal Alexander. It read 'The wounded and the sick from the battlefields of Italy owe much to the staffs of the ship which carried a large proportion of them in comfort and safety. The part you played in the Sicily landing, the Anzio beach head, at Ancona and Bari, has been most praiseworthy'.

The *Leinster* came home with distinction. Captain Wilson was awarded an OBE and a Lloyd's War Medal; another OBE, one MBE and three BEMs were recorded on an oak memorial plaque which the ship carried for the rest of her postwar career on the Irish Sea. Before she could be refitted for peacetime service those who worked in her at Queen's Island toiled long and hard to cleanse her accommodation from the still pervading smell of blood. She belongs to this chapter because her future fortunes were bound up with the Belfast Steamship Company and we shall meet her again.

The *Lady Connaught*, reconstructed as a hospital carrier by Barclay Curle, served in the English Channel after D-Day. She would lie off the Normandy beaches, embark and carry the wounded to Southampton, turn around within several hours and return to the beaches on a virtually nonstop basis. Her medical and nursing staff were entirely American and Negro stretcher bearers carried the wounded ashore. Her crew received little relaxation although the British Sailors' Society at Southampton did their best with short film shows on board. On 18 June 1945, Captain John Hawthorn brought the *Lady Connaught* back to Belfast where for the second time in five years she faced an uncertain future.

The company's old *Magic*, now the *Killarney*, was not too aged to see active service. In September 1939, the 'Shining brass work and whitened decks gave way to battleship grey' and she was on war service once more. In May 1940, under the command of Captain R Hughes, she received orders to proceed to assist in the rescue of the army from Dunkirk. Entering a port with smoke rising from blazing oil dumps and under constant attack by German aircraft, she tied up alongside the breakwater. Her passage home was enlivened by fire from German artillery in Graveline. She escaped serious ill effects as a result of evasive tactics and a smoke screen. Unfortunately, one shell did hit the after end of the boat deck, killing eight and wounding thirty. She reached Dover safely and was back for another round of ferrying exhausted troops from the field of battle to safety in England. For the rest of the war she was used as a depot and accommodation ship at Rosyth and was towed back to Liverpool's Trafalgar Dock early in 1946.

The *Longford* and the *Louth* both spent time in the Channel at the D-Day landings, as we have already noted. The *Longford* was employed finally on the Tilbury to Ostend trooping 'shuttle'.

A Reconciliation

In the midst of conflict there was one item of peace to record for 1944. Negotiations were successfully concluded for the purchase by Coast Lines Limited of the Belfast Mersey and Manchester Steamship Company which was the final form of the competition mounted first outside the conference and then within it by Samuel Lawther and the Mack brothers. The purchase price was agreed at £200,000.

Following Samuel Lawther's retirement in 1909, the Belfast and Mersey and Belfast and Manchester Companies, now within the conference, plodded unspectacularly across the

The reconstructed *Lady Connaught* leaves Dieppe. She has lost her dummy second funnel while round ports have replaced her rectangular saloon windows and there are solid bulwards on her foredeck in place of rails. (McRoberts/Merseyside Martime Museum)

Irish Sea. They built up a steady clientele. Sisal and hemp came into Belfast in their ships and went out again as finished products from the well-known Belfast Ropeworks Company. Messrs Davidson's Sirocco Engineering Works in Belfast sent their famed tea-making machinery on the first stages of its journey to all parts of the world in the holds of the *Fleswick* and *Manchester*. Then on the other side of the Irish Sea and up the Ship Canal, Isaac and James Mack had many business contacts, especially in the unbleached cloth trade in Manchester.

From 1929 the combined firms experienced a renaissance. At Liverpool, Charles G Mack (son of Isaac) and Harold B Mack (son of James) had entered the business whilst there was new blood in Belfast in the shape of L R Briggs who had married Stanley Lawther's daughter and become a partner in S Lawther and Sons.

The end of the old order was finally signalled in 1932 when Isaac Mack died full of years and achievements in temperance, the African Missions and Bootle Corporation on which he had served for forty-five years as councillor, alderman and mayor.

Meanwhile, the younger generation planned an onslaught on the cattle trade. First of all, the Belfast and Mersey and Belfast and Manchester Companies were combined in 1929 into the Belfast, Mersey and Manchester Steamship Company. The carriage of cattle started in February 1930. In preparation for this, the steamer *Saltees* had been bought from the Clyde Shipping Company in 1929 to become the *Stormont*. She was able to carry 220 head of cattle and was registered in Belfast in the name of the Belfast, Mersey and Manchester Steamship Company. The new dynamism in S Lawther & Company was sufficient to entice a young man called Arthur Moore from the Maysfield Goods Depot of the Great Northern Railway (Ireland). Experienced in the shipping of cattle, he was to play a key role in the growing challenge which the Belfast, Mersey and Manchester Company posed to the Belfast Steamship Company in the decade of the 1930s. He was later to become managing director of the Belfast, Mersey and Manchester Company.

The shipping of cattle was a weakness in the Belfast Steamship Company's traffic arrangements. Because of the length of the passage to Liverpool, it was not possible to carry cattle in the express steamers as they had no time to call at Woodside Lairage before going to the stage or docking. We have already alluded to the use of the Londonderry steamer for the cattle trade but perhaps this was not really sufficient provision. It was as if Samuel Lawther's words were ringing out again forty years on ... 'I see the opening, I'm going to take advantage of it and what is more, I mean to make it a success ...'. It must be said, however, that at boardroom level, once again, the running was made by the Macks in Liverpool.

In 1933, the Mersey Company bought the Clyde Shipping Company's *Rathlin* which became the *Greypoint*. The *Manchester* could now be disposed of for scrap. In 1936 the Clyde Shipping Company's *Pladda* was acquired and became the *Mountstewart*. The *Fleswick* was then sold for further trading.

Basking in the publicity of the Prince of Wales' passage in the *Ulster Prince* to open Parliament buildings at Stormont on 16 November 1932, the Belfast Steamship Company could hardly have been pleased at the sight of a saucy but prominent advertisement inserted in the *Commemorative Supplement* issued by the *Belfast News Letter* for that day. 'Fast Cargo Service', 'Livestock carried', proclaimed the Mersey Company, drawing the Loyal public's attention to its three sailings per week to Liverpool and Manchester from that very Donegall Quay on which Royalty had just stepped.

Little wonder that the Belfast, Mersey and Manchester Company was watched closely and jealously from round the corner on Donegall Quay. So much so that a very senior official of the Belfast Steamship Company, looking out of his office window towards the Mersey Company's berth, saw what looked like white smoke rising from between the masts of the *Stormont*. Racing into a surprised main office, with perhaps a little pleasure mixed with excitement, he is reported to have shouted, 'The Mersey boat is on fire, why don't they let us run the company?'. In fact, both his statement and wish were doomed to disappointment for nothing more lethal had occurred on board the *Stormont* than a spillage of bleaching powder in her hold which became wet and gave off a white vapour. Far from letting anyone else run their business, the Mersey company later stiffened the competition by adding Bromborough Dock to their Mersey loading berths and Lever Brothers to their customers. During the war years Northern Ireland's margarine ration arrived on a Monday morning in Belfast in the hold of a Mersey steamer.

Sir Alfred Read had been conducting negotiations during 1938 with Fisher Renwick, Bristol Steam Navigation and Palgrave Murphy. Only the first named were to join the Group as a result. But a measure of Sir Alfred's concern at the competition from the Mersey Company was his report to the Board that of all negotiations those with the Belfast, Mersey and Manchester Steamship Company were first in priority.

Nothing more was heard of negotiations until 1944, when these were resumed energetically between Sir Alfred Read and Captain Nutting on behalf of Coast Lines and Harold Mack on behalf of the Mersey company.

The terms were that the Belfast, Mersey and Manchester Company was to remain independent but its trade incorporated with that of the Belfast Steamship Company. In recognition of this, Harold Mack and L R Briggs were to join the Board of the Belfast Steamship Company. In fact, Mr Briggs

Another view of the *Lady Connaught* leaving port. (Imperial War Museum)

decided to emigrate to Rhodesia but Harold Mack did join the board. Though there was rationalisation, expecially where the Manchester trade was concerned, the Belfast, Mersey and Manchester Company, S Lawther & Sons and J J Mack and Sons had an astonishing resilience and many years were to pass before the flags and funnels of the Mersey Company vanished from the Irish Sea.

In fact it would not be an exaggeration to say that Harold Mack continued to be somewhat of a thorn in the flesh for the Belfast Steamship Company, albeit as a member of the 'family', for some time.

The crowded and trying years of war brought a kaleidoscope of events to the company which it is impossible to chronicle in full. For example, Atlantic convoys were a regular event when, battered by winter weather, they brought ships into Belfast with their stow broken down. Their urgently needed cargo had to be restowed and the ships sent on their way to Liverpool or, sometimes, their cargo was reloaded on ships owned or chartered by, or allocated to, the company. In all this, the war years have concentrated for the most part on the ships and the men who sailed them. But ashore, Sir Alfred Read emerged from the war in his seventy-fifth year, tired and debilitated from the bombing of London which caused frequent moves of the Coast Lines headquarters to places of greater safety.

During the war years, government, as it always does when it has a need of the merchant marine, led the nation in a sentimental invocation of the British sea tradition which had played the major part in feeding and supplying Britain and defeating the enemy. Afterwards, this would all be forgotten. The coming peace would be rugged in a different way from the war but it would be no less daunting.

XI

A Daunting Peace

There was a widespread belief that shipowners made a fortune from the war. Like individuals here and there, some may indeed have done so but it was not true for the Coast Lines Group. For example, they were only able to declare a dividend of 4 percent minus tax for 1943. Men and ships had given of their best during the war but so, in all fairness, had the shipowners. Government terms for requisitioned ships had been far from satisfactory. Worse still, owners were left to find the difference themselves between 1939 prices and postwar replacement prices. This was particularly keenly felt by the Belfast Steamship Company with only one surviving express steamer from prewar days. To replace the *Ulster Prince* was going to take an outlay of £500,000 in 1946, almost twice her prewar cost. The company received from government a mere £260,000 for her loss.

The urgent task of restoring cargo and passenger services to prewar standards and improving on them was a far more difficult task for the company in 1945 than that which it faced in 1918.

Work would shortly resume on the new Waterloo Entrance lock at Liverpool which would enable the express passenger service to be operated by two ships instead of three. But the completion was several years away at least. The most economical solution to the problem facing the company was a second vessel to sail opposite the *Ulster Monarch* and the continued use of older tonnage until the Waterloo Entrance was ready. This was what was done.

The 'new' vessel was to hand in the *Leinster*, already well known to us and no stranger to the Belfast/Liverpool service. She had returned to Belfast for refit in June 1945. It is no reflection on this fine vessel to say that she and her sister had not proved entirely suitable

to the requirements of the Dublin/Liverpool trade during their brief prewar service. The provision for passengers had been too generous on a route where carryings were marked by seasonal variations even more pronounced than from and to Belfast. They both lacked facilities for the carriage of cattle which was such an important constituent of the British and Irish Steam Packet Company's business to the Mersey. A wise decision was taken by the Coast Lines Board to transfer the *Leinster* to the Belfast Steamship Company and re-equip the B & ISP Company's passenger service with new composite ships carrying cattle as well as cargo and a smaller number of saloon passengers. They were to be owned and registered in Dublin from the outset, unlike their predecessors.

So it was that on 27 February 1946, the *Leinster* passed from the ownership of Coast Lines Limited to that of the Belfast Steamship Company for a consideration of £300,000. For the second time in her career Liverpool was wiped off her stern and was replaced, this time, by Belfast while at the same time she assumed the name of *Ulster Prince*.

The 'new' ship was compatible with the *Ulster Monarch* with whom she was to enjoy a partnership of over twenty years. Differences there were: externally, the *Ulster Prince* had 3ft more beam and 20ft more length, a raked stem, a stepped bridge front, a longer poop, rectangular ports on 'A' deck and a single, pear shaped funnel which could be floodlit at night. Internally her decor was brighter and her suite rooms were on the boat deck for'ard of the smoke room. Reputedly a little slower than her older consort, she was undoubtedly the better sea boat of the two and certainly the finest ship the company ever owned.

She would have to work hard to earn her keep for her new owners. Harbour and light dues were based on a ship's net tonnage and

The *Ulster Prince* going astern in the Victoria Channel, approaches Donegall Quay in 1946 or 1947. (Captain W Grogan)

Captain Joseph Wilson, OBE. (PRO (NI)/BSS Co)

that figure for the *Ulster Prince* included spacious lounges, smoke room, restaurant and a high proportion of single berth cabins. From July to September 47 percent of the annual total of passengers was carried on the Belfast/Liverpool service, leaving, in effect, 75 percent of the passenger accommodation unused for the rest of the year. Her capacious holds had been designed with prewar dockers' working hours in mind. Postwar conditions at Belfast, in particular, with shorter hours meant that it would be difficult to utilise to the full her cargo capacity.

It was entirely appropriate that the *Ulster Prince*'s wartime master, Captain Joseph Wilson OBE, should command her in peacetime. Modest and reticent to a fault, few of his passengers on 28 February 1946, when the *Ulster Prince* left Belfast for the first time in her new guise, would have known how many hundreds of men and women from the *Lancastria*, *Warwick Castle* and *St David* owed their lives to 'Captain Joe'.

Passenger services had operated nightly from 18 December 1945, when the *Louth* had joined the *Longford* on the express service. Both the veterans had worked hard, rarely docking in Liverpool, and now with the advent of the *Ulster Prince* the *Longford* could be withdrawn for a thorough refit in Liverpool prior to reopening her owners' Dublin/Liverpool passenger service. Sailings were now adjusted to four nights per week in each direction with the *Ulster Prince* sailing on Mondays and Thursdays from Belfast and Wednesdays and Saturdays from Liverpool

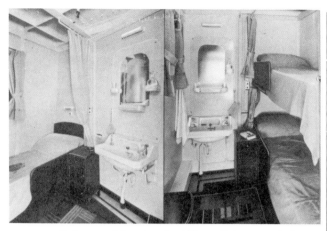

Saloon cabins in the *Ulster Prince* ex-*Leinster*. (BSS Co)

The smoke room of the *Ulster Prince* ex-*Leinster* showing saloon staircase looking aft. (BSS Co)

and the *Louth* sailing on Tuesdays and Fridays from Belfast and Mondays and Thursdays from Liverpool. Captain R J Gray, who had reopened the passenger service in the *Longford* on 18 June 1945, was in command of the *Louth*. The latter vessel had her hull painted black by this time but it would be some months before her upperworks glistened white again.

Repeated references to financial matters can be tedious but without them the postwar pattern of operation can hardly be appreciated. The world into which the *Ulster Prince* thrust her elegant stem on 28 February 1946 was hardly encouraging. In that year, compared with 1938, there had been an overall increase of 112 percent in working costs.

Loading and discharging expenses were nearly three times what they had been in 1938 and, to make matters worse, turnrounds at the ports had slowed to such an extent that five vessels were needed in 1946 where three sufficed in 1938.

A more balanced and economical express service would be possible by getting the *Ulster Monarch* refitted as soon as possible. Hand bills offering a nightly service by the two motor ships from 1 August 1946 were prepared but proved too optimistic. In the event the *Ulster Monarch* made her first sailing after her refit on 9 August when she left Belfast under the command of Captain R J Gray.

She was largely unchanged from her prewar appearance. Her entrance saloon on 'B' deck was now finished in light oak and was a pleasant and appropriate foil for the distinctly brighter aspect of the *Ulster Prince*. Both ships had their cabins painted in light green and this matched the green curtains and quilts supplied. As we have noted, Lady Read was believed to have been responsible for this finish. Green paint was replaced by white in 1950 after Sir Alfred's retirement from the chairmanship. A more practical new feature installed in both ships was the provision of 7,500cuft of refrigerated space for food products.

There had been nightly sailings during August 1946, but these reverted to four sailings per week in each direction from 1 September. From 1 October 'sailing tickets' were dispensed with. These had been introduced in wartime to regulate the number of passengers travelling and were issued free of charge then and for some years after. Their use was restricted to peak periods in postwar days.

Postwar conditions and the amount of cargo offering meant that there was great pressure on the available cargo capacity, much of which was made up by obsolete vessels. The company's position was not assisted by the decision of the main board of Coast Lines to transfer the company's most modern cargo vessel *Ulster Duke* to the British Channel Islands Shipping Company on 1 August 1946 for the sum of £47,615. She was renamed *Guernsey Coast*. Unfortunately, a near sister which had been ordered from the same builders at Ardrossan and launched as the *Ulster Duchess* was delivered to the company on 9 September 1946, only to be transferred to the Channel Islands Company on the same day and renamed *Jersey Coast*. Although little consolation at the time, both ships were later to return to the company.

The Belfast, Mersey and Manchester Steamship Company, now a subsidiary of the Belfast Steamship Company, had been just as short of tonnage in the closing period of the war and the early months of peace. Sailing for them had been the Gdynia registered Polish motor ship *Slask* while the much smaller Hessle built motor ship *Empire Fanal* was another 'stranger'. She had been built in dry dock, a novelty at the time, and was registered in Hull. Competitors were not slow to exploit tonnage shortages and resort was had to chartering the Clyde Shipping Company's *Rockabill* which made a number of sailings in 1945 with cattle between Belfast and Birkenhead.

Misfortune visited the Mersey Company on 20 November 1946, when the *Stormont* under the command of Captain Percival Peacock was making her way up the Mersey on a flood tide. She was keeping close to the Liverpool side in order to make a wide sweep across the river to stem the tide and berth at Woodside Lairage. She had sailed the previous night from Belfast with 208 head of cattle, eight horses, 30 tons of tea-making machinery for Calcutta despatched from Messrs Davidson's Sirocco Engineering Works, a large consignment of electric motors from Messrs Hugh J Scott, 1,000 cases of Nestles milk, 120 tons of potatoes and other foodstuffs. Disaster struck when the *Stormont* was about to execute her turn. Outward bound in the river was the Donaldson Atlantic Line managed steamer *Empire Brent*, with 900 Canadian war brides and children on board for Halifax. She had been better known as the *Letitia*, sister of the *Athenia* sunk at the outbreak of war. As the *Stormont* crossed the liner's bows a collision became inevitable. The *Stormont* was rammed on her port side and despite the efforts of Captain Peacock to beach his ship and the tugs which came to her aid she heeled over on to her port side on Pluckington Bank which extends the length of the South Docks from close to the landing stage to Herculaneum Dock. Early morning ferry passengers were the hapless witnesses of the struggles of the *Stormont*'s livestock cargo in the flood tide, many of whom perished. The ship's company of seventeen survived but, sadly, despite a valiant search, the ship's two kittens were lost.

The *Stormont* was righted and beached at low tide alongside the Albert Dock wall but was abandoned to the underwriters two days later. In subsequent High Court proceedings she was found to blame for the collision, a severe blow for her owners in addition to the total loss of a ship, elderly yet valuable at a time of tonnage shortage. The loss of her cargo and potential damage to goodwill was a serious item.

The *Empire Brent* sustained damage above and below the waterline on her bow and was dry docked after disembarking her passengers. She was able to resume her voyage some days later.

An immediate replacement came in the shape of the veteran *Wicklow* from the British and Irish Steam Packet Company. Built in 1895, she had the distinction of being the sole survivor of the City of Dublin Steam Packet Company's fleet. On transfer to the British and Irish Company in 1919, she had been renamed *Lady Wicklow* until March 1938, when she reverted to *Wicklow* once more. A useful cattle carrier, she was not renamed by the Mersey Company when she was transferred to them later, on 1 October 1947, at the surprisingly high valuation of £22,500. By 14 August 1948, her value was only £3,200 when she went to the British Iron and Steel Corporation for breaking up.

The policies of Mr Atlee's Labour administration which took office in July 1945, had serious implications for the company and the Coast Lines Group. They were committed to the nationalisation of the railways and this was bound to call in question, sooner or later, future relations on the Irish Sea. Just as the formation of the LMSR had meant the ending of a closer co-operation with the Midland Railway for traffic via Liverpool than had existed with the LNWR, so the company would eventually lose its close ally, the Great Western Railway.

A more immediate blow was the govern-

Reginald Berkeley, appointed General Manager and Director, Belfast Steamship Company, 1947. (R W Berkeley)

Arthur Moore, Managing Director of the Belfast, Mersey and Manchester Steamship Company and latterly Director of Ulster Ferry Transport. (Arthur Moore)

ment's intention that the state would operate all British air transport services. As early as November 1945, the government announced that the railway and shipping companies would have no financial share in the state owned corporations to be formed. The Minister, Lord Winster, expressed the hope, gratuitous in the circumstances, that the railway and shipping companies would co-operate with the new organisations. The government proclaimed that air travel would become a normal mode of travel for the masses and not a luxury for the few. It was unfortunate that the government could not see its way to compensate the company for more than physical assets acquired. More unfortunate that in their pursuit of making air travel available to the masses they felt it necessary to initiate a policy of subsidy which was bound to damage the passenger carryings of the Belfast Steamship Company, itself unsubsidised, and not generously compensated for the losses incurred in the war effort.

Another more localised policy of the government which was to trouble the company a great deal in the immediate future was the decision to give Lieutenant Colonel Frank Bustard what was in effect a subsidy in starting his roll-on roll-off freight services which were to be in direct competition with the Belfast/Liverpool route.

At the end of 1946, Sir Alfred Read relinquished the managing directorship of Coast Lines and associated companies including, of course, the Belfast Steamship Company. He was to remain an active and involved chair-

man until the end of March 1950. He was succeeded as managing director by M Arnet Robinson, who was a native of Stanmore, Middlesex. He had been commissioned in the King's Royal Rifle Corps and the Royal Flying Corps in the 1914-18 war. After leaving the army, he had some deep sea shipping experience before joining Sir Alfred's newly established Coast Lines organisation. A keen yachtsman and ornithologist, he was serving as general manager at Liverpool prior to his new appointment.

At home in Belfast, the war had dealt severely with Samuel Berkeley's health. At its conclusion he had been awarded the CBE in recognition of his public services in war and peace. He was not fated to enjoy this honour for long as he became seriously ill in 1946 and died on 20 February 1947. To him must go a great deal of the credit for making the modern Belfast Steamship Company a formidable commercial force on the Irish Sea, respected by the railway companies, unlike them trading at a profit in its shipping operations, and esteemed by the shipper and traveller. He had been a man for his times which had demanded firm and resolute management coupled with rigorous cost control and no quarter given to the occasionally arrogant senior officers of the LMSR.

The new general manager was Samuel Berkeley's only son, Reginald. Destined originally for a banking career, Sir Alfred selected him as one of his cadets in a scheme of management training in the Coast Lines Group modelled closely on the traffic apprentice schemes of the four main line railway companies. The difficult days ahead would call for an entirely different technique in management from those employed in prewar days. It is fair to say that the task facing the young new general manager was possibly more difficult than that which faced his father who was able to enjoy a degree of autonomy which postwar conditions did not allow his son.

The opportunity was taken in 1947 to rationalise the Belfast to Manchester trade and this resulted in the Mersey Company withdrawing altogether from Manchester but continuing to serve Liverpool (Trafalgar Dock), Birkenhead (Woodside Lairage) and

The Greypoint **ex** *Rathlin* **(PRO (NI)/BSS Co)**

Bromborough. The Belfast Steamship Company now assumed sole responsibility for the Manchester trade and commenced a twice weekly service between that port and Belfast.

Two ships, already past their quarter century, came to the company for use on the Manchester trade at £1,000 each. They were, first, the *Cambrian Coast*, originally G & J Burns' *Gorilla*, launched at the Govan yard of Harland & Wolff. She was a sibling of the company's *Ulster Coast* but had borne three other names apart from *Gorilla* before becoming the *Ulster Merchant*. From 1925-29 she had been the *Cumberland Coast*, then from 1929-1933 the City of Cork Steam Packet Company's *Kinsale*, since when she had been the *Cambrian Coast*. The *Ulster Mariner* had been built by A & J Inglis in October 1922 as the *Ayrshire Coast* and had been content with this throughout her career save for a spell from 1923-25 when she had been the Burns and Laird Line's *Spaniel*.

Further attempts at economy in working the Belfast, Mersey and Manchester Company initiated by the Belfast Steamship Company were firmly resisted by Harold B Mack. Concern had been expressed at the amount of commission being paid to S Lawther & Sons in Belfast and J J Mack & Sons in Liverpool for managing the company. The logical suggestion was made that the three firms, all owned by Coast Lines, should be merged and so save management expenses and enable the Belfast Steamship Company to operate at a greater profit. Not only did the Board of Coast Lines thwart these suggestions from Belfast but Mr Mack was able to persuade them to transfer the ownership of the shares in the Mersey Company from the Belfast

Steamship Company to Messrs J J Mack & Sons. In a fashion the Mack family had at last achieved their ambition of being the sole proprietors of a cross channel liner service, even if it was a subsidiary of Coast Lines.

Staying with the Mersey Company for the moment, they received during 1948 a replacement for the *Wicklow*. She was a smaller steamer named *The London Queen*. The Burntisland Shipbuilding Company had built her in 1933 for the London and Channel Islands Steamship Company which Coast Lines had acquired on 1 October 1936. From 3 December 1946 the *London Queen* had been owned within the Group by British Channel Traders Limited. She was given the name *Stormont* by her new owners.

A different ship was added to the Mersey Company's fleet on 2 September 1948 when the Clyde Shipping Company's *Eddystone* was purchased for £80,000. Dating from 1927, this former coastal liner was a fine acquisition with a gross tonnage of 1,550 and a horsepower of 1,800. She had a spacious saloon, unfortunately not required for her new owner's trade but, more importantly, plenty of accommodation for live cattle. She was renamed *Brookmount*.

A dangerous new competitor appeared on the Irish Sea on 20 May 1948 in the shape of Lieutenant Colonel Bustard's Atlantic Steam Navigation Company which commenced to operate a roll-on roll-off freight service between Preston and Larne after successful operation of similar ventures between Tilbury and Rotterdam, Antwerp and Hamburg. Wartime experience had shown how useful

The *Ulster Castle* ex *Lady Kildare* in the Mersey. (McRoberts/Merseyside Maritime Museum)

The *Ulster Hero* ex *Lancashire Coast*. (McRoberts/Merseyside Maritime Museum)

the Admiralty-built landing ship tanks (LSTs) had been during the invasion of Europe. In fact, no merchant ships need have been employed at all if there had been enough of these craft, for the transport of tanks and vehicles was a task for which conventional merchant ships were not well suited. Between July 1944 and May 1945 inclusive, 43 percent of the total of vehicles carried across the channel for the British and US sectors combined went by LST.

In 1945, Frank Bustard was 60 and returning to civilian life from the army. He was a Liverpool man who had once been passenger manager and a director of the White Star Line and became one of the human casualties of the Cunard–White Star merger of 1934. He possessed great drive and imagination and it was no fault of his that the Atlantic Steam Navigation Company which he had founded in 1936 to foster low cost ocean travel failed to buy the Red Star Line and failed to establish itself on any deep sea route for City financial

interests and government had been implacably hostile. His imaginative approach to sea transport enabled him to appreciate the possibilities of using LSTs for the cross channel conveyance of laden lorries and the moribund Atlantic Steam Navigation Company was poised for a resurrection as the vehicle for his enterprise.

Alfred Barnes, Minister of Transport at the time, was sympathetic to Bustard's ideas and the Admiralty was keen that employment be found for the LSTs so that they would both be serviceable and available in any future emergency. The result was that very favourable charter terms were arranged. The hire for each ship was believed to be approximately £500 per week and Bustard was later to record his debt to the Labour government, without which he was convinced that the revolution in sea transport which he initiated would never have taken place, certainly at that time. Government provided the ships but Bustard and his backers had to raise the money for fitting them out and providing crew accommodation on board. The first sailing from Tilbury to Rotterdam had taken place on 11 September 1946 and it was not long before it occurred to Bustard that Ulster would be a profitable target for his next operation since there were uniform regulations governing the use of road transport vehicles in Great Britain and Northern Ireland and no customs barriers. Two terminal ports suggested themselves at once, Preston and Larne. Both ports had been losing money for some years and were keen to have the additional trade and to give undertakings to improve their facilities.

The most serious challenge ever mounted against the Belfast Steamship Company began on 20 May 1948 when the LST *Empire Cymric* sailed down the Ribble with a modest cargo for Larne of vehicles and returned with an even more modest one of two lorries. She was the apparently unlikely start of an adventure which was eventually to revolutionise Irish cross channel shipping and boost the annual value of trade through Larne from a mere £4 million in 1948 to £104 million within the decade. Not only did the *Empire Cymric* and her sisters offer the trader carriage of goods in his own lorry if need be, freedom from the damage and delay all too often inseparable from postwar rail transit, she also offered simplicity in freight charges in place of the complexity of the conference rates structure. The nature, weight, cubic capacity or value of the consignment was of no interest to Bustard but only the space which the vehicle or container occupied on the deck. The shipper might carry, if he pleased, 'Gold bricks or carrots'.

Almost without exception new competitors on the Irish Sea have foundered for lack of financial backing to sustain the enormous cost of running a liner service which they have habitually optimistically underestimated. With a rare exception or two new challengers have sought to offer the same type of service as the established line whilst undercutting rates; a mixture which is doomed to failure. Innovation is the key to successful competition because it will usually bring the financial backing which mere competition will not attract. The Mack brothers and Samuel Lawther almost sixty years before had successfully competed with the Belfast Steamship Company because they were able to provide a regular cargo service in a vessel exclusively devoted to cargo and fitted, for its day, with the most modern appliances, ie the *Manchester*. She had been followed some years later by the *Fleswick*, another modern cargo ship. The competition had eventually forced the Belfast Steamship Company to reconsider its policy of not operating separate cargo vessels. Bustard's venture demanded a response with the same type of equipment offering the same type of service. Sadly, the response from the main Board of Coast Lines was initially misguided and latterly inexplicable.

Sir Alfred tended to regard the Irish Sea as belonging to him. The normal type of competitor received short shrift: 'This opposition must cease', 'You are to see that it is killed-... dead' was the terse memo sent to the assistant general manager in Belfast in 1946. The occasion was the competition mounted with chartered tonnage by Patrick Thompson & Company of Liverpool who offered twice weekly sailings to Belfast as well as to Dublin for a few months and may be remembered for their engaging telegraphic address, 'Uwan-

tus'. Accordingly, 'Run him off' was a fair assessment of his strategy in meeting the challenge from Bustard who was to prove a much wilier foe than Patrick Thompson & Company.

Good intelligence was essential to fight any enemy and to this end covert surveillance of the Bustard operation was decided on. Officials, notably J Hughes, traffic manager at Liverpool for Coast Lines and the Belfast Steamship Company, were despatched on espionage missions to the ports. The spies were soon unmasked and were asked if they were getting all the information that they needed, invited to stand in a more comfortable place less exposed to the elements and offered tea or coffee. Mr Hughes and his colleagues recommended that the roll-on roll-off principle be adopted as the best way of meeting the competition. Why was this not done?

The reasons are complex. Undoubtedly Sir Alfred resented Colonel Bustard's intrusion into his domain and there is evidence to suggest that he disliked him personally. As an old Anchor Line man Sir Alfred may not have thought highly of Bustard's prewar plans for low cost Atlantic travel which might have hit that company from which he had received his early training.

It is more likely that Sir Alfred was incensed that the government was subsidising competition with very cheap charters whilst refusing to compensate adequately existing shipowners for the loss of vessels on war service yet expecting them to restore facilities for traders and passengers.

Bustard had lost £52,874 in the first year of operation. His lack of tangible assets and lack of substantial financial backing may have induced a complacency in Sir Alfred and his colleagues that was not justified. It was known that the newly created British Transport Commission had declined to subscribe capital and that Courtaulds, just commencing manufacturing in Northern Ireland, had also declined to assist. On the other hand Messrs Bahr, Behrend & Company of Liverpool and Messrs McCalla of Belfast were acting as forwarding agents whilst at Larne, the Shamrock Shipping Company were general agents. The well-known firm of McGregor, Gow and

Company of London had contributed £3,000 to the venture as a gesture of goodwill. On the board of directors of the Atlantic Steam Navigation Company was Gilbert Szlumper, a former docks and marine manager for the Southern Railway and later its general manager.

There had been a failure to appreciate the determination of the ports of Preston and Larne to make a success of the new service. Surprisingly, the Northern Ireland government had made a grant of £100,000, a sizeable sum for those days, to Larne harbour for the improvement of berthing facilities for the roll-on roll-off service. If there are objections to government subsidies for shipping operations there should be even more for selective subsidies to favoured operators.

It does not seem as though Sir Alfred objected to new technology as such. The evidence is to the contrary. There is certainly some evidence that the newly formed British Transport Commission with rail and road interests in its substantial portfolio, did not behave towards Sir Alfred with quite the openness and integrity that might have been expected in responding to the new competition. We shall return to this later.

The year 1948 saw the disappearance of the main line railway companies from 1 January. They were replaced by the British Transport Commission operating through the Railway Executive. The same date thus saw the end of the Belfast Steamship Company's relationship with the Great Western Railway. With it went that distinguished railway's agent who had enjoyed office accommodation in the Belfast Steamship Company's head office and so went also the automatic routeing of all unconsigned traffic for the north of Ireland from GWR stations via Birkenhead and the company's route. No more would advertisements appear in travel guides exhorting passengers to, 'Travel to Ulster by the Great Western Railway – the most picturesque route via Birkenhead–Belfast'.

Through services were never resumed from former Midland Railway stations to Liverpool (Central). Doubtless British Railways could claim that their own service from Heysham was not directly served by trains from these stations. British Railways was doing no more than perpetuate, for different reasons, the prewar antipathy which the LMSR had displayed towards putting traffic on the rails of the Cheshire Lines Committee. In those days the company had been reproved by Euston more than once for delivering traffic consigned to Midland stations to the CLC Goods Depot at Huskisson Dock instead of to the LMSR at Sandon Dock. The reasons from now on would be rationalisation of routes within British Railways and this might not all work to the company's advantage.

There was one advantage from all this for the Coast Lines Group. The last general manager of the Great Western Railway, Sir James Milne, declined the offer made to him of the chairmanship of the Railway Executive. Instead, he sought an outlet for his talents in the wider business world and the Group were fortunate to secure his services as a director. In a sense there was a perpetuation of the link between the former GWR and the Belfast Steamship Company.

Afloat again at last, in 1948, nightly services were resumed for the summer season as the result of the commissioning of the B & ISP Company's new motor ships *Munster* and *Leinster* which entered service on 5 April of that year. From 1946, the *Longford* and *Louth* had coped valiantly with summer torrents of holidaymakers escaping to Ireland from the postwar rigours of rationing. Now one of them was available to supplement the Belfast Steamship Company's sailings. It was the *Louth* which returned to her old haunts from 31 May 1948 wearing the funnel colours and flying the flag of her original owners. On 1 October 1948, after she had retired to lay up in Liverpool for the winter, she was transferred back to the ownership of the company at a valuation of £1,000 and renamed *Ulster Duke*, once more registered at Belfast. The *Longford*, a still sprightly 42-year-old, continued to serve her Dublin owners sailing, a little incongruously, along with their ultra-modern composite vessels.

The veterans of 1906, like all other vessels in the Coast Lines fleet, had been equipped with radar. Extensive trials had taken place with the MV *Atlantic Coast* early in 1946, before the Group had adopted radar for all its vessels. The menace of fog in the Mersey

The *Lady Killarney* after her refit in 1952. (McRoberts/Merseyside Maritime Museum)

The *Lady Killarney*: passenger accommodation plan. (Coast Lines Ltd)

approaches could never be eliminated but at least dislocation of services had been reduced to a minimum.

In 1946, the Coast Lines Group had taken part in the official trials of the Decca system of navigation in co-operation with the Ministry of Transport. By 1948, the Decca 'navigator' employing the concept of hyperbolic navigation using transmissions from shore radio stations had become a standard fitting in all the vessels, irrespective of age, of the Coast Lines Group. In retrospect, some might query why the *Lady Connaught* (the former *Patriotic*) had not been cast in the role of relief ship on the Irish Sea routes from Liverpool pending the completion of the Waterloo Entrance? She had lain at Queen's Island, Belfast, since July 1945, while her future was mulled over. The extensive nature of her reconstruction as a hospital ship and the considerable refrigeration capacity installed for that role eventually assured that future. She would replace the *Killarney* as a cruising yacht in home waters. She was beautifully fitted out for her new career with a restaurant seating 100 on the main deck and a spacious entrance saloon combining the main staircases to the main and promenade decks into which was built a chief steward's office for the reception of passengers. She even had a card room provided on her lower main deck

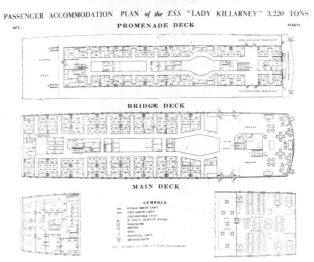

and a timbered smoke room on her boat deck. With her hull painted buff, the same shade as that used on the prewar *Munster* and *Leinster*, a funnel of the same colour, white upperworks and green boot topping, she left Belfast for Liverpool under the command, appropriately, of Captain Peter Mullan. Without his courage and seamanship, she would simply have been just another wartime wreck awaiting clearance in the Mersey approaches. She was renamed *Lady Killarney*, perhaps a little awkwardly combining her own and her predecessor's names.

In March and April she maintained the Dublin/Liverpool sailings for her owners whilst the *Longford* and *Louth* were on survey. In so doing, she made a brave splash of colour on a grey austerity ridden Mersey where she frequently lay at anchor in the Sloyne before docking. During this period, on 31 March, she was transferred from the ownership of the B & ISP Company to that of Coast Lines Limited but her days as an Irish Sea liner were over when she finished her stint on the Dublin/Liverpool service.

Several factors lessened her usefulness as a relief vessel. Her passenger accommodation, eminently suitable for cruising, was no longer suitable to the needs of a two class passenger service. Also her belting had been removed so that launches could be used conveniently when she was at anchor in Scottish lochs. The most serious impediment to her use on regular passenger service was her engine bed plate, bent by the mine explosion in 1940, which now inhibited her speed.

The *Lady Killarney* enjoyed great success as the last British vessel solely dedicated to cruising in home waters. Her buff hull proved as impracticable with her as it had with the prewar Dublin vessels and gave place to green after three seasons. Finally, in 1952, her hull was painted black with the Coast Lines' white chevron superimposed. Lord Pirrie had been prophetic when he had spoken of her possessively as his yacht when she was still the *Patriotic*. Amid much lamentation from her regular clientele she was withdrawn after her 1956 season and disposed of to breakers at Port Glasgow. From 1950 her master had been Captain J B Wright RNR, a Belfast Steamship Company man and a future senior master.

The *Lady Killarney*'s predecessor, the *Killarney*, spent some months of idleness in wartime grey drabness in Trafalgar Dock, Liverpool, following her release from naval service. To most observers it seemed certain that the next voyage she would make would be her final one. Surprisingly, the old *Magic* had a trick up her sleeve yet for she was sold on 17 March 1947 for £23,000 to the Bury Court Shipping Company Limited (Vergottis Limited) for trading under the Greek flag in Aegean waters where there was an acute shortage of tonnage. Renamed *Attiki* she left Liverpool on 26 April 1947 for Piraeus. She was soon renamed *Adrias* under the ownership of the Epirotiki Steamship Navigation

Company. Her long career came to an end on 6 October 1951 when, with 700 passengers aboard, she was wrecked in heavy weather on the east end of Falconera Island.

The company was affected by a change within the executive organisation of Coast Lines Limited following Sir Alfred's vacation of the managing director's chair. The burden of the change was to transfer much of the corporate 'decision making' at Group level from London to Liverpool. A Liverpool Committee of Management was formed and the affairs of all the cross channel companies in the Group now became the concern of the newly formed Liverpool Board. Though Reginald Berkeley was a member of the Board, the new organisation does seem to have removed the cutting edge of the general manager's former direct access to the chairman and managing director in London with no intermediary involved in Liverpool. The influential Harold B Mack was also a member of the Liverpool Board.

A nightly passenger service was maintained through the summer of 1949 with the aid of the *Ulster Duke*. Between 15 July and 26 August, duplicate sailings were offered on Friday nights from Liverpool and Saturdays from Belfast. One mid-October forenoon the *Ulster Duke* seemed to remember that when she was the *Graphic* her owners had had a score or two to settle with the LNWR, and its successors who would never agree to run Belfast boat trains to Riverside Station. Moving into Prince's Dock from the Half-Tide Dock she collided with the swing bridge carrying the railway lines to Riverside Station over the dock passage. The bridge was thrown out of alignment by several inches and four British Railways tank locomotives and two complete boat trains were imprisoned for a day at Riverside.

Through the 1950s plenty of conventional cargo was available to the company and the live cattle trade was buoyant. There was a deceptive air of prosperity but the slow turnround at terminals and steady increase in terminal charges should have been sending warnings to the Coast Lines Board that the days of break bulk cargo handling were numbered and they had better look to new methods. They would ignore what was happening at Preston at their peril. On 17 February 1949 the veteran *Ulster Star* had gone to the British Iron and Steel Corporation (Salvage) Limited, for £1,250 whilst the *Ulster Castle* of 1920 followed her to the same buyers for £3,000 on 6 June 1950.

None of the newcomers to the fleet at this time was youthful but they represented a tendency to larger vessels to try and cope with traffic requirements. On 1 July 1948 the *Lancashire Coast*, dating from 1920, came at a valuation of £1,000 and became the second *Ulster Hero*. She had been launched as the *Princess Olga* by Sir R Dixon & Company Limited, Middlesborough, for Langlands of Liverpool. Her owners had been purchased by Coast Lines and they soon renamed her the *Princess Olga*.

Two sisters were transferred on 27 August and 3 September 1949, respectively. They were the *Avon Coast* which became the *Ulster Star* and the *Medway Coast* which became the *Ulster Duchess*. Both were valued at £1,000 and had originally been in the fleet of Fisher Renwick, Manchester–London Steamers Limited, which had been acquired by Coast

The *Ulster Mariner* ex *Ayrshire Coast*. (McRoberts/Merseyside Maritime Museum)

The *Medway Coast* ex *Sentry* later *Ulster Duchess*. (Captain W Grogan)

The *Graphic* returns to her original owners as the *Ulster Duke*. (McRoberts/Merseyside Maritime Museum)

Lines in 1939. The *Avon Coast* had been built in 1923 by W Dobson & Company as the *Sapper* and the *Medway Coast* in 1924 by the Tyne Iron Shipbuilding Company as the *Sentry*. They had cost Coast Lines £20,000 each on 1 April 1939.

Towards the end of 1949, Sir Alfred's attitude to Colonel Bustard's competition had changed from 'run him off' to beating him at his own game. However illogical and out of character his original reaction had been he was never an opponent of new technology as his prewar interest in air services had shown. He now proposed to British Railways that they start a joint service with LST vessels from an unspecified Lancashire port to Northern Ireland. There is no recorded response to this proposal. Nor is it clear whether or not Sir Alfred was aware that the comptroller of the British Transport Commission, Sir Reginald Wilson, was having discussions with Bustard at the same time. Though nothing tangible emerged from the discussions they undoubtedly paved the way for the agreement of 1954 by which the Transport Commission agreed to purchase the Atlantic Steam Navigation Company. One would hesitate to describe Sir Reginald's actions as devious but the impression is given of a certain lack of frankness on the part of the Transport Commission which may have misled the Board of Coast Lines after 1950 when Sir Alfred had left the scene. Unfortunately, the Board was to make it all too easy for the Commission to achieve a notable coup by acquiring Bustard's company.

Sir Alfred and his Board had much to absorb their attention in 1949 when the dream of nightly passenger services to Belfast and Dublin operated by two vessels each took a mighty step towards realisation. On 29 March 1949 the present Queen, then Her Royal Highness Princess Elizabeth, accompanied by the Duke of Edinburgh, opened the Waterloo Entrance lock. Some months would elapse before the express ships could use it but at least it was in place at a final cost in the region of £1,000,000. Not only had the lock with its gates, sluices and culverts to be constructed but a new deep water approach channel had to be dredged involving the removal of 140,000 tons of sandstone and overlying silt.

The old West Waterloo–Victoria Docks Passage and its tongues had to be removed and the Scherzer rolling lift bridge which spanned it moved to a newly constructed Victoria–Trafalgar Dock Passage. Then there was much dredging to be done in West Waterloo Dock before an ample turning basin was available at the inner end of the lock.

The lock itself was 450ft long between the outer and inner pair of gates and 65ft 6in in breadth. An intermediate pair of gates enabled the lock to be subdivided into two compartments of 135ft and 315ft respectively for smaller vessels; sad that it was all to have such a comparatively short life.

The actual opening ceremony was performed by the Dock Board's tender *Galatea* which cut through a blue ribbon across the lock and was the first vessel to enter it. Aboard were the Princess and her consort to whom Sir Alfred Read and Arnet Robinson had been presented before the *Galatea* cast off from the landing stage. The Belfast Steamship Company's *Ulster Prince* had been placed at the disposal of the Dock Board for the day. With 300 guests aboard, Captain Wilson brought her to the entrance of the lock astern of the *Galatea* but remained outside. The *Galatea* made her way through the central docks to Salisbury Dock where she re-entered the Mersey and rejoined the waiting *Ulster Prince* which was in company with the Wallasey Corporation Ferry *J Farley*. Together they went down the river to the Gladstone Dock where the Royal party disembarked to inspect the port radar station.

The old South Entrance dating from 1868 had to remain in use for the time being so that ships could still enter Prince's Half-Tide Dock from the river. The contemporary North Entrance had already gone, engulfed in the new works. Without Sir Alfred's foresight and determination, the whole scheme would never have been undertaken and he received a well deserved tribute from his fellow directors after the official opening.

The Waterloo Entrance became fully operational in March 1950. Unfortunately, what should have been an occasion for celebration was marred by an unofficial strike of crews which was soon settled when the men realised that they were going to enjoy better leave

conditions than under the previous operating practice. A disadvantage which could not be overcome so easily was that half an hour had to be added to the quay to quay passages to cover the time taken in working through the lock. The Belfast sailing time was advanced to 8.30pm, whilst that at Liverpool became 9.30pm.

Though the new entrance was a great engineering achievement seamanship of a high order was demanded from the masters, officers and crews of ships using it. For example, an inward bound vessel worked through the lock and then went ahead on a head rope so that her stern could be swung out into the turning basin in Waterloo Dock. Next she went astern through West Waterloo Dock, threading her way through the passage to Prince's Half-Tide Dock which she crossed before negotiating the passage to Prince's Dock. Both passages were narrow and were not in alignment with each other and a head rope had to be used in passing through both. Then there was the approach to the berth stern first at Prince's Dock South West.

An outward bound vessel still had to be 'heaved off' the dock side at her berth before going ahead through the passages. When it came to leaving the Entrance lock, a westerly wind combined with an ebb tide created difficulties in getting her off the dock wall and on occasions a tug had to be summoned to pull her off. A standing arrangement, accordingly, was made with the Alexandra Towing Company to have a tug on hand on

Prince's Dock in 1948 or 1949. At the Dublin berths the *Munster*, astern of her the *Longford*, ex *Lady Connaught* ex *Heroic*, under sailing orders. At the Belfast berth the *Ulster Monarch*, astern of her can be seen the masts of the *Ulster Duke* ex *Graphic*. (J Y Grogan)

sailing nights. Harold B Mack, whom we have met before, was a director of the Alexandra Towing Company.

With the new Entrance operational, the *Ulster Duke*, which had helped to maintain a nightly service throughout from June 1949, was laid up for the winter.

Certain members of the Board, Percy Wharton and Arnet Robinson in particular, renewed a plea for a relief ship to be ordered specially for the Irish Sea liner services. Whilst Sir Alfred remained as chairman, it seems that no encouragement was given to this particular idea. It is possible that Sir Alfred may have had his doubts about the viability of such a project. However, Sir Alfred decided to retire from the chairmanship as soon as the Waterloo Entrance became operative. His withdrawal from the coastwise shipping scene which he had dominated for over thirty years was the end of an epoch. He was succeeded by Captain A R S Nutting OBE, MC who was a man of many parts, being chairman of Cantrell and Cochrane, and a director of Guinness, the Guardian Insurance Company and the Westinghouse Brake Company. Most significantly he was a former Governor of the Bank of Ireland and had been so at the time when that

The second *Greypoint* ex *Fastnet*. (McRoberts/ Merseyside Maritime Museum)

great Irish financial institution came to the rescue when Sir Alfred ordered the *Ulster Monarch* and her sisters. He had been on the Board of Coast Line for many years, latterly as vice-chairman.

Sir Alfred's departure saw some immediate changes. The new chairman and his fellow directors immediately addressed themselves to the provision of a relief cargo and passenger vessel which could be used by all the Group companies. Ostensibly the decision to order had been delayed because the *Louth* (*Ulster Duke*) and *Longford* had been put through special surveys in 1948. Another change which may have been coincidence was that the saxe blue stripe, 'Lady Read Blue', disappeared following Sir Alfred's departure, but only from the Belfast Steamship Company's vessels.

The requirement for a new relief vessel was based on the need, as the Board saw it, to maintain services at a high quality while the various Irish Sea liners were off for survey and overhaul. Group policy called for a very thorough annual overhaul, including a great deal of work in the engine room. The result was an excellent standard of maintenance and a not unmixed blessing in that the vessels had a remarkable longevity. The policy also meant that each liner was absent for a month in the year from her usual route. This was considered worthwhile to achieve an annual depreciation rate of 5 percent on each well cared for and long-lived ship.

The cost of the proposed vessel was estimated at £785,000, but soon increased to £816,000. To meet this, Group indebtedness

Bank was increased to £2,000,000 and Sir James Milne negotiated a loan from the Ship Mortgage Finance Corporation for £400,000 at 4¾ percent per annum.

Other attempts were made to bring in cash such as disposing of the Carrollstown Estate near Trim in Co Meath, for any offer over £60,000. Sir Alfred Read would not have cared to take this step for it had been an agricultural venture in which he had taken an especial interest. Latterly, it had been limited to supplying the needs of the B & ISP Company vessels from Dublin as British Ministry of Food regulations prevented the victualling of the *Lady Killarney* in Dublin prior to her cruises, as Sir Alfred had originally intended. In any event rationing had now ceased in the United Kingdom. No satisfactory offer for the estate was received and it was still unsold in 1965 when the B & ISP Company was eventually disposed of to the Irish government.

A rational economy was a decision to dispose of the *Ulster Duke*. She was sold for £23,000 to Italian owners and left Liverpool under tow of the Dutch tug *Hudson* on 8 March 1951, bound for Spezia. Her purchasers ignored advice to sail her out under her own power and not to tow her. A week later, in a gale in Finisterre Bay, the old *Graphic* rebelled against the indignity of being towed away by strangers to a foreign land and capsized and sank, this time for ever. Unfortunately, three out of the six men aboard her perished.

The *Longford* was to be used as relief vessel for both the Belfast Steamship Company and B & ISP Company routes pending the completion of the new vessel. Fuller utilisation of the *Longford* was achieved by chartering her to the Butlins organisation for the summer months of 1951 and 1952 during which she made special sailings between Liverpool and Dublin in connection with their Mosney holiday camp.

The Coast Lines chairman's wife, Mrs Nutting, named the long debated 'relief ship' *Irish Coast* and sent her down the ways at Harland & Wolff's Queen's Island yard on 8 May 1952. She was handed over to Coast Lines Limited on 16 October 1952. Noticeably beamier than the *Ulster Monarch* or *Ulster*

Prince she was 341ft 6in long on a moulded breadth of 51ft 6in.

A smart and sturdy looking ship, she had a handsome profile at a time when good looks were taken for granted and these were much assisted by her large black funnel with the white chevron on it.

She was the first ship to be equipped with stabilisers to sail on the Belfast Steamship Company's route, though these were intended to minimise rolling rather than eliminate it and were of the electro-hydraulic Denny-Brown variety. It was her misfortune

The *Irish Coast*. (McRoberts/Merseyside Maritime Museum)

The *Longford* towards the end of her life. (PRO (NI)/BSS Co)

to be something of a nomad throughout her sixteen year long career on the Irish Sea. Her initial routine was to spend October and November in each year running from Belfast to Liverpool; December, Cork to Fishguard; January and February, Dublin to Liverpool; March and April, Glasgow to Belfast; May, her own overhaul. The summer and autumn were spent on the Glasgow to Dublin service.

Her decor and furnishing was executed by Heaton Tabb & Company Limited, who had created the comfortable ambience which characterised the Belfast Steamship Company's vessels. She accommodated 242 saloon passengers in the midships house on three decks, promenade, 'A' and 'B'. There was the usual spacious entrance saloon which was panelled in White African mahogany and lacewood whilst a carved representation of the Coast Lines' ensign adorned the chief steward's bureau.

White was also the predominant colour of the sycamore furniture in the restaurant whilst gold predominated in the satinwood panelling of the bulkheads. The chairs were upholstered in deep crimson leather which was reflected in the damask patterned curtains. Each table, glittering with its Walker &

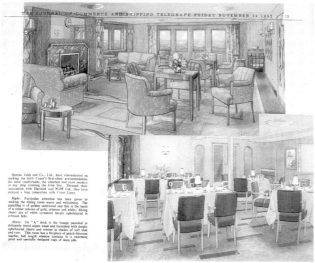

An early morning view of the *Irish Coast*. (Captain W Grogan)

Interior views of the *Irish Coast* from Journal of Commerce Special Supplement. (Jocast Ltd/ Lloyds List)

room. The 'A' deck ports were round save for the two special state rooms which had windows.

Although the passenger accommodation was arranged on three decks, a very attractive cocktail bar was placed aft on the sun deck above the promenade deck. It was recessed into the after end of the funnel and adorned with early nineteenth-century sporting prints.

There was much improved accommodation in the steerage to sleep 146 passengers in two and four berth rooms as well as large separate sleeping cabins for men and women. A smoke room and cafeteria was provided.

With ample cargo capacity, four-footed passengers were catered for in the main 'tween decks and in Numbers 2 and 3 lower 'tween decks. She could carry 348 head of cattle and eight horses.

Captain J Wilson, the Belfast Steamship Company's respected senior master, took the *Irish Coast* on a short cruise, including Dublin, Glasgow and Liverpool in her itinerary. On 1 November 1952 he took her out on her

Hall silverware, had an individual lamp with a gold and crimson bordered shade.

On 'A' deck the lounge was furnished in soft rose and pastel blue with full length print curtains and bulkheads in tinted willow wood whilst a realistic looking log fire 'burned' in a peach blossom marble surround and hearth. Chestnut wood panelled the main smoking room on the promenade deck, chestnut leaves patterned the curtains whilst coral leather upholstered the main seating round the 'walls' with coral and blue hide settees and armchairs dispersed elsewhere in the maiden voyage from Liverpool to Belfast.

As the *Irish Coast* left the Mersey on her maiden voyage the *Longford*, forty-six years her senior, had already cleared Belfast Lough on her last commercial voyage. Though flying the flag of the B & ISP Company, it was fitting that the old *Heroic* should end her days on the service for which she had been built. Fitting, too, that with gallant service under the White Ensign to her credit in the First World War, she should be commanded on this poignant occasion by Captain Tom Wrigley OBE, who had served with distinction under the same ensign in the Second World War. After discharging at Liverpool, the *Longford* was laid up in Birkenhead's Morpeth Dock and advertised for sale. Italian ship-breakers were interested in her but the Ministry of Transport would not agree to a sale to foreign interests and she was reported sold the following January to the British Iron and Steel Corporation for £27,000. She was broken up later in the year at Barrow.

The wisdom of building the *Irish Coast* is open to question. Even as the *Irish Coast* was commissioned it was becoming increasingly clear that the future lay in roll-on roll-off services which in little more than a decade would make the *Irish Coast* obsolete. Her luxurious saloon passenger accommodation would be available to the Belfast Steamship Company and the other cross channel companies at a time of year when passenger utilisation was at its lowest. She was, however, a very expensive investment for the summer season on the Glasgow/Dublin service. Coast Lines' policy was to time charter her to the Belfast Steamship and other companies with hire calculated on a daily basis. It is surprising that a composite ship of her type was considered at all in view of the inability of dockers at the terminal ports to load or unload a full cargo into or from the holds of the express steamers in postwar working conditions.

It had been this very reason which had dictated alterations to the *Ulster Monarch* during her overhaul at the end of 1950 when the *Irish Coast*'s order had been under placed. The *Ulster Monarch* had always been a tender ship but sailing in winter weather with much of her cargo capacity empty emphasised the

Blue Ensign broken on the poop of the *Ulster Prince*, 1954. (Captain P G Lynch)

tenderness. To remedy it, her funnels had been reduced in height; her main mast removed from the after well deck and a short main mast stepped in place of it at the after end of the 'midships house. Rectangular openings in which rails were fitted were made in the promenade deck bulwarks. Lest these alterations should appear too fastidious, a surprising factor had been discovered which was contributing to her tenderness. Over the years accretions of paint had added appreciably to her top weight, whilst to the end of her career her stability was assisted by redundant Belfast granite street setts as ballast.

Nevertheless, Coast Lines were intensely proud of the *Irish Coast* and sent her to the Coronation Naval Review in May 1953. Without a ship of their own present on this occasion, the Belfast Steamship Company was represented in the person of Captain J Wilson who was invited in his final year at sea to command the *Irish Coast* for this cruise with invited guests aboard. He was by now also senior master of the Coast Lines Group.

On 27 February 1954, Captain Wilson took the *Ulster Prince* out of Belfast for the last time, closing a notable seagoing career with the company. He was to retire to Bangor, Co Down, where his wiry physique and alert mind carried him to his centenary, without doubt the only master in the company's service ever to attain that age or to have the rescue of so many lives at sea to his credit.

His successor in command of the *Ulster Prince* was the senior relieving master, Captain E B Clark RNR. He was the great grandson of a Liverpool privateer, Captain Byrne, who had sailed out of the Mersey in the late eighteenth century. Captain Clark had the distinction of holding his extra master's certificate which he had gained at the early age of twenty-five. He served his apprenticeship with Elder Dempster and was fifth officer in the White Star liner *Adriatic* before joining the Belfast Steamship Company. He had been commissioned in the Royal Naval Reserve since 1928 and during the war commanded the French destroyer *Arras*. After this, he spent three years in the Mediterranean on special and secret duties working from Gibraltar with Naval Intelligence. His final appointment in the navy was that of commanding officer of the fleet repair ship *Ausonia*, a former Cunard liner. During the war he had landed eighty secret agents in enemy occupied countries and picked up 400 escaping agents and servicemen.

There was a sequel to Captain Clark's appointment to the *Ulster Prince*. Soon after he assumed command, the Blue Ensign of the Royal Navy Reserve was broken at the *Ulster Prince*'s stern at Belfast. This was believed to be the first time that the Admiralty had granted a warrant to fly the Blue Ensign to a merchant ship engaged in the home trade or cross channel service. It was certainly the first time that such a vessel had been commanded by a master holding the rank of captain RNR, to which Captain Clark had been promoted at the end of 1953. At that time, Queen's regulations required a proportion of officers and ratings to be on the active list of the Royal Naval Reserve before the warrant would issue and the *Ulster Prince* was able to fulfil this requirement. The regulations were later changed and allowed captains holding RNR commissions to fly the Blue Ensign in their own right. It should be said that the company's senior relieving master at the time, Captain J B Wright, had also been promoted to captain RNR, in the same promotions list as Captain Clark.

Colonel Frank Bustard's service from Preston would simply not go away during these years in the early 1950s. Bustard would need capital to develop and expand but such was the potential of his new technology that it should have been clear to the Coast Lines'

Board that sooner or later someone would supply that capital. Unfortunately, the Board members were conservative in outlook, dedicated to maintaining what they saw as high standards. They were lulled into a false sense of security by the generally high volume of trade at this period and by their ability so far to pass on the escalating costs which traditional methods and practices were incurring. It is possible, too, that the Coast Lines Board had been influenced by the difficulties which the Belfast Steamship Company had been experiencing since they had introduced container traffic in 1948. They had complained to the Irish and British conference of alarming losses caused by poor loads, difficulties in returning empty containers, additional cranage costs and increased harbour dues and they wanted increased remuneration for carrying containers. British Railways would not agree to this but there is some evidence that the Belfast Steamship Company and the whole Coast Lines Group were a little sour on new technology at the time.

There was more correspondence between the Coast Lines Board and British Railways who were known to be interested in a purchase of the Bustard operation. Perhaps a little disarmingly, British Railways had expressed the view that the competition was only of 'nuisance value'. In response Coast Lines showed disinterest coupled with the view that there was 'nothing to buy'.

In April 1954, the British Transport Commission, in a move of surprising swiftness, purchased the Atlantic Steam Navigation Company and placed it under the wing of its subsidiary British Road Services. News of this does not seem to have percolated immediately to the Board of Coast Lines. A discussion subsequently took place within the ambit of the Irish and British Traffic Conference in October 1954, on the subject of the purchase by the British Transport Commission of the Atlantic Steam Navigation Company Limited. It was hard hitting and the Belfast Steamship Company and its associates on the Irish Sea expressed their concern to the conference that they had loyally followed conference policy in encouraging transit to and from ports by rail and now were faced with the acquisition by British Railways' parent of their most potent and dangerous competitor dedicated to through transit by road and roll-on roll-off ferry operations.

An impartial observer might be forgiven for saying that the Coast Lines Board by their refusal to face coming change had brought much of the trouble upon themselves. Yet any sympathy with the British Transport position must be tempered by the patent duplicity which they practised. Wearing their British Road Services 'hat' they were prepared to foster traffic outside the conference by the Atlantic Steam Navigation Service; wearing their British Railways 'hat', they opposed in conference any proposal by the Coast Lines Group Companies to use road haulage operated by their own subsidiaries on the British side on the hypocritical ground that this was contrary to conference regulations. The proposal had only been made because of the undeniable fact that the British Transport Commission were serving their various sea services by road as well as by rail. In the not too distant future this unreasonable attitude of the British Transport Commission would lead to the Belfast Steamship Company setting up a new subsidiary to deal with container traffic. There were some within the company who felt that the time had come to break with British Railways and the conference and the traditional type of passenger service and commence a roll-on roll-off operation with purpose built tonnage. This would have been a radical and most expensive option but the long term consequences would have been beneficial.

In the meantime, the conventional cargo services were augmented by five interesting ships in the years 1953 and 1954. First of all came the *Hebridean Coast* from the Aberdeen Steam Navigation Company. She was Dutch built in 1938 for the Tyne Tees Steamship Company, at that time outside the Coast Lines Group. She was named the *Sandhill* and was a mere 195ft in length. She had plenty of wartime adventures and had spent three days in Dunkirk harbour prior to the evacuation bringing in much needed supplies and discharging under continual bombardment. Around her fires had blazed whilst opposite to her lay two unattended ships, one loaded with ammunition and the other with petrol.

The *Brookmount* at Liverpool. (PRO (NI)/BSS Co)

She had been in the Irish Sea later in the war and on a voyage from Belfast to Preston in January 1941 was severely damaged by a mine near the English coast. Disabled she had drifted helplessly for two days until taken in tow near the Northern Ireland coast. Then in November 1941, off the west coast of Scotland, fire broke out in her after 'tween decks and she was carrying 800 tons of high explosives... She was noteworthy as the first foreign built ship to be owned by the company by whom she was named *Ulster Chieftain*.

Then came the *Ulster Drover* in 1954. She was no stranger either to these waters as she had originally been the *Sligo* built in 1930 for the Sligo Steam Navigation Company. Following the acquisition of the Sligo trade by Coast Lines she had become the *Lairdsdale* in 1936.

Next, in November 1954, the *Jersey Coast* and *Guernsey Coast* returned from the Channel Islands to become the *Ulster Weaver* and the *Ulster Spinner*. They enabled the coal burning *Ulster Merchant* and *Ulster Mariner* to be disposed of for breaking up and their British Polar diesels brought modern tonnage at last to the Manchester trade which they served until it was discontinued at the end of April 1963. Interestingly, their single screws were driven in opposite directions from each other and it is thought that their engines were originally intended for one twin screw vessel.

The fifth vessel was the most attractive

Publicity postcard from a painting by John S Smith of *Ulster Pioneer*. (BSS Co)

from the ship lovers point of view to enter the fleet but was the least necessary and the wisdom of this purchase must be called in question. She was the steamer *Drover* of 1,660 gross tons and 270ft in length with a horsepower of 1,526. She had borne that name for a very short time. In fact, it was hardly dry upon her bows before she was purchased. It had come to the company's ears that the Vestey Group were contemplating entering the Irish Sea cattle trade. Rumour became fact when they purchased the steamer *North Down* from Messrs G Heyn & Sons, Belfast, and renamed her *Drover*. She was none other than the Clyde Shipping Company's Glasgow/London liner *Copeland* built at Dundee in 1923 by the Caledon Shipbuilding and Engineering Company.

After a cruise for her owners and guests involving a sail inside Skye and a 'turn round Oban Bay' she led a blameless and uneventful life until the outbreak of war. She then served as a rescue ship in the North Atlantic and Russian convoys. As she was a fine sea boat with a deep well deck for'ard and bulwarks level with the 'midships sheer she was well suited to this work. She had two cranes for'ard and these carried the motor rescue vessels which were so essential.

In 1946, she was sold to G Heyn & Sons of Belfast. The Clyde Company had discontinued passenger carrying to London and the *Copeland* was no longer suited to their requirements. She was renamed *North Down* and registered at Belfast in the name of the

North Continental Shipping Company Limited making sailings on their account from Belfast and Dublin to Amsterdam, Rotterdam and Dunkirk. She did well on this service and was popular with passengers for whom a piano, bolted to the deck, was provided in her spacious saloon. Later in the prosperous early 1950s, Messrs Heyn found it more profitable to employ her carrying cattle between Belfast and the Mersey.

She had been laid up in Belfast when the Vestey Group bought her and was bought from the Blue Star Line (part of the Vestey Group) for £17,000 and registered in the Belfast Steamship Company's name as the *Ulster Herdsman*. She underwent a refit in Liverpool which cost £65,000 instead of an estimated £25,000. Nevertheless, she looked as handsome a steamer as could be seen anywhere when she sailed out into the Mersey on her trials and one could forget that she was over thirty years of age, coal fired, and there were such monstrosities as roll-on roll-off ferries up the coast at Preston.

The *Ulster Herdsman* spent much of her career on charter to the B & ISP Company. On one such charter in 1958 she co-starred with James Cagney and Don Murray in *Shake Hands with the Devil*, a United Artists' production made at the late lamented Ardmore Studio. Berthed at Custom House Quay she featured in a gun battle between the IRA and 'Black and Tans'.

Two motor ships for the Belfast/Liverpool cargo service joined the company's fleet in 1955. They were the *Ulster Pioneer* launched from Brown & Company's yard, Greenock, on 24 February 1955 and named by Mrs Reginald Berkeley *Ulster Pioneer*. Her near sister was launched from the yard of A & J Inglis on the Clyde by Lady Brookeborough, wife of the then Northern Ireland Prime Minister, and named *Ulster Premier*. She had a plaque in her saloon recording her sponsorship. The two new ships enabled the *Ulster Duchess* to be sold for £11,500 to the British Iron and Steel Corporation for scrap. These were two fine ships and the company had publicity postcards prepared depicting them at sea. But they were uncompromisingly traditional. Container services had already begun and we have talked enough of what

Dangerous competitor, *Empire Gaelic* enters Larne. (Michael P L Costeloe)

was happening at Preston. Mild misgivings were expressed among management in Belfast at the large investment in tonnage which might soon be obsolete. The two ships commenced a thrice weekly service between Belfast (York Dock) and Liverpool on a schedule which only demanded three round trips per fortnight and three nights at sea per week from each vessel.

It is fitting that we take leave of the Belfast Steamship Company in 1955, bathed in perhaps a deceptive aura of prosperity but there were long shadows over its break bulk cargo operations and there must have been some unease on the passenger side that air traffic had increased in volume by tenfold in the past decade.

The company had been unfairly treated in the immediate postwar years by the Labour government and then by the Conservative government which had allowed the state owned Transport Commission to use public money to buy out Colonel Bustard at a time when the state-owned steamship routes to Ireland were admitted to be losing money. But these things were in the past now; the company had been outsmarted by the British Transport Commission but it was time, more than time, that the whole Coast Lines Group looked to the future.

Perhaps it was a sign of the times that the man who had built up a complex network of steamship companies independent of the railways at no cost to the public purse should pass to his rest on 8 March 1955 at Lisbon,

where he had lived modestly since his retirement. He had not always been right. He could make unreasonable demands on those closest to him which taxed their ingenuity. 'Get me a case of Champagne', was a request to young Reginald Berkeley, reasonable enough were it not past midnight and the venue a charity ball in Belfast. The problem was solved by nocturnal diplomacy with Belfast's Grand Central Hotel. 'Lady Read wants a dog, you are to get one.' 'What kind?' 'That's up to you, but if she does not like it you will be in trouble, and if it lifts its leg indoors you will be sacked.' Dr Ernest Reader discharged this embarrassing assignment by purchasing a pedigree Samoyed.

Alfred Read left behind a modest enough £27,216 gross. Royal Mail Lines brought home his body. After a short service in the chapel of the Missions to Seamen in Southampton, on 23 March 1955, his body was put aboard the MV *Adriatic Coast* which put to sea in worsening gales and buried him as he would have wished in the coastal waters which he loved.

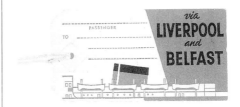

XII

Of Containers and Car Ferries

Roll-on roll-off operations were pioneered by Noah, so it has been said, and not by Frank Bustard and others, as we might have thought. Strangely, no such ancient lineage can be found for the notion of packing cargo in a box at the consignor's premises and despatching it by land and sea to the consignee's address without intermediate handling of the contents. Coastwise shipping, and Irish shipping in particular, can lay claim to being very early users of this method. Prior to 1914 biscuits were shipped from Dublin to London in large boxes from the manufacturer's premises direct to the distributors' depot without intermediate handling at the dockside.

Pilferage, breakage and excess handling, such as horizontal movements in ships' holds, were endemic problems in traditional cargo handling. One way to reduce these adverse factors and to speed up transit was to extend the use of the container and this was the philosophy on which the use of the railway container was based. The Belfast Steamship Company had been well accustomed to carrying these 8ft by 8ft boxes for the sea portion of their journeys before 1939. Operators were placed in a dilemma in the 1950s. There were plenty of complaints from traders of damage to goods in transit and of delays. One man was quoted as saying that it was '... quicker to get a man with a wheelbarrow to push goods from the Midlands of England to Liverpool and row them across to Belfast than to use the ordinary rail and sea transport'. The volume of cargo moving across the Irish Sea was large. Something had to be done and the solution at Board level was, as we have seen, to build larger and more economical but traditional vessels. They would alleviate the problems and reduce operating costs but offered no long term solution to slow turn-rounds and inefficient cargo handling methods.

It is all too easy to say what should have been done. A large scale and sudden transition to total container operation would have been devastatingly expensive but to do nothing would have been ruinous in the long term. Apart from the provision of containers themselves expensive modifications would have been necessary to ships and new purpose-built tonnage would have been needed in addition. On shore large areas for the storage and marshalling of containers for loading would have been necessary and, lastly, investment in cranage to handle containers from ship to shore would have been inevitable.

The best solution was that adopted by Board and management of a gradual change-over for it has to be remembered that despite strident complaints from traders, commerce and industry were no more ready for the container revolution than the most conservative of shipowners and would continue to demand traditional break bulk cargo facilities. Where the Coast Lines Board are open to criticism is in their continued heavy investment in traditional type ships long after a question mark had been placed over them and in their slowness to come to terms with the need for a full roll-on roll-off service for freight vehicles as well as passengers' cars. When receipts are more than satisfactory it is very difficult for the directors of a public company to persuade shareholders that they must forego dividends in order to invest for the future. Private companies, on the other hand, with a road haulage core making an entry into a specialised form of shipping, are not so troubled by shareholders to whom they must account. Nationalised undertakings, too, have no dividends to pay although they may have difficulties in persuading political masters to sanction investment. In the 1950s shareholders in Coast Lines had seen the dividend for the year on their ordinary shares

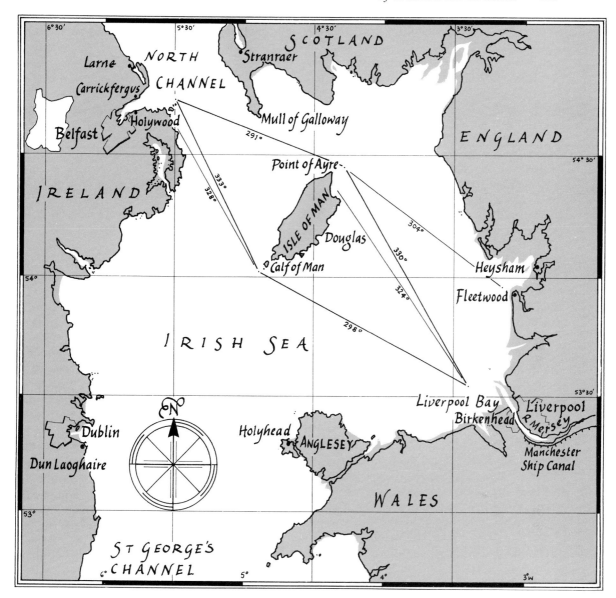

rise from 7½ percent for 1953 to a steady 10 percent for 1955 and 1956. They would see little sign of a crisis in their company but the shipowner who fails to take a long term view of his business does so at his peril.

The Belfast Steamship Company had not operated its own containers at all until 1948 when representations from Reginald Berkeley to the main Board bore fruit and he was authorised to spend £10,000 on containers. The company's traffic manager, R A McDowell, selected a firm in Bangor, Co Down, to make the containers. They had made poultry houses but never containers.

However, they did all that was required of them and the containers when delivered were similar to the railway 8ft by 8ft boxes. A similar order was received from the Belfast, Mersey and Manchester Steamship Company. The containers were carried on the ordinary break bulk liner services to Liverpool and Manchester. They fulfilled a need but like all transitional arrangements the partial use of containers in a largely traditional cargo handling situation proved expensive. They carried two tons of cargo and weighed 15cwt unladen. If a return load could not be found, not only had a heavy box to be handled and carried on the vessel but dock dues on 15cwt of 'cargo' had to be paid. The hatches of the traditional cargo steamer were far from suitable for the reception of containers. They tended to be roughly handled by dockers who were disinclined to attach tackle to the four hooks with which each container was provided. When only two hooks were used the container was often strained and damaged. The dockers also demanded extra payments for handling containers. In the previous chapter we saw that the Belfast Steamship Company unsuccessfully tried to persuade the Irish and British traffic conference to allow an extra charge for the carriage of containers. A solution to the damage problem was initiated by the Mersey company which introduced aluminium containers and banished the incubus of claims for damaged goods in wooden containers, no longer watertight. The immediate future would see the introduction of larger more economical containers which in their turn would make specialised ships and cranage imperative.

The present all-container operations by the company were some way off in the future. In 1953 they had their first experience with such an operation when they were involved with British Railways in an experimental service from Belfast to Barrow and then to Preston. This involved British Railways 'A' type containers which were forwarded by rail to their English interior destinations. The service seems to have been a temporary measure pending the installation of extra cranage at Heysham harbour although Messrs Henry Tyrer & Sons were appointed agents at Preston. A recent addition to the Coast Lines Group, the Zillah Shipping Company (Messrs W A Savage, managers) provided their SS *Caldyfield*, dating from 1921, for this trade and she was followed by other and larger ships in the Group. It was hardly a very modern operation with Clydesdale horses toiling down to the quays with containers on their wooden drays for loading into a 32-year-old coal-burning steamer.

The gauntlet was unequivocally thrown down by a new competitor in the following year, 1954. Anglo-Continental Container Services of London had been sending containers to Northern Ireland for some time by the

vessels of the Atlantic Steam Navigation Company from Preston. Now they had chartered their own vessel to carry containers on a regular service between Larne and Preston. By 1955, this dangerous new foe had three chartered vessels offering eight sailings per week between Preston and Larne and by 1956 the Dutch flag MV *Clipper*, newly-built at Groningen, appeared. She was claimed to be the first vessel built for the exclusive carriage of containers. An unhappy parallel with competition of long ago was that the Belfast agents for Anglo-Continental Container Services were Lawther and Harvey now, of course, no connection with S Lawther & Company.

The ACCS competition hurt and so did competition from another new entrant using chartered tonnage, Northern Ireland Trailers Limited. Both these concerns were outside the conference and both charged rates including container charges which were as much as 20 percent below the conference rates. The Belfast Steamship Company was bound by conference regulation to make a separate charge for containers.

The end of the British and Irish traffic conference in its traditional form was rapidly approaching. The company was prepared to support it loyally but was confronted by the British Transport Commission expecting its railway undertaking to be protected by conference regulations, which placed restrictions on the company's freedom to meet competition from new entrants whilst the commission claimed the freedom to support its own sea services with the resources of British Road Services. This was not fair. Although the Atlantic Steam Navigation Company, as a subsidiary of the British Transport Commission, joined the conference in 1956, no progress whatever could be made on the thorny question of harmonisation of rates. From now on the company's container traffic was frequently forwarded to English inland destinations by road using one or other of the Coast Lines road transport subsidiaries. Indeed, the situation was to lead to the establishment in 1959 of a new subsidiary company of Coast Lines Limited to cater specifically for container traffic between Belfast and Liverpool with road haulage in England as

part of an inclusive 'transport package' un-
trammelled by conference regulations requir-
ing carriage by rail to be fostered.

The disposal of assets by the Board of
Coast Lines where possible continued.
Throughout 1955 apparently abortive overtures were made to the government of the
Republic of Ireland with a view to the
disposal of the British and Irish Steam Packet
Company. It would be another ten years
before a sale could be accomplished. Since
the establishment of the Irish Republic in
1949 in place of the former Irish Free State,
the Dublin company had been gradually
moving away from the Group organisation.
Irish based unions represented the ratings and
led inevitably to separate superintendents in
Dublin. Much of the commercial success of
the Belfast Steamship Company and B & ISP
Company between the wars had been based
upon a sharing of terminal charges and
facilities at Liverpool. This situation no longer applied as much as formerly and an
increased burden was thrown on the company as a result. One effect of the changes was
that catering and other ratings who did not
wish to join Irish based unions had to be
absorbed as far as possible, and paid, by the
Belfast Steamship Company. As the years
went on, other factors were to lend a greater
urgency to the sale of the B & ISP Company.

Staying ashore, the Liverpool offices of
Coast Lines were involved in a momentous
move on 1 January 1957. The lease of the
office space occupied in the Royal Liver
Building expired on 31 December 1956. In
nearby Water Street, a new building was
rising on the site of Colonial House destroyed
by enemy action in the recent war. The
Reliance Marine Insurance Company was the
owner of the new building and Arnet Robinson, group managing director, was on the
insurance company's board. For £17,000 per
annum Coast Lines secured the use of the
third and fourth floors and a semi-basement
which became a spacious and attractive passenger booking office. Not since the days of
Langtry & Herdman had the Belfast steamers
possessed a Water Street address.

Between 1954 and the move to Water
Street, facilities for passengers at both terminal ports had been immeasurably improved. A

The *Scottish Coast*, a luxury Coast Lines could
not afford but a most attractive one. (Mc-
Roberts/Merseyside Maritime Museum)

new office block had been built at Prince's
Dock South West at a cost of £75,000 and
included in its ground floor were a waiting
room, ticket offices and buffet and a left-
luggage office plus a covered pedestrian
approach. At Belfast the Missions to Seamen
moved to Corporation Street and their former premises on Donegall Quay were purchased for £5,000 by the company. Expenditure
of £10,000 produced offices, a passenger
waiting room and left-luggage facilities.

The cargo fleet was augmented on 1 March
1956 by the Dutch built motor ship *Clyde
Coast*. On the small side, she was renamed
Ulster Senator and was not an unmixed blessing to her new owners for she had to be
re-engined in 1957 at a cost of £35,000, just
£626 short of her prime cost when delivered
new by her builders on 12 July 1938.

On the threshold of technological change
of a far reaching nature in cargo handling, the
Coast Lines Board made a regrettable investment decision in 1955 when they placed an
order with Harland & Wolff, Belfast, for a
combined passenger and cargo vessel to cost
£1,130,000. It was a step which was to place a
great strain on Group finances, including the
Belfast Steamship Company.

The new vessel was to replace the Burns
and Laird steamer *Lairdshill* employed on the
Glasgow to Dublin service. It was by any
standard an extravagant provision for the
Glasgow/Dublin service which had a limited

future for passengers and depended for its viability upon the continuation of the live cattle trade, something which could not be relied upon in view of the continuing calls for shipment of meat 'on the hook'. When the new ship was eventually launched, it was announced, perhaps by way of justification, that her first task would be to relieve the *Ulster Monarch* on the Belfast/Liverpool express service when the celebrity retired temporarily for an extensive overhaul. For most of her life on the Irish Sea she would be employed in the Burns and Laird fleet but initially she was owned by Coast Lines Limited and registered at Liverpool. The Ship Mortgage Finance Corporation was applied to for assistance but the Board found it necessary to raise a further half million by way of a rights issue to finance this and other items of capital expenditure. There were arguments for building the *Irish Coast* and arguments against but this ship was 'a luxury that Coast Lines could not afford'.

For better or worse, the new ship was launched on 21 August 1956, by Lady Glentoran, wife of the Northern Ireland Minister of Commerce whose family, incidentally, had purchased Drumadarragh House, Doagh, Co Antrim, from the executors of Charles Langtry in 1862. She was named *Scottish Coast* and was the last in a line of thirteen motor ships commencing with the *Ulster Monarch* in 1929 which had been built to the same general design for the Coast Lines Group. At her launch Captain Nutting observed ruefully that she had cost more than the combined cost of the *Ulster Monarch* and her two sisters twenty-seven years before.

Painted in the colours of the Belfast Steamship Company and proudly flying the company's flag, the *Scottish Coast* sailed on her maiden voyage from Belfast to Liverpool on 4 March 1957. She was commanded by Captain D F Owens OBE, senior master of the Belfast Steamship Company who had been in the service of the company since 1921 and commanded the *Ulster Monarch* during the Norwegian evacuation in 1940.

The *Scottish Coast* followed closely upon the dimensions and general arrangement of the *Irish Coast*. The correctness of the decision to build her apart, she was a delight to ship lovers and one of the most attractive ships ever to sail between Belfast and Liverpool.

Given the *Scottish Coast*'s good looks, was it right to base the layout of her passenger accommodation on a design first introduced twenty-eight years before? It was not. In five years' time the company and others in the Group would be criticised for the inadequacy of the second class accommodation offered in its ships. As far back as 1941 the position of the steerage passenger, so far as access to the lifeboats was concerned, was criticised by Captain P Mullan in a report made to the Admiralty following the mining of the *Lady Connaught*. The criticism was not heeded in the *Scottish Coast*'s design.

There were detail differences from the *Irish Coast*. For example, she had two pairs of electrically driven derricks on her foremast instead of one. She berthed 246 saloon passengers, four more than in the older vessel, but she berthed 144 second class passengers, two fewer. In her saloon restaurant a Highland theme could be discerned in her panelling, doubtless considered appropriate for the Glasgow/Dublin trade. Her large streamlined funnel had outlines in rivets which would enable the Coast Lines chevron or the Burns Laird stripe to be painted on easily. In fact, she never did wear her owners' colours. On the other hand, her aluminium lifeboats each jauntily sported a miniature Coast Lines ensign in addition to her name and port of registry. Manoeuvrability and sea kindliness were assisted by a bow rudder and Denny-Brown stabilisers. She had two complete steel decks, and eleven bulkheads divided her hull into twelve watertight compartments.

She was the last traditional Irish Sea passenger ship to be built. There would never be another ship built with such a spacious saloon restaurant in which eighty-two passengers could dine in comfort and watch the passing scene through deep windows. She never looked better in her all too short life in the Group than during the four months which she spent on charter to the Belfast Steamship Company, demonstrating that strong, simple colours impart the Grace of God to a ship. The *Scottish Coast* took up duty with Burns and Laird Lines on their Glasgow/Dublin service in July 1957 and was

discreetly reregistered in their name on 30 November 1957, but she still carried *Liverpool* on her stern.

Within twenty-four hours of the *Scottish Coast*'s maiden voyage a less comely vessel went down the ways at Denny's yard at Dumbarton. She was named *Bardic Ferry*. Designed for the Atlantic Steam Navigation Company's services from Preston to Larne and Belfast, she was the first fruit of the acquisition by the British Transport Commission of Colonel Frank Bustard's pioneering enterprise. Bustard had retired from the managing directorship in the previous year but it was he who had been responsible for her design and layout. Her significance lay in her main deck which could accommodate between sixty and seventy commercial vehicles driven on and off through a stern ramp and in her long weather deck aft where twenty-five to thirty containers could be carried. She was fitted with Denny-Brown stabilisers provided for the benefit of her cargo rather than for the fifty-five passengers accommodated in two classes, the first class in spacious luxury.

The *Scottish Coast* was an expensive testimony to the excellence of the past. The *Bardic Ferry*, to be joined five months later by a sister, the *Ionic Ferry*, was the pattern for the future.

That other dangerous competitor, ACCS, added a third chartered vessel to their Preston/Larne service at the same time. This was the newly built Dutch MV *Goodwill* able to carry fifty-five 5-ton containers, and they now boasted that heavy freight could be delivered in 24 hours from Belfast to London and that with less danger of damage or pilferage. Furthermore, ACCS were able to offer trad-

ers the same tariff in 1958 that they had used five years before.

The British Transport Commission bought ACCS in June 1958, displaying once more the curious split personality that pervaded the commission and made them difficult bedfellows with the Belfast Steamship Company on the Irish Sea. On the one hand, through their subsidiary British Road Services, they were exploiting the new freedom given to road haulage by the Conservative government which came to power in 1951 and fostering this freedom through roll-on roll-off operations; on the other hand, through British Railways, they had built in 1956/57 three very traditional Irish Sea packets for the Heysham/Belfast mail service. As far as ACCS were concerned, the charters of their three Dutch owned vessels were transferred to Transport Ferry Services as the services of the Atlantic Steam Navigation Company were now styled.

At this time the port of Preston was handling approximately half of all the Anglo-Irish unit load traffic. Road haulage operators had well established depots in the Preston area and this would have implictions for the Belfast Steamship Company and Coast Lines when they started at last to fight back in earnest.

When the *Scottish Coast* made her maiden voyage on 4 March 1957, the *Ulster Monarch* returned to her birthplace in Belfast. It was the second time in her long career that she was to have an extensive overhaul and be replaced by a new vessel designed for another route and registered in the name of Coast Lines at Liverpool. She was to undergo a very extensive mechanical overhaul and to have an extension to her generating capacity installed. The three new turbine steamers on the Heysham service were uncompromisingly traditional but had vastly improved second class accommodation which banished the term 'steerage' from that service. It was essential that improvements be made at once to the *Ulster Monarch*. In fact, the whole after part of the ship was stripped and the second class lounge redecorated in the style of the *Irish Coast*. A deckhouse on the poop similar to that on the *Irish Coast* was also planned. This was never provided, probably due to the *Ulster Monarch*'s tenderness. The *Ulster Prince* was provided with a deckhouse of this type during her 1960 overhaul.

The intention was not only to bring the *Ulster Monarch*'s second class facilities up to date but to give the ship a possible further ten years of working life. Improvements and extensions made to the second class accommodation were to prevent the handling of cargo from the starboard side of the after hold but as the ship now always lay port side on at both Belfast and Liverpool, this was no disadvantage.

Coast Lines intended to send the *Irish Coast* on the West Highland cruises from Liverpool for the 1957 and succeeding seasons. Advertisements appeared in periodicals, including *Punch*, depicting the *Irish Coast* at anchor in a Scottish loch but it was not to be.

The veteran Burns and Laird steamer *Laird's Isle*, which sailed between Ardrossan and Belfast on the summer daylight service, was forty-five years of age and required a special survey. Necessary work to pass her would have involved prohibitive and totally uneconomic expediture. She was withdrawn and sold for scrap. The *Irish Coast* replaced her and although she was unable to equal the older vessel's 21 knots, she proved a reasonable substitute on the daylight service. The West Highland cruises were never resumed from Liverpool. From 1958, the British Railways steamer *Duke of Lancaster* offered short cruises from Heysham to the West Highlands, among other places, in the spring and early summer. The Belfast Steamship Company's

Captain J B Wright, who had been master of the *Lady Killarney*, accompanied the *Duke of Lancaster* as pilot when she cruised in Scottish waters. Coast Lines Group Companies also acted as agents for these cruises.

Traditional attitudes were still a long time dying within Coast Lines. In 1958, the share capital of the old established Glasgow firm of William Sloan & Company, which operated liner services with coal-fired steamers from Glasgow and Belfast to Bristol Channel ports, was acquired by Coast Lines. This purchase made no sense at a time when such routes were doomed to an early demise by the relentless march of containerisation and was no help to the serious problems facing the company and others in the Group. An ominous development in 1957 was a fall in profits for the year 1956 to £1,145,808 from the £1,549,876 attained in 1955. The Indian summer of good profits from traditional cargo operations was coming to an end. It has been remarked that there was an undoubted resentment in both the Belfast Steamship Company and Coast Lines that road hauliers seemed able to charter their own tonnage on the Irish Seas and make very good profits even though they were not traditionally shipowners. Many found it hard to accept that a ship was now no more then 'a bridge over the water' and that the skill in making money from cargo operations was now transferred from sea to land.

But change there had to be and the trading community were shortly to see a welcome determination in the Coast Lines Board and in the Belfast Steamship Company to fight back, matched by a welcome new spirit in the port of Belfast that the drift of cross channel trade to Larne must be halted and reversed. The result was the establishment at the end of 1958 of Link Line Limited which would cater exclusively for unit loads, and offer door to door transit.

The Belfast Steamship Company could not mount this operation under its own name. As a member of the Irish and British traffic conference it was bound by Regulation 30 forbidding member steamship owning undertakings from encouraging road services on either side of the channel to the detriment of other parties to the conference, meaning the railways. Coast Lines Limited was not a conference member, nor was its latest offspring, so there would be no breach of Regulation 30 if road transport was used to the exclusion of rail. The Group was simply placing itself in the same position as the British Transport Commission who shamelessly exploited the dichotomy between their British Road Services and their British Railways.

Some of the old flair in presentation seemed to return to the Coast Lines Group with the launch of the Link Line. The name was pithy and to the point. The house flag was yellow and black, quartered with yellow at the upper hoist and yellow at the lower fly. It was identical with signal flag 'L' in the International Code of Signals, save for the initial letter 'L' displayed in black on each yellow quarter. The ensign could be read as a riposte to those who thought that the container revolution had bypassed the Coast Lines Group for signal flag 'L' on its own means 'You should stop. I have something important to communicate'.

Link Line Limited had its head office at Donegall Quay, Belfast, where Reginald Berkeley and his assistant general manager, Albert Robinson, were directors. N E Harper was appointed manager. The new service was able to draw on the support of Coast Lines haulage companies such as Thomas Allen Limited and the Liverpool Cartage Company. A vital ingredient in the success of Link Line was the firm of Ulster Ferry transport. This concern had been founded in 1956 with the idea of catering specially for Northern Ireland's egg packers. At first they had used the Atlantic Steam Navigation Company's transport ferry service where they had been receiving discounts of up to 20 percent on conference rates. They now agreed to give their exclusive patronage to the new service and despatched 10,000,000 eggs per week from Northern Ireland. This amounted to one-third of the total trade of Link Line Limited. Ulster Ferry Transport itself was later to join the Coast Lines Group in a deal which would include over 200 trailers, 100 containers and flats, a number of English-based tractor units, together with depots in Larne, Lisburn, Liverpool, Preston, Glasgow and Cardiff.

Apart from eggs, machinery, textiles, tobacco, feeding stuffs and canned and frozen goods made up the balance of the Link Line trade. The nature and quantity of the cargo carried was a significant commentary on the extent to which the generation of business had moved from the shipowner to the road haulier.

The loading berths were at Spencer 'A' Quay, Belfast, and East Victoria Dock, Liverpool, which were equipped with Butters 15-ton electric derrick cranes with 120ft jibs to handle the cargo units. The aluminium alloy containers had a capacity of 900 cuft and were of 12 tons capacity, three times that of the units currently in use on the general cargo services. Scruttons Limited handled all stevedoring.

New tonnage was not constructed for the service and Link Line Limited never owned any ships itself, chartering them from its parent, Coast Lines Limited. Two modern motor vessels owned by the Zillah Shipping Company Limited were on hand and would be more usefully employed on the new service than on the coastal and short sea tramping trade where prospects were poor. These were the *Brentfield* and *Birchfield* built in 1955 and 1956, respectively, which were transferred to Coast Lines on 4 December 1958, to become the *Spaniel* and *Pointer*.

Both ships were sent to Ardrossan and had their after hatches plated over to give flush decks whilst their gear was removed to enable containers or vehicles to be accommodated. Below, deep tanks between the fore and after holds were removed giving one clear and unobstructed hold. Main masts were replaced by lighter masts stepped on the monkey island above the bridge. The funnel markings for vessels chartered to Link Line Limited were black with a red chevron piped with green superimposed. A service speed of 11½ knots and the use of the Waterloo Entrance at Liverpool made a regular nightly service easily attainable. (At Preston there were severe constraints imposed by tidal restrictions.)

The service opened on 21 January 1959 when the *Pointer*, under the command of Captain P Miller, and the *Spaniel* Captain N Blundell, set sail from Belfast and Liverpool, respectively.

The establishment of the Link Line was a notable coup for the Belfast Steamship Company and the Coast Lines Group which seemed to have been losing the container war so far. Later in 1959, British Railways commenced a service, which had been planned for some time, between Heysham and Belfast but the initiative had passed from them. In fairness, it should be stressed that their service commenced with the first British purpose-built container vessels, the motor ships *Container Venturer* and *Container Enterprise*.

A third vessel joined the Link Line operation in 1959. This was the *Saxon Queen* owned by the Coast Lines tramping subsidiary, Queenship Navigation Limited. She had been built as far back as 1939 at Bowling by Scott & Sons who had launched her as the *Yewmount*. Coast Lines bought her in 1947. She was never fully converted for container operation so that her appearances on services between Belfast and Liverpool were few. She was repainted in the Link Line colours and re-named *Lurcher*. She spent much of her time far from Spencer 'A' Quay, one voyage in 1959 taking her from the Thames to Odense, Oscarshamm and Calmar before returning to Liverpool and Preston.

At 5.15pm on 21 January 1961 the *Lurcher*, outward bound for Glasgow with generals, including two heavy machinery lifts of 140 tons each for Colville's new steel works at Glasgow, was in collision in fog off New Brighton with the Greek motor ship *Stamatios G Embiricos*. The *Lurcher* sank in 7 minutes in 60 ft of water, fortunately without loss of life. Captain M B Leask and his crew of eleven were rescued due to the prompt action of the tug *Vangarth*. The *Lurcher* herself was raised on 24 February and beached but her career was over and she was abandoned as a constructive total loss. She was later broken up at Preston.

Northern Ireland Trailers, which was the last 'independent' container firm on the Irish Sea at that time to operate its own ships using chartered tonnage, was acquired by Coast Lines in 1959. It operated between Preston and Larne and Ardrossan and Larne. Major G B MacKean, chairman of Northern Ireland Trailers, was also chairman of Larne Harbour Company. This concern continued to trade as

an entity from its operational headquarters at Albert Edward Dock, Preston. For the reasons given above, it was not possible to move its English terminal from Preston to Liverpool; to have done so would have provoked strong resistance from road hauliers using the service.

Reshaping of the company's services across the Irish Sea to match the container age meant that well tried traditional services and traditional ships which had acquired personalities of their own far removed from the concept of 'a bridge over the water' were to fall rapidly before the new all conquering technology. On 31 December 1959 the Belfast, Mersey and Manchester Steamship Company at last ended its independent existence. Its cargo and livestock services were merged with those of the Belfast Steamship Company to form a new organisation called the 'Belfast and Liverpool Joint Service' offering traders who required 'break bulk' services at least two sailings per day in each direction.

Arthur Moore turned the key on fifty-four years of sometimes tempestuous and always rugged independence and fifteen years of far from docile membership of the Coast Lines Group when he left the Mersey Company's offices in Ann Street, Belfast, for the last time. They had forsaken their Corporation Square office in 1952 and it was to nearby Donegall Quay that Arthur Moore went to join the management team of the Belfast Steamship Company. He was to conclude his career in transport later with a directorship of Ulster Ferry Transport. In Liverpool, Harold B Mack, third shipowning generation of his thrusting and enterprising family, retired from the maritime scene at the same time to farm at Malpas, south Cheshire.

Though the old Mersey Company was no more, their memory seemed indestructible for ships bearing their names and funnel colouring continued to cross the Irish Sea for some years.

In the five years up to 1960, the Mersey fleet had been modernised. The steamer *Mount-stewart* had been sold to BISCO for scrapping on 23 November 1955, yet something of her survives still in Belfast. Her bell, engraved with her original name *Somerset Coast*, became the font in the chapel of the Missions to Seamen in Corporation Street. The *Greypoint* followed the *Mountstewart* to BISCO for scrapping on 28 August 1957. In mid-September 1959, the *Brookmount* left Belfast for the last time for an unfamiliar landfall: Barrow, where only the shipbreakers awaited her.

The first motor ship joined the Mersey Company on 10 November 1955, when the Ardrossan-built *Southern Coast* became the *Colebrooke*. Well known in Belfast, she was handed over to William Sloan and Company nearly four years later, on 5 October 1959, to give a younger image to that company's still venerable fleet as the *Forth*. On 30 June 1957, the *Essex Coast*, also from Ardrossan and not quite two years old, became the *Mountstewart*. There had never been such a modern ship in the Mersey fleet since the *Fleswick* joined the fleet new in 1900. The last ship to join was the Denny-built ten-year-old Burns and Laird motor ship *Lairdsben* which became the *Brookmount* in September 1959. A Sulzer engined vessel with good cattle and general cargo capacity, she was lively in a seaway, a quality which did not endear her to all mariners. To assist with the still busy cattle trade, the *Ulster Herdsman* was chartered in the summer of 1959 to take the place of the first *Brookmount*.

The last survivors of the Mersey fleet, the motor vessels *Brookmount* and *Mountstewart*, were re-registered in the name of the Belfast Steamship Company on 1 January 1960. On the following 22 March the *Brookmount*'s near sister, *Lairdsmoor*, dating from 1948, also Denny-built, was transferred to the ownership of the Belfast Steamship Company and renamed *Colebrooke*. The cattle trade continued to be prosperous in the early 1960s though it was soon to decline. In the meantime, economy was sought by increasing the carrying capacity of the *Colebrooke*. She was taken in hand by Grayson, Rollo and Clover of Birkenhead at the end of 1962. A 22 ft section was inserted in her midship body, increasing her length and gross tonnage and, incidentally, improving her seakeeping qualities which had been no better than those of her sister. She was now able to carry 550 head of livestock, an increase of 125, with new pens

The *Ulster Weaver* outward bound from Manchester. (J Y Grogan)

The *Ulster Weaver* in the Manchester Ship Canal. (Captain W Grogan)

for a further 388 sheep and eight horses. In fact she carried neither sheep nor horses in the extra pens after her return to service in February 1963. The last ship to be given a 'Mersey' name was the *Stormont* which joined the Belfast Steamship Company's fleet in 1963. She had been built by G Brown on the Clyde in 1954 as the *Fife Coast* and became the *Fruin* in Sloan's fleet in 1958.

The next victim of the onward march of unit load operations was the Manchester trade on which the Belfast Steamship Company had been unchallenged for little more than a decade and a half. The service closed at the end of April 1963, and the murky waters of the Ship Canal knew the *Ulster Weaver* and *Ulster Spinner* no more. The former remained with the company on the general cargo services to Liverpool until 30 June 1964, when she became the *Kentish Coast*. She was sold in 1968 to Kuwaiti owners. The *Spinner* remained with the company until 1968 when she was sold to Beirut interests.

Manchester traffic was made up into unit loads in a new depot at Milewater Road, Belfast, which was in fact short lived. It was carried nightly by Link Line or 'Joint Service' vessel to Liverpool and forwarded by road to a depot in Salford. The shipper got a better service but the romance had gone.

The Link Line's Belfast/Liverpool Unit Load Service was going from strength to strength and accordingly demanded further investment. On 2 May 1961, the first of two purpose-built vessels went down the ways at Ardrossan. Named *Buffalo* by Mrs W McCoubrey, wife of the general manager of the associated B & ISP Company, *Buffalo* was delivered at midnight on 6 December but did not enter service until the following month. Her consort came from the Bristol yard of Charles Hill & Sons. She was launched on 11 July and named *Bison* by Mrs F R Hooker, wife of the Coast Lines secretary. Both ships made their maiden voyages in January 1962, with Captain Peter Miller commanding the *Buffalo* and Captain Stanley Newton, the *Bison*.

The new ships had a deadweight capacity 50 percent greater than that of their predecessors and new matching shore facilities were needed. A new berth was provided at Liverpool at North Trafalgar Dock and both here and at Belfast 25-ton cranes were installed.

On board the sisters, containers could be carried on the upper and 'tween decks and vehicles in the hold. The 'tween deck was not continued for the whole length of the vessel so that vehicles with high loads could be accommodated in the hold. The two hatches were fitted with MacGregor hatch covers operated by two 3-ton electrically driven winches. The lifeboats were of glass fibre construction and practically every member of the regular crews had single berth cabins. Separate accommodation was also provided for relief officers and ratings.

The superseded *Pointer* and *Spaniel* were placed on a new Link Line Unit Load Service from Belfast to Ardrossan. Both vessels were transferred to the ownership of Burns and Laird Lines with Glasgow registration on 1 January 1965 but without change of name.

There was no place left now for the *Ulster Pioneer* and *Ulster Premier* on their easy going schedule and they left the company's fleet eventually in December 1964. The *Ulster Pioneer* went to William Sloan & Company on 20 December to become the *Talisker* with Glasgow as her port of registry. Her sister went to the same owners on Christmas Eve and became the *Kelvin*. They had found useful additional employment in their final years with the company coping on a 'lift-on lift-off' basis with accompanied motor cars which could not be accommodated on the passenger vessels in the height of the season.

Services to and from Derry had continued on a placid course since the war. The *Ulster Drover* had been sold to the breakers in February 1960, and replaced by the twin-screw Burns and Laird motor ship *Lairdswood*, a sprightly twenty-three year old, which became the *Ulster Sportsman* on 3 October 1959. She had always carried Belfast on her stern so no change was needed here on her transfer to the company's fleet. Apart from general cargo, she could accommodate 290 head of cattle. The Northern Ireland Ministry of Finance had provided a loan of 60 percent at low interest rates towards her construction costs of £51,616 in 1935.

As at Belfast, other vessels from the Group put in appearances at Derry from time to time. So, the MV *Antrim Coast* found herself sailing from the Foyle on 6 May 1961, bound for Douglas, Isle of Man, under the command of Captain E Maddrell, himself a Manxman and one of the Belfast Steamship Company's masters. She had a cargo which earned her owners £780 in freight and consisted of the twin-articulated diesel railcars Numbers 19 and 20 from the recently closed County Donegal Railways. They were destined for service on the Isle of Man Railway and the *Antrim Coast* was the only vessel which could accommodate them and berth at Douglas, where tidal conditions allowed only 2 hours for unloading on each tide.

That same year, 1961, was to see the comparative tranquillity rudely shattered by the announcement in July that Messrs Rainey Brothers of Larne had formed Anglo-Irish

Short sea liner, convoy rescue ship, cattle carrier and film star – the *Ulster Herdsman* berthed at the North Wall, Dublin. (Michael P L Costeloe)

Transport Limited with the intention of offering a unit load service between Londonderry and Preston. They had secured a berth at McFarland Quay together with the use of a 25-ton crane and had undertaken to install a new 15-ton jib crane. Rainey Brothers' *Loch Linnhe*, with a carrying capacity of thirty-one containers, would offer twice weekly sailings in each direction.

The Coast Lines Group could not allow such an impudent challenge to pass without response but they were in a difficulty. Rainey Brothers had stolen a march on them and there was no suitable berth available in Londonderry for another unit load operation. But the Group had an under-utilised asset nearby in the shape of a substantial shareholding inherited from the former Laird Line in the Portrush Harbour Company. Reginald Berkeley was chairman of that company and it was Portrush that offered an immediate solution.

In its present form Portrush Harbour dated from a private Act passed in 1827 for improvements at the expense of forty named men and women headed by Lord Mark Kerr who formed themselves into the Portrush Harbour Company. The works were carried out largely for the benefit of the Borough and Port of Coleraine situated up the River Bann which posed navigational difficulties at the time. The harbour enjoyed reasonable prosperity and the Laird Line, which took a financial interest in it, had regular weekly sailings to Liverpool and a summer service to Ardrossan, neither of which had survived the First World War.

Portrush was an awkward harbour to enter and leave when any kind of sea was running. A 'run' was created by a heavy sea racing past the entrance causing a constant movement of great force in and out of the harbour and creating hazards for ships moored there. A ship entering the harbour in such conditions had to drop anchor to swing round and it was vital that there be no miscalculation. Leaving the harbour in a gale was a tricky business as a ship had insufficient way on her as she cleared the harbour mouth and a heavy sea would push her to leeward and into shallow water.

Before any service could commence a survey was carried out by Captain P G Lynch RNR of the Belfast Steamship Company, who found to his surprise that the leading lights were not in alignment. A 25-ton Butters crane was installed which unfortunately had to be painted every three months due to the type of paint initially used, and a groupage depot was established in Londonderry to deal with small consignments and make up full container loads from them. The Coast Lines Board had decided to purchase the remainder of the shares in the harbour company and the townspeople saw a new age of commercial prosperity dawning.

The practical consummation of all the planning and work came on 16 September 1963 when the MV *Wirral Coast*, painted in Link Line colours, berthed at Portrush at 5.30 pm after a difficult entrance in choppy conditions. She was loaded with containers, flats and trailers and her arrival prompted the Portrush Urban District Council to give a luncheon to mark the inauguration of the new service and the apparent renaissance in the port's fortunes.

The early 1960s were full of changes, sometimes sudden and often bewildering.

One which had become inevitable was the end on 1 April 1962 of the Irish and British Traffic Conference. It was replaced by the Irish and British Traffic Association but this body, a mere pale reflection of its predecessor, played no part in the fixing of individual rates and restricted itself to questions of general policy. The old conference was much maligned in its day by traders and travellers. Provided that the members obeyed the spirit as well as the letter of the rules it conferred benefits on all users of the Irish Sea liner services by providing them with good standards of accommodation and attempting to ensure that the operator could earn enough to maintain and replace the capital equipment which he used. It has yet to be seen that a 'free for all' in rates will be to the long-term advantage of traders and passengers, whatever the short-term advantage might be.

In this changing world there could be regret but no surprise when the forty-year-old *Ulster Herdsman*, last coal-burner and indeed last steamer in the Belfast Steamship Company's fleet, was sold for demolition on 7 October 1963. Her good looks had been marred in later years by the shortening of her masts for the Manchester Ship Canal. On charter to the B & ISP Company and inward bound from Dublin on 16 March 1960, she sustained slight damage in the Mersey in a collision with Pacific Steam Navigation Company's motor ship *Kenuta*. She ended her days at the yard of Haulbowline Industries, Passage West, Co Cork.

The Belfast Steamship Company's passenger service enjoyed reasonable patronage in the early 1960s despite competition from air services supported still by subsidy. Unfortunately, a committee appointed by the Minister of Transport at Westminster to enquire into shipping services to Northern Ireland and known as the 'House Committee', from the chairman's name, had reported on 26 October 1962. It did not spare the passenger facilities offered by the company, nor those of the associated Burns and Laird Lines from Glasgow to Belfast. The ships were referred to disparagingly as of prewar construction and design and compared most unfavourably with the Heysham/Belfast steamers of 1956/57 and with the, admittedly superb, ss *Caledonian*

Princess which had entered service in December 1961, with drive-on drive-off facilities between Stranraer and Larne.

The House Committee did not concern themselves deeply with the level of operators' profits other than to say that they appeared fair and reasonable. They found it difficult to disentangle the shipping undertakings of the British Transport Commission from their other activities. Had they been able to do so a fairer picture of the Coast Lines Group's activities might have emerged, for in 1959 the Commission had admitted to a Tribunal of Inquiry in the Irish Republic that they were losing money on their conventional services from which it follows that these had been provided up to that time at the taxpayer's expense. No such burden was imposed by the Belfast Steamship Company nor the Coast Lines Group, nor did they receive any subvention from the government.

Despite the element of subsidy in the British Transport Commission's services, and especially in the services being provided by British European Airways at that time, the company could not feel complacent over the situation revealed by House. From the public point of view, the policy of a 5 percent annual depreciation on the passenger ships gave their vessels an antiquated reputation which they did not entirely deserve. However, even allowing for the standard of maintenance of the Coast Lines Group which was second to none on the Irish Sea, the standard of second class accommodation could not be defended. Here again, the perpetuation of the *Ulster Monarch* design in a ship as modern as the *Scottish Coast* was unwise. More imprudent had been the heavy expenditure on relief ships, and even the expenditure on the *Ulster Monarch* must be questioned.

The Belfast Steamship Company's patrons would shortly expect sophisticated specialised ships with extensive purpose-built shore facilities to match. The capital cost was frightening even to a company backed by the resources of the Coast Lines Group. At the moment, investment priority was directed towards the expansion of unit load operations. Europe could not be ignored by any transport company which wished to stay in business. The Group had established Link

Line (Continental) Limited in November 1962. This was closely associated with the Tyne-Tees Shipping Company which had joined the Group in 1944. A service was commenced between Newcastle and Rotterdam offering three sailings a fortnight. Shortly after this venture, Coast Lines, again through the medium of the Tyne-Tees company, formed North Sea Ferries in association with five other partners, one of whom was the General Steam Navigation Company. This company was, of course, part of the mighty P&O Group and the alliance with Coast Lines would bring to that great shipping company's notice the extensive road haulage network in the United Kingdom which Coast Lines had built up as coastwise shipping declined.

A welcome inflow of £3,606,922 to Group coffers in 1965 cleared the way for ordering new passenger tonnage on the Belfast/Liverpool service. This windfall came from the sale, as from 1 January 1965, to the Irish Government of the British and Irish Steam Packet Company. Negotiations had continued to achieve this end throughout 1964; indeed, as we have seen, the topic of sale had been on the Coast Lines' agenda in one form or another for thirty years and culminated in legislation in Ireland in 1965.

Between 1948 and 1960, £2,750,000 had been spent on new tonnage for the B & ISP Company and its subsidiary, the City of Cork Steam Packet Company, far more than for any other Group company. The Irish cattle trade faced an uncertain future and the Dublin/Liverpool passenger service was at a disadvantage in comparison with the Holyhead route for destinations other than to Liverpool and its hinterland.

The Belfast/Liverpool service, in comparison, was the most direct sea route from Northern Ireland to most English destinations. The short sea crossings to the Province involved an unacceptably tiresome land journey depositing the traveller at a remote haven in southwest Scotland. That said, the balance of economics was swinging against an overnight service where the passenger ate at most two meals on board and slept the rest of the time. Short sea routes in daylight hours enabled operators to extract money from the traveller for meals and shipboard entertain-

The *Ulster Sportsman* ex *Lairdswood*. (Captain W Grogan)

View of Princes Dock from Royal Liver Buildings. *Scottish Coast* is on the left; the *Munster* on the right and the City of Cork S P Coy's *Glengariff* in Victoria Dock in the distance. The graving dock is now a cargo berth unofficially known as the Gut. (Coast Lines)

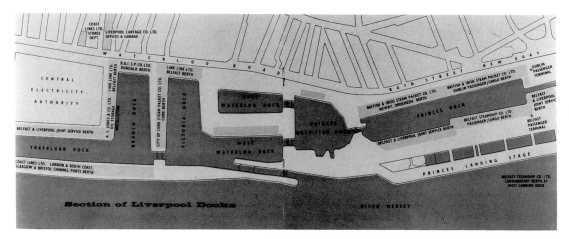

Section of Liverpool Docks

The Liverpool berths of the Coast Lines Group. (Coast Lines)

ment in a relatively short passage time without having to provide sleeping accommodation. The cross channel passenger ship was becoming not merely 'a bridge over the water' but simply a floating garage with a casino attached and minimal meal facilities.

None of this boded well for investment on the B & ISP Company's passenger services. Only in later years would United Kingdom legislation make it possible for Holyhead to be used by operators other than British Railways and their successors. Events since the sale of the B & ISP Company to the Irish government have proved the wisdom of the Coast Lines Board's decision to sell. Commercial considerations apart, the action of the Irish government was courageous in attempting to guarantee that some at least of its sea communications with the United Kingdom would remain under Irish control and give employment to Irish seafarers. The heavy losses, and painful economies in consequence, which have occurred in recent years lie outside our scope but one could wish that similar courage and vision had been displayed by the British government acting in the place of the suspended government of Northern Ireland in 1981. Far less in the way of funding would have been needed than was required ultimately in the case of the B & ISP Company, but we shall come to this in the next chapter.

A consequence of the sale of the B & ISP Company was the transfer to the Belfast Steamship Company of responsibility for the continuance of the Newry/Liverpool Unit Load Service. The company's name appeared soon after this in prominent white letters on the shed at Albert Basin, Newry. The service was discontinued shortly afterwards.

An order was now placed with Messrs Cammell Laird and Messrs Harland & Wolff for two car ferry vessels to be built, one at Birkenhead and one at Belfast, at a cost of £1,940,976 each. Design responsibility for the new ships was placed with Cammell Laird.

Extensive preparatory work ashore was put in hand at once. At Belfast an angled quay extension at No 4 shed, Donegall Quay, was constructed with a loading ramp for the new service. A further ramp was constructed for the intended year-round Ardrossan/Belfast daylight service of Burns and Laird Lines. The south end of Clarendon Dock was filled in and designated as a marshalling area 6,400 sq yds in extent.

At Liverpool, a marshalling area of 10,000 sq yds was achieved by filling in that portion of Prince's Dock South West alongside No 10 shed. Historically, this had been part of the passage which once linked Prince's Dock to the vanished George's Dock, had since served as a dry dock and latterly as a loading berth. The ramp was sited at the north end No 10 shed.

At both Belfast and Liverpool the ramps consisted of steel bridges 76 ft in length and 17 ft wide and had a maximum downward gradient of 1 in 11. They were operated by electro-hydraulic machinery and an operator was located in a conveniently positioned

Donegall Quay in the early 1960s. (Captain W Grogan)

cabin to make the adjustments in height necessary to suit the level of the ship's car deck depending on whether she was light or loaded at both terminals and additionally taking account of tidal conditions in Belfast.

In Prince's Dock, two concrete dolphins were constructed to position the ships in a longitudinal direction and provide support for the housing machinery to operate the loading ramp. The quay alongside No 9 shed was extended by 450 ft and widened by 24 ft. For the moment we shall leave the new ships taking shape at Birkenhead and Belfast and the preparations for their entry into service.

While these momentous events were taking place there had been changes in the board-room of Coast Lines and the Belfast Steamship Company. Captain R S Nutting had died at his Surrey home in March 1964. Arnet Robinson, managing director and vice-chairman, had been knighted on 16 July 1963. In his capacity as chairman of the Mersey Docks and Harbour Board he had the honour of receiving Her Majesty the Queen in December 1962, when she opened the £20,000,000 Langton Dock Entrance. His succession to the chairmanship of Coast Lines and associated companies was virtually automatic. It is no criticism of Sir Arnet to say that he was determined to maintain the traditional

high standards of the saloon passenger services in the Group. But whether this determination was quite the prescription needed for the future success of those services is open to doubt.

In Belfast Reginald Berkeley had occupied the chair of the Belfast harbour commissioners for some years. In the Queen's Birthday Honours List for 1959 he was awarded a CBE.

Still in Belfast and away from the ships, half a century's association with Belfast's prestigious Donegall Place came to an end on 14 December 1965, when the city passenger office was removed to 94 High Street. The solid oak panelling and counter from Donegall Place were transferred to the new office. They had been at Donegall Place since the office at 7a was re-opened in July 1920. It is believed that they were purchased in July 1919 at the auction sale, held at Harland & Wolff's, of the furnishings intended for the great White Star liner *Britannic*, sunk in the Zea Channel in the Aegean four nautical miles west of Port St Nikala on 21 November 1916. The *Heroic* picked up many of the survivors from the stricken liner so it was appropriate that some of her intended furnishings saw

The *Brookmount* of 1959. (McRoberts/ Merseyside Maritime Museum)

service in the offices of the *Heroic*'s owners.

The company's visible presence in the heart of suburban Belfast amidst the most fashionable shops was a prime asset at a time when the passenger had to be wooed and cajoled away from the embrace of the airlines. Unfortunately, the new High Street site made less impact on the city centre shopper.

Even as the *Wirral Coast* was landing her first cargo at Portrush in September 1963, talks were well advanced between Coast Lines and Rainey Brothers, and an outline agreement had been reached to dispose of the harbour. Early in 1964, a final agreement was struck for Coast Lines to acquire a controlling interest in Anglo-Irish Transport Limited.

Coast Lines Group Unit Load operations now obtained access to McFarland Quay, Derry, and services to and from Portrush harbour could be brought to an end. No time was lost in disposing of Portrush harbour and the outline agreement reached with Messrs Kennedy, removal and haulage contractors, was carried into effect. Ultimately, the harbour came into the ownership of Coleraine Borough Council on 6 July 1978.

With all cargo operations from Derry 'unitised', the conventional cargo liner service to Liverpool could be dispensed with. Although she was not the regular vessel on the service, the last such sailing was made by the *Brookmount* on 27 September 1965. The *Ulster Sportsman* remained with the company until 19 December 1966, when she was sold to foreign buyers.

The motor ships *Lancashire Coast* and

Cheshire Coast, dating from 1953 and 1954, respectively, were transferred from Coast Lines to the Belfast Steamship company on 29 September 1965. No change was made in name or registration and for the first time the company owned ships that were registered in Liverpool. In exchange for this pair the *Mountstewart* and *Stormont* were transferred to Coast Lines in the same month, again without change of name or port of registration. The *Lancashire Coast* and her sister were Clark-Sulzer engined shelter deckers with three hatches and a deadweight capacity of 1,400 tons. Their deck gear was capable of handling hoists of up to 10 tons. They acquired a reputation of being good timekeepers on any service in which they were engaged. Both were well known in Belfast from which port they had once sailed to the northeast of England on the former Antrim Iron Ore run. The Antrim Line had been bought by Coast Lines, together with their last two ships, on 1 August 1929. In 1961 the *Lancashire Coast* and her sister were placed on the Belfast/London station in succession to the Clyde Shipping Company which had sold its trade and goodwill but none of its ships to Coast Lines.

The *Lancashire Coast* was to remain on the Belfast/Liverpool service intermittently until May 1980. During this period she was transferred again to the ownership of Coast Lines on 1 December 1967, returning to the company's ownership in 1972. In 1968/69 she was demise chartered to the Prince Line and assumed the name *Trojan Prince*. The *Cheshire Coast* had similarly been returned to Coast Lines ownership but before this, on 8 May 1967, she had been chartered to T & J Brocklebank by whom she was renamed *Malabar*. On 19 October of the same year the Prince Line took her on charter and gave her the name *Spartan Prince*.

The Dutch-built *Ebba Robbert*, dating from 1959, had been bought by Coast Lines in 1963 for Link Line service. She was named *Terrier* and had a hull strengthened for navigation in ice. She was given a refit in Greenock in June 1965 and fitted with an ingenious system of hinged arms fitted to strengthening struts on the ship's side which increased her capacity from seventeen units in the hold to twenty-three, in addition to the fourteen which she

The *Ulster Prince* at her berth in Prince's Dock. (Coast Lines)

could carry on deck. The hatch combings were raised by 4 ft to accommodate the extra containers in this first application of such a system to a home trade ship. Turnround was speeded up by the fitting of Velle single pull hatch covers which halved the time for covering and uncovering the hold. The *Bison* and *Buffalo* had their container capacities increased at the same time from fifty-eight to sixty by means of rolling beams fitted in No 1 hatch.

In the following year, 1966, another ship from the Coast Lines fleet joined the Belfast/ Liverpool Unit Load Service. This was the MV *Dorset Coast*, built at Ardrossan in 1959 for the Dagenham to Cork service, then an important liner trade in connection with the Ford Motor Company operations. She went to Smith's Dock, North Shields, for conversion to unit load operation earlier in the year. For the first time in Britain, chain operated Erman type steel sliding 'tween decks were fitted to her hold between the two permanent decks, enabling her to carry forty-four containers. She took up duty at the end of 1966.

The Belfast Steamship Company's freight services had undergone a transformation with unit load operations accounting for more and more of the volume of cargo carried each year. With this had gone hand in hand a much more intensive utilisation of tonnage and a drastic reduction in turnround times with the aid of the latest technology. By 1966, the company was poised to rejuvenate its passenger operations with the new drive-on drive-off vessels when it received a cruel and undeserved blow. The National Union of Seamen called a strike in that year which had devastating consequences for British shipping in general.

The background to the strike lay in dissatisfaction with leave, working hours, conditions and pay. This had been particularly notable in the North Atlantic steamers based at Liverpool and Southampton. Unofficial strikes had occurred in 1955 and 1960, spearheaded by the unofficial National Seaman's Reform Movement, a group which was aided by the Seamen's International Union based on the American West Coast. The Belfast Steamship Company's passenger services had been unaffected in 1955 but were stopped in 1960 in the month of July, of all times, with consequent irreparable damage to passenger revenue for that year.

In 1965, an agreement on wages and hours had been concluded between the National

The *Irish Coast* at Glasgow. (Coast Lines)

Union of Seamen and the employers. However, in subsequent elections to the Executive Council of the Union no fewer than fifteen prominent members of the unofficial reform movement or its sympathisers succeeded in obtaining seats. It should be said that only one in thirteen of the union's members had been able to vote due to the nature of seafaring. The stage had been set for confrontation and a strike was called with effect from midnight on 15 May 1966, following the rejection by the owners of demands for increased pay, leave and reduced hours. Intervention from the then Prime Minister, Harold Wilson, and the promise of a Court of Inquiry failed to mollify the union.

The dispute was bitter and continued amid accusations of Communist influence from the Prime Minister and statements from an Executive Council member, James Slater, on 5 June, that the time had come 'to hit the shipowners hard'. In vain on 18 May had Sir Maurice Laing, President of the CBI, pointed out that the end result of the strike would benefit foreign competitors and in vain did he warn that the nation appeared to be 'hell bent on committing industrial suicide'.

After forty-seven days the union adjourned the strike for twelve months and accepted the offer of a Court of Inquiry. The Belfast Steamship Company and the Coast Lines Group had been severely affected. The *Ulster Prince* had lain alongside at Belfast and the *Ulster Monarch* at Liverpool for practically seven weeks. Deep sea shipowners had not been as much affected as their ships only became strike bound when they reached a British port and only 26,000 out of 65,000 seamen had been on strike throughout the dispute. Cross channel shipowners were the immediate victims of the strike. The Coast Lines Group suffered an £800,000 loss of profits. The next few months were to see an intensification of the effort to dispose of non-essential assets and a programme of retrenchment.

Investment, however, was not neglected and in 1966 the well-known Liverpool specialised and general haulage company Jarvis Robinson Transport was acquired. This added an extra eighty vehicles to the Coast Lines Group's already extensive road haulage interests. The Carrollstown Estate in the Irish Republic was disposed of and so were wharves in the Tees area as well as 25 percent of the Group's interest in Anglo-Irish Transport Limited. The Atlantic Steam Navigation Company was the purchaser of the latter asset. Also disposed of was Coast Lines' African venture, Thesen's Steamship Company of Capetown.

Of immediate moment to the Belfast Steamship Company was the decision not to put the *Ulster Prince* and *Ulster Monarch*

The *Ulster Monarch* as many will remember her. (PRO (NI)/BSS Co)

through their surveys on October and November 1966. Instead they would be withdrawn after the conclusion of their voyages from Liverpool to Belfast early in October. The *Ulster Monarch* arrived in Belfast on 3 October and returned immediately to the Mersey with sadly empty decks to await disposal. Her consort followed her on 8 October.

Pending the delivery of the new passenger and vehicle ferries in the following year, the *Irish Coast* and *Scottish Coast* were chartered to keep the service going. Though these two ships were near sisters, they had never sailed opposite each other on any service. Regrettably, the opportunity was not taken during their charters to paint them in Belfast Steamship Company colours, nor did the company's familiar red pennant with a white circle even grace their main masts. There was no money for such trivia in the hard post-strike world but both ships looked a little dejected while they filled the gap in the service.

The *Ulster Monarch* was sold on 8 December 1966 to Van Heyghen Frères of Ghent, where her sister, the *Ulster Queen*, had ended her days nineteen years before in undeserved obscurity. Such occasions are sad and when the *Ulster Monarch* set sail on her last voyage, men's memories went with her, even men's lives. Below, Chris Murphy, her fourth engineer, had spent over thirty-seven years of

The *Ulster Monarch* leaves Belfast on 1 October 1966 on her last passenger voyage. Mr and Mrs Derek Neill and Mr J D Hamilton bid farewell to Captain Lucas. (*Belfast Telegraph*)

The *Bison* after handing over at Bristol 1961.
(Captain W Grogan)

his life in her, from her entry into service through peace and war, and had been awarded the DSM for his part in the Sicily landings in 1943. Some would recall gentler prewar days when Minnie from Donegall Quay, a feline exemplar of intensive working, crossed regularly backwards and forwards in the galleys of the *Monarch* and her sisters, skilfully changing ships in Liverpool and even reputedly fitting in a Liverpool/Douglas sailing and back before returning to Belfast that night. Others might recall the *Monarch* in her comparative youth one night in 1934, logging a steady 20 knots from Belfast to Liverpool to catch a 5 am tide.

As soon as she cleared the Bar, on her final voyage the *Ulster Monarch*'s engines were worked up to give a steady 18 knots which she maintained to Start Point. It was an emotional moment when her crew took a last look at her before boarding the coach at Ghent on the first stage of their journey home.

The *Ulster Prince* has been renamed *Ulster Prince I* in October 1966, to release her name for one of her successors. She languished in Morpeth Dock until 11 April 1967, when she also was bought by Van Heyghen Frères, but

she was to cheat the breakers for she was almost immediately resold to the Epirotiki Steamship Company of Greece who renamed her *Adria*. A year later she became the *Odysseus* with Limassol as her port of registry.

Engaged in liner and cruising services in the Aegean and Mediterranean, the *Odysseus* (ex-*Ulster Prince*) was chartered in 1970 to Michael Deeley-Peter Yates Films Limited to play a key role in the making of *Murphy's War* starring Peter O'Toole and Sian Phillips. This was an adventure drama based on a novel by Max Catto in which the Irish survivor of a U-boat attack in the dying days of the Second World War becomes drawn into a relentless struggle against a German submarine. For the old ship, this meant a long voyage from the Piraeus out to the Orinoco River in Venezuela. There, in 100°F, she cruised up and down the river, housing the film crew, production offices, cutting room, make-up departments, etc.

In 1976 the *Odysseus* arrived at the Kyle of Lochalsh for use as an accommodation ship by workers building an oil rig platform at Loch Kishorn. Curiously, as in the days of her youth, her hull was once more arrayed in yellow. She was laid up in Glasgow in 1977 and sold for breaking up at Faslane in 1979.

Before the new passenger vessels entered service in 1967, a significant change affecting Link Line Limited took place when its road and shipping interests were separated. The latter were transferred to Coast Lines Limited, from whom its ships had already been chartered. The Link Line head office was removed from Belfast to Liverpool at the same time. One result of all this was to create a blurring of functions and responsibilities between the Belfast Steamship Company and its 'parent' Coast Lines and accentuate perhaps the tendency to top-heavy management of the Belfast/Liverpool service.

On and from 20 April 1967, the Belfast Steamship Company ceased to accept cargo in anything but unit loads. Any goods offered not already in a unit were made up by the company into unit loads so that break bulk cargo handling finally came to be end. Unfortunately, even before this final development the end had also come for the company's team of draught horses, oftimes prize winners at the Belfast Spring Show. There was no place for animal power in the unit load era.

The new *Ulster Prince* entered the water at Harland & Wolff's Musgrave Shipyard on 13 October 1966, and was named by Lady Erskine of Rerrick, wife of the Governor of Northern Ireland. On the following 1 December, Lady Robinson, wife of the chairman, launched the *Ulster Queen* from Cammell Laird's Birkenhead shipyard.

The *Ulster Prince* sailed on her maiden voyage on 19 April under the command of Captain J B Wright OBE, RNR (Retd), soon to be senior master in succession to Captain E B Clark. The son of a former commodore of the Elder Dempster Line, Captain Wright was the last master in the company to be entitled to fly the Blue Ensign by virtue of his rank as a captain RNR. He was, on the other hand, the first master in the Coast Lines Group to control the engines of his ship from the bridge. It was a poignant occasion for Captain Wright whose father had taken the then new Elder Dempster liner *Adda* out on her maiden voyage almost exactly forty years before. The chief engineer of the *Ulster Prince* was Arthur Luke DSC whom we have met before serving in the previous *Ulster Prince* when she met her end in Nauplia Bay in 1941.

The *Ulster Queen* sailed on her maiden voyage on 6 June under the command of Captain William Lucas. Both ships set a precedent in that they were the first owned by the company to make their maiden voyages from Liverpool rather than Belfast. No doubt this was not unconnected with the extensive berthing trials necessary at Liverpool before they could enter service.

They were the first ships owned by the company to have all welded hulls. Their twin screws were driven by two Crossley-Pielstick type turbo-charged 12-cylinder diesel engines providing a service speed of 17½ knots. In a situation where dimensions were tightly restricted this type of machinery offered the advantage of a low headroom and lent itself to automated control. The designer of the original Pielstick engine had been responsible for the propulsion machinery installed in the German pocket battleship *Admiral Graf Spee* of River Plate fame and her two consorts. Manoeuvrability in enclosed waters was assisted by a bow thrust unit while a bow rudder and twin spade stern rudders made the ships easier to handle than their predecessors. The age old custom of heaving the ships off the quay at Belfast and Liverpool ended, as did the need for water men to take the heaving lines.

The car deck accommodated 120 cars and had a turntable at the fore end. Entry was by means of a hydraulically operated stern door. At the after end of the deck a small number of high sided vehicles could be accommodated. Lifts took car drivers and their passengers up to the accommodation.

Single and double berth cabins were provided for 288 passengers in the first class, including four cabins-de-luxe. The main restaurant was on the starboard side of the first class accommodation with a cafeteria on the port side whilst a smoke room/bar, writing room and lounge were also provided. Air travel had influenced the lounge which had aircraft type seating and that influence permeated to travel tickets which now strongly resembled air tickets in place of the Edmondson type card tickets previously used. The second class showed a great improvement over previous ships with a large lounge, smoke room/bar and cafeteria. There was berthing accommodation for 140 passengers in two, three and four berth cabins.

They were good looking ships in an age when the cult of ugliness was beginning, but this is the best that can be said for them.

XIII
Misalliance

The new ships started to earn dividends for their owners almost at once. In the summer season of 1967, the carrying of accompanied motor cars rocketed to a figure 75 percent over that for 1966. There were high hopes that this would be no summer flash in the pan but that a steady year round business could be had from mainland based representatives with their sample laden cars.

Burns and Laird Lines started their daylight all year Ardrossan/Belfast Car Ferry Service with the Cammell Laird built *Lion* on 3 January 1968. A little less in length and a little more in beam than the company's new twins, she was certainly faster. Her two Crossley Pielstick engines developed 5,500hp each, gave her a speed of 20 knots and enabled her to make the crossing in 4¼ hours. A one class ship, she could carry 160 cars at the height of the season when her moveable 'tween decks were in position. She carried all her cargo on wheels. Units which were not so equipped were transferred to special ship trailers before being put on board. Apart from her daily round trip to Belfast, she later made a trip without passengers each night to Larne and back.

In anticipation of her advent the Glasgow/ Belfast motor ship *Royal Scotsman* had been withdrawn on 29 September 1967 and sold to the Hubbard Explorational Company Limited on 2 November. The *Scottish Coast* took her place. Then on 30 December 1967 the *Royal Ulsterman* made her last sailing from Glasgow and was sold in the following March to Cammell Laird of Birkenhead as an accommodation ship. For a few months a conventional cargo/passenger service was maintained between Glasgow and Belfast, three nights per week in each direction, by the *Scottish Coast*.

In retrospect, it seems a pity that the three new car ferry vessels were not compatible with the ramps at all three ports involved, making it possible for more intensive use of the *Ulster Prince* and *Ulster Queen* to be made from the outset, as, for example, by making an additional Belfast/Ardrossan sailing. Had the two Liverpool vessels been given a little more speed and with compatible ramps, a third vessel for the Ardrossan/Belfast service might not even have been necessary.

However, the essential ramps were in place and the ships were attracting additional passenger business but that business would only be retained and developed if facilities at the terminals matched the ships they served. At Belfast, the new passenger facilities were not ready until 1968.

The new building on Donegall Quay was opened officially on 14 March by the Right Honourable Brian Faulkner MP, Northern Ireland Minister of Commerce, and fated to be the Province's last Prime Minister. What was expected by a generation used to airport departure lounges was supplied in full by the large comfortable waiting room with its information and booking offices, including one for the Hertz car hire organisation, on ground floor level. Above were a snack bar, bookstall, toilet accommodation, nursing room and viewing platform from all of which covered walkways led off to mechanically operated gangways giving access to the ship.

Future car ferry pasengers were not to be left without a tangible reminder of the past. Before she had left Belfast for the last time, the carved wooden 'monstrosity' which surmounted the newel at the head of the staircase in the *Ulster Monarch*'s first class smoke room was removed. This mythical beast had been regarded as a lucky mascot by all who sailed in the *Monarch* during the war and was destined for a place of honour in the new terminal.

The second *Ulster Queen* is launched by Lady Robinson at Cammell Laird's Yard, Birkenhead, 1 December 1966. (PRO (NI)/BSS Co). Right: Sir Arnet Robinson.

Facilities as good as at any airport silenced critics, but some older travellers would, illogically perhaps, look back to a time when the gentle clink of harness, as patient Clydesdales shook their manes, and the smell of hay was a prelude to mounting a green wooden gangway away from the exciting bustle of the shed to the bright warmth of a panelled entrance saloon fragrant with lavender polish.

The *Scottish Coast* acted as relief vessel for the car ferries during their 1968 and 1969 overhauls. The days of month long absences had gone and a ten day overhaul period for each ship now sufficed. The *Scottish Coast* had been refitted in 1965 to enable her to carry twenty-five motor vehicles on a drive-on drive-off basis by means of a 'Gull wing' ramp on the port side for'ard. This facility had proved useful on the summer Ardrossan/Belfast daylight service on which she had replaced the *Irish Coast* in 1965. Her employment between Glasgow and Belfast on a regular basis came to an end on 1 October 1968 when the service was withdrawn, save for a temporary restoration in the summer of 1969. She was returned to the ownership of Coast Lines Limited on 1 November 1968.

How stood the Belfast Steamship Company, then, in 1968, with the car ferry operation in place and break bulk cargo services consigned to oblivion? Could it be said, in the words of the President of the Chamber of Shipping for 1966, that there had been no 'standing still', no complacent '... relying on a long tradition of service as ensuring vigorous survival in the future?' How had they coped with the demand for roll-on roll-off freight operations? 'Expertise born of the past will always be a great asset provided that it is harnessed to new thinking and new techniques.' Had there been enough new thinking and new techniques? The answer must be 'no'. The 'expertise born of the past' showed up in an excessive conservatism on the part of the Coast Lines Board which ensured that the *Ulster Prince* and her sister were no more than cross channel passenger ships with a limited facility for vehicles.

The low headroom on the car deck, due to the second class accommodation above, prevented the ships from playing any part in the imminent ro-ro revolution and deprived them of the opportunity to earn a worthwhile living in the lean winter months.

To be a success a car and vehicle ferry ship has to be designed around the car deck. Indeed, the needs and requirements of the lorry driver must have priority in ferry design. Had these factors been heeded, the ships would have needed greater headroom in the car deck and this would have meant greater beam and difficulties with the crucial dock passages at Liverpool. These, the Mersey Dock and Harbour Board at the time would

M.V. "ULSTER PRINCE," BELFAST STEAMSHIP CO. LTD.
LIVERPOOL/BELFAST CAR FERRY SERVICE

The third Ulster Prince (1967). (BSS Co)

not agree to widen. But there were alterna-
tives such as seeking a new berth down river
even though this would have meant abandoning Prince's Dock, so convenient to the city
centre, the Mersey Tunnel and main line
stations. Perhaps the more radical step of
moving to another port should have been
considered.

Compromises are rarely satisfactory. The
new ships attempted to be all things to all
men: drive-on drive-off facilities for the passenger accompanied motor car; vastly improved second class accommodation; first
class retained to please the company's traditional clientele. An even worse compromise
with the past was narrowly averted, for the
original design specification provided for two
holds for'ard to handle 450 tons deadweight
of cargo. Mercifully, this potentially disastrous feature was altered at the time of the
Ulster Prince's launch to enable the hold space
and foredeck to be utilised for the carriage of
unit loads. It was not altered in time to
prevent the erection of largely unnecessary
cranage at the terminals. An American invention, of which much was made at the time of
its installation, called the 'Stackertruck
Hoverpallet', which lifted a unit load of up to
4½ tons about ¹/₁₅th inch off the deck by
means of a cushion of air, was used in the
holds so that one man could easily move units
from place to place.

It would have been wiser to have built one
class ships or at least ships that could easily
have been converted to one class operation.
As it was, the saloon passenger missed the
spacious open decks, gracious furnishings

and the Bibby-Tandem cabin arrangements
which ensured that most state rooms had a
porthole. The resulting two class accommodation was higher in capital cost, wasteful
in space and inefficient in earning power.

As 1968 wore on, farewell was taken of an
old friend as the Irish Coast was sold to Greek
interests on 16 August 1968. Group overhaul
policy no longer needed a special ship for
relief purposes and the B & ISP Company,
now made their own arrangements. Still in
Coast Lines ownership, the Irish Coast had
spent her last few months before her sale on
Burns and Laird services. According to one
commentator, she was the subject of a
scheme to operate a transatlantic service to
Montreal from Greenock in 1969 under the
name Eros but the plans came to nothing. She
was employed instead on the cruising service
of the Epirotiki concern, being named suc-
cessively Orpheus, Semiramus II, Achilleus and
then Apollo.

At the end of 1968, Sir Arnet Robinson
stepped down from the chairmanship and
managing directorship of Coast Lines and
associated companies, closing half a century
of service to coastwise shipping. He was also a
director of Grayson, Rollo & Clover, the well
known Mersey ship repairers, Martins Bank,
and was joint deputy chairman of the Reliance Marine Insurance Company. Following his retirement, he was elected first president of Coast Lines Limited.

The new chairman was K W C Grand who
had been on the Board since 1962. He
became, incidentally, the eighth chairman of
the Belfast Steamship Company and as a
former Great Western Railway officer was to
be the last example of the 'auld alliance'
between Paddington and Donegall Quay
forged more than a century before. John
Turner became managing director of Coast
Lines Limited on 1 January 1969, and was the
last to hold that office.

Changes soon followed. The creeping assi-
milation of the Belfast Steamship Company
into Coast Lines Limited came to an end. A
new subsidiary was formed, called 'Coast
Lines (Management) Limited', charged with
operational responsibilities for five divisions
organised on a functional basis. Could there
have been an echo here of the former Trans-

port Commission's Railway Executive which was organised on a similar functional basis and with which Mr Grand would have been familiar? Be that as it may, one of these divisions was designated 'Irish Shipping'. Included in it were the Belfast Steamship Company, Burns and Laird Lines and all Coast Lines vessels on unit load services on the Irish Sea. Reginald Berkeley was managing director and the division was managed from Donegall Quay, Belfast.

The Coast Lines Group had survived the

The second *Ulster Queen* in service. (BSS Co)

Prince's Dock in 1967. The *Munster* at the Dublin berth, ahead of her the *Inniscarra*, *Ulster Prince* at Belfast Car Ferry berth, ahead of her the *Brookmount* and nearest to the camera on right, *Cheshire Coast*. (J Y Grogan)

revolution sweeping through cross channel transport even though it had stumbled badly. Others had pulled out of the race or were faring even worse than Coast Lines. The Clyde Shipping Company had already vanished from the coastwise scene; the dismal recent record of the Isle of Man Steam Packet Company depicts a Board that was quite unable to come to terms with change. The North of Scotland, Orkney and Shetland Shipping Company Limited had reportedly been looking for somebody to buy them out in 1961 because they had over-committed themselves to new conventional ships. 'If Coast Lines did not buy the company for a song, they certainly got a bargain', according to E M Turner (no relation of John Turner), Aberdeen manager of P&O Ferries, speaking in 1979. He was referring to the bid of £1.1 million which had won control for Coast Lines of the North company early in 1961. It

now comes into our story for it had tonnage available in the winter months to relieve the *Ulster Prince* and *Ulster Queen* during their overhauls. In 1970 and 1971 the MV *St Clair* forsook her Aberdeen/Lerwick service and spent approximately three weeks on the Belfast/Liverpool service. She had been built by the Ailsa Shipbuilding Company at Troon in 1960 and was a graceful little vessel, said by some to resemble the Royal yacht *Britannia*. She had Denny-Brown stabilisers and refrigerated cargo space but could only cope with twenty-nine passenger cars on a lift-on lift-off basis. Commercial vehicles were beyond her scope and she had insufficient speed to connect with the 7.55am Liverpool

The *St Clair*. (J Y Grogan)

(Lime Street) to London (Euston) Pullman Express. The hopeful anticipation was that passengers would find her an 'interesting vessel'.

Unsuitable as she was, the *St Clair* enabled the *Scottish Coast* to be disposed of in the autumn of 1969. She was sold to the Kavounides organisation for whom she cruised as the *Galaxias* in Mediterranean waters. Later, she was reported as operating 'fly' cruises in the Canaries and to North Africa. She was reported as lying at Vancouver in 1987 after which she was apparently sold to Golden Cruise Tours of Acapulco. Now named *Galaxy*, she was the subject of an unsavoury report in 1988 of passengers having to be flown home from Panama with US State Department assistance after crew riots, faulty air conditioning, unflushed toilets and engine problems. She had reached a sad pitch in a career that through no fault of hers had been all too short on the Irish Sea. There she had closed an era of unhurried comfort and reliability which the *Ulster Monarch* had opened forty years before and now had no place in the jet age.

The colourful past could not provide the means for survival in the future. Much that was prosaic and visually unprepossessing could. When the *Lancashire Coast* returned from her Prince Line charter, she was sent to Harland & Wolff's Belfast yard for an extensive refit. Her derricks and hatch coamings were removed, the hatch openings were plated over and a new exposed deck was raised over the former upper deck. Two hatchways with hydraulically operated steel hatch covers were provided and beneath the deck for'ard to port a gull wing door was fitted, enabling cars and cattle to be loaded from portable shore ramps. In her new uglier but much more profitable guise she sailed for the first time from Liverpool on 24 June 1969.

Ulster Ferry Transport, which had only recently become a wholly owned subsidiary, was not as profitable as Coast Lines wished so a decision was taken to amalgamate it with Link Line Limited. As we have seen, the latter had ceased to operate ships in 1967 and its activities now largely duplicated those of Ulster Ferry Transport. The new combined undertaking was styled 'Ulster Ferry Link Line Limited', and commenced business on 1 January 1970.

Conventional ships had no future in a modern cross channel transport operation and the *Brookmount* was sold in 1970 after ten years' faithful service to the Belfast Steamship Company. She was, of course, the last survivor of the Belfast, Mersey and Manchester Company's ships. She went in 1970 to Rosade Lines SAL of Beirut who renamed her *Pierre Rodolphe*.

Marketing of the passenger business through 1970 did much to offset the effect on passenger carryings of the civil unrest in Northern Ireland. This was a problem which was to beset the company for the rest of its operational existence and was to receive scant sympathy from the government. Emphasis was placed on the company's greatest asset: the possibility of a comfortable night's sleep in a floating hotel so that the passenger could face a day's business or the start of a holiday free from fatigue. Travel agents were exhorted to book passengers the 'civilised way' under the slogan, 'We are selling your clients down the Mersey!' In the national press there were advertisements inviting prospective travellers to 'Join the Sleep-In' and a 'Sleeping Beauty' commercial was sponsored on TV.

By 1970, the Coast Lines Group had become 25 percent owners of North Sea Ferries and General Steam Navigation (part of P&O) held a similar stake. Close relations with General Steam Navigation, whose ambitious executives were keenly aware of the huge Coast Lines road transport organisation and

The *Scottish Coast* in Burns and Laird colours laid up in Birkenhead, 1968. (J Y Grogan)

mindful of the EEC, which the United Kingdom was shortly to join, probably created the atmosphere in which a message reached John Turner. It invited him to call on Sir Donald Anderson, chairman of P&O.

John Turner duly called on Sir Donald and found his assistant Ford Geddes also present. It was he who had delivered the message from Sir Donald. Mr Turner was asked if Coast Lines would like to join the P&O family? The approach was based on the friendly relationship which existed between them and Turner was assured that if the Coast Lines Board did not agree to join P&O there would be no question of a takeover bid.

The proposal for a friendly union was eventually consummated in August 1971, when P&O purchased the share capital of Coast Lines Limited for a consideration of £5.6 million worth of P&O deferred stock. The transaction was given retrospective effect to 1 January 1971. The only hitch in the otherwise smooth course of negotiations which at one time threatened the proposed takeover concerned the valuation of Ulster Ferry Link Line which had failed to perform in accordance with expectations.

Inevitably, one asks was the takeover necessary or was it even desirable? It was probably not necessary. Coast Lines could have continued and could have financed the expansion and development that would have been necessary in the future.

Carry on they might have done but a rights issue would have been necessary. Then a bid might have been made on terms that the shareholders would not have been able to refuse. Indeed, even while the talks with P&O were under way an approach was made and withdrawn when the situation was explained to the bidder. Whether it was desirable or not is a more difficult question to answer. At board room level P&O still presented a very traditional face. 'Gorgeous it was, no doubt, with a string of jewels embedded in the east, but getting heavy and sluggish with age.' Possibly, an invitation from P&O with such a reputation might have seemed to offer at the time security in the comfortable embrace of a large Group which knew how to cherish its assets. Beneath the surface the executive team of P&O were striving to break the old image which the company had enjoyed. The Belfast Steamship Company was soon to find that they had joined a family which expected adequate returns based on five year projections from its progeny and which lacked sentiment in any shape or form for businesses which seemed unlikely to perform adequately in the future. Early in 1972, danger signals had been hoisted when Reginald Berkeley in Belfast received a letter from an executive of P&O in London. The writer asked for Mr Berkeley's views on more profitable employment for the *Ulster Prince* and *Ulster Queen* than their existing service. As managing director of the Belfast Steamship Company, Reginald Berkeley had the right to approach his chairman directly and did so. Ford Geddes, in office since August 1971, replied reassuringly. He had given instructions that Mr Berkeley, who had much to contend with in the troubled conditions of Northern Ireland, was not to be troubled in that way again.

The *St Magnus* ex *Ulster Sportsman* ex *Dorset* ex *Donautal*. (P&O)

Donautal at Liverpool. (J Y Grogan)

Ford Geddes was not destined to be chairman for much longer.

An early overt sign of P&O control was the transfer of the *Bison* and the *Buffalo* from the former Link Line Belfast/Liverpool Unit Load Service. They were sent to the Hull/Rotterdam service of North Sea Ferries in which P&O now held a 50 percent interest and were renamed *Norbank* and *Norbrae* respectively.

The *Norbank* reappeared in the Mersey when she was chartered to the MacAndrews/United Baltic Corporation joint 'Macpack' container service to Spain. In April 1979 she was sold to the National Suriname Shipping Company of Paramaribo.

The *Norbrae* (ex-*Buffalo*) had a spell in P&O's London/Continental trade as the *Roe Deer*. She was sold in 1977 to Harvey Containers of St Johns, Newfoundland, by whom she was renamed *Newfoundland Container* and used in the Canadian East Coast trade.

The Belfast/Liverpool (Trafalgar Dock) Unit Load Service was maintained after the departure of the *Bison* and *Buffalo* by the *Spaniel* and *Pointer* who had been ousted nine years before. They had been reregistered in the name of the Belfast Steamship Company at Belfast and painted in the company's colours in 1971. The service ceased in 1973.

With the long shadows of the P&O takeover already falling, the Belfast Steamship Company had taken what seemed like a confident step into the future. Management, convinced of the inadequacy of the *Ulster Prince* and *Ulster Queen* and at the same time of the urgent need to get into the ro-ro freight market, saw that the answer lay in chartering suitable tonnage. With the blessing of the Coast Lines Board, the company made use of the services of a Glasgow firm of shipbrokers who secured for them a charter of the 1,000 ton *Donautal*, barely a year old. Registered in Lubeck, she was owned by the Hamburg firm of J A Reinecke. As she was built at Bremerhaven, she had in all a strong Hanseatic lineage and was the first peacetime charter of a foreign flag vessel by the Belfast Steamship Company and went into immediate service in February 1971 between Belfast (Donegall Quay) and Liverpool (South Nelson Dock), making three sailings in each direction per week. She was bought in 1974 and renamed *Ulster Sportsman*, being the last ship to be registered in the name of the Belfast Steamship Company. Unfortunately, she never had a chance to prove her real worth on the service. Her top deck was only suitable for lift-on lift-off operations and dockers at Liverpool refused to load her. In

1976 she left the company (or 'P&O Ferries' as it had then become) on bare boat charter to Truck Lines for their operations out of Poole and was renamed *Dorset* by them.

The *Donautal*'s almost identical sister, *Saaletal*, was chartered in June 1971. After brief service on the Ardrossan/Belfast run she started a new ro-ro service in October 1971 from Belfast to Heysham, jointly with British Rail. It is likely that British Rail was not entirely uninfluenced by national politics in this venture. Edward Heath's Conservative government was in the process of compelling the Transport Holding Company, successors to the British Transport Commission, to disgorge the Atlantic Steam Navigation Company from its maw. A sale took place at the end of 1971 to European Ferries. Without the new joint service, the whole state-owned transport undertaking of which British Rail was a part would have had no freight ro-ro services from England to Northern Ireland. The joint service continued until 1978 when the partnership was dissolved. A ro-ro service continued as a purely British Rail operation to Heysham. It ended on 31 December 1980, with low freight rates and shortage of freight being blamed. In fact, Sea Link, as the British Rail shipping operation was then called, were carriers only, selling no more than space on their ships. There was no attempt at a total transport operation.

On the threshold of the P&O takeover, the Coast Lines headquarters staff at Liverpool was facing a crisis. The coasting liner trade had been extinct for some seven years, leaving many executives and staff with little option but to duplicate management's function in Belfast were it not for the continuing extensive passenger and freight agency for the B & ISP Company, owned, of course, by the Irish government since 1965. Now the Irish company had given notice of its intention to end the agency agreement. To develop its sales and marketing potential in England it quite properly considered its own organisation to be essential. No fewer than 156 Coast Lines staff were engaged on B & I agency work in Liverpool and other places. Eventually, the vast majority of these were transferred to the employment of the B & ISP Company; an operation that was only completed after P&O

had assumed control. This diminution of staff commenced the inevitable rundown of Coast Lines headquarters at Reliance House and the eventual departure of cross channel staff from Water Street to Prince's Dock South West.

Meanwhile, all was not well at Beaufort House, headquarters of the Belfast Steamship Company's new foster parents in the City. The old dynasty of forward looking but traditional shipowning directors who had invited Coast Lines to join the family fell at a stroke in November 1972, brought low by an ill judged attempt to diversify. The proposed purchase of Bovis, the building and civil engineering group, at what was thought to be an excessive price brought about the 'palace revolution'. Ford Geddes and six other directors resigned. Lord Inchcape, an existing P&O director, assumed the chairmanship.

The 'palace revolution' became the occasion to put into effect a report from the McKinsey organisation on P&O's management structure. Ironically, the study leading to the report had been commissioned at Geddes' suggestion. P&O was reorganised into five operating divisions in 1972 and Dr Rodney Leach joined the P&O organisation from McKinsey where he had been instrumental in drawing up the recommendations in the report. He was to exercise an unhappy influence over the future of the Belfast Steamship Company. However, it must be said that in 1972 P&O's own financial position after the 'palace revolution' was such that its very existence was at stake.

Amid all this maelstrom of change, Reginald Berkeley CBE JP retired from the managing directorship of the Belfast Steamship Company on 29 November 1972, bringing to an end forty-five years of service to the company. He was only the fifth general manager in the company's 120 years. The new managing director of the company was Harold McMurray, formerly assistant general manager and before that general manager of Anglo-Irish Transport Limited.

Before Mr Berkeley's retirement, the company had an unpleasant reminder of the near impossibility at times of trying to carry on business in a community bedevilled by political instability and torn by civil strife. On 21 July 1972, twenty-two bomb explosions took place within a radius of one mile of Belfast city centre, causing nine deaths and 130 injuries. One of these bombs was planted in a car outside the company's head office in Donegall Quay and caused considerable damage but mercifully no casualties.

Another ro-ro charter party was entered into by the company in February 1973, which uniquely demonstrated the growing complications of shipowning. The ship concerned was the *ASD Meteor* intended for the Belfast/Heysham joint service. Larger than the *Donautal* and her sister, she was a maritime mongrel, having been built in Norway in 1971 for Finnish owners. Bought in the same year by World Wide Shipping of Monrovia, she now flew the Singapore flag, was managed by Bernhard Schepers of West Germany and had German officers and a Portuguese crew. A useful ship, she was only too typical of a tendency to drive ships from the British registry and cast their crews ashore on the streets.

In 1972 a movement began within the P&O Group which would soon gather pace to threaten the Belfast Steamship Company's Belfast/Liverpool passenger service and finally extinguish it altogether within a decade. This was the formation of Ferrymasters (Ireland) Limited. An offshoot of the vigorous and thrusting Ferrymasters Limited of Felixstowe, formed in 1956, this concern offered shippers a unique package deal undertaking all documentation and customs clearance as well as operating extensive tractor fleets, not only in England but also in the Netherlands, Belgium and Denmark. Shrewdly, Coast Lines Limited had acquired an interest in Ferrymasters and it was now a wholly owned subsidiary of P&O. Operating initially from Preston to Larne, Ferrymasters chartered the German built *Embdena* completed in Emden the previous year. She was then chartered to Anglo-Irish Transport for their Preston/Londonderry service. Due to the devaluation of the pound against the Deutschmark, the charter became less attractive and the *Embdena*, which had borne the name *British Unit* for a time, was bought for the Belfast Steamship Company's service for which she was renamed *Ulster Merchant* in November 1973.

Ferrymasters inaugurated in June of that year a new Fleetwood/Larne container service using the chartered MV *Amuthon*. Not only was there significance in the arrival of Ferrymasters but there was deeper significance in their use of Fleetwood. The truth was that though Preston had carried the torch for much of the new technology in cross channel transport, deep seated silting problems in the Ribble, beyond the aid of dredging, made further development there impossible.

In November 1973 the British Transport Docks Board began work on a roll-on roll-off terminal at Fleetwood. The Wyre port was about to experience an astonishing resurrection which would make it the principal freight port for Northern Ireland.

In the following year, 1974, P&O invested £8 million in two 2,250 ton deadweight ro-ro vessels which were building for Stena Line AG of Gothenberg in the specialist yard of J J Sietas of Hamburg. Designed by Knud Hansen of Copenhagen, the ships were equipped with fin stabilisers, had a fixed internal ramp and a 32 ton freight elevator between the main and lower decks. They had no passenger certificates and with accommodation limited thus to twelve drivers they were able to carry hazardous consignments on their upper decks.

In addition to buying the ships building for Swedish owners, P&O invested £1.25 million in ro-ro units of various kinds to be used with the new ships. In December of 1974 a new organisation called 'Pandoro', providing a total transport operation for shippers to Ireland, was established with headquarters at Altrincham. Northern Ireland Trailers and Ferrymasters (Ireland) as well as Ulster Ferry Transport were absorbed into the new organisation. Not all of the expenditure was to serve Northern Ireland as one of the two ships was to sail on a new Fleetwood/Dublin service to be operated jointly with the B & ISP Company.

Fleetwood was as well placed as Preston for motorway connections and for the depots established in the northwest of England by many hauliers. Larne was at the pivot of the modern trunk road network planned by the former Northern Ireland government. Fleetwood/Larne was a logical priority for investment by the P&O Group and simply followed on the foundation laid by Coast Lines on a pattern dictated by the road haulage industry.

The first of the new ships was named *Bison* at Larne by Mrs McMurray, wife of the Belfast Steamship Company's managing director on 11 February 1975. She made her maiden voyage in the same month from the Royal Seaforth Dock, Liverpool, to Belfast loaded with trade cars. After several more such voyages she took up duty on the Fleetwood/Larne services. Her sister, *Buffalo*, commenced sailing from Fleetwood to Dublin in the following month. Meanwhile, the Belfast Steamship Company's passenger business was well maintained despite a perceptible lack of interest on the part of P&O. The great and the famous now winged their way across the Irish Sea but some still preferred the comfort of the ship and saw good sense in arriving fresh for a business engagement after a comfortable night's sleep.

The service was not carried on without difficulties due to the civil unrest. On 20 July 1974, the *Ulster Queen*, under the command of Captain Peter Lynch RNR, was alongside at Donegall Quay when a caller to Belfast's *Irish News* at 8.15am warned of three bombs on board. A small bomb later exploded in a lounge on the port side but the damage was not severe and the vessel was able to sail for Liverpool that night. It was thought that the device had been smuggled on board the previous night at Liverpool. However, the ships continued to sail without interruption and in December 1974 the two millionth passenger since the introduction of the car ferry service was recorded.

The comparative prosperity of the passenger business and the rapid expansion of ro-ro freight services was achieved against a difficult background. On the one hand shipping in general was going through a period of cyclical fluctuation without a proper boom and with a background of stagnation. Whilst this had only an indirect effect on the company and P&O unit services in general, there was no doubt about the direct effect of the sharp increase in world oil prices which took place in the same period. A hard look at speed had to be taken by all operators and the accelerated schedules introduced soon after

the commissioning of the *Ulster Prince* and *Ulster Queen* which had made a Belfast departure time of 8.45pm possible were withdrawn. From 1 January 1975 the Belfast departure time reverted to 8.30pm and at Liverpool there was a similar reversion to 9.30pm from 9.45pm.

National inflation was reflected in wages afloat and on the dockside. Regrettably, a bone of contention between the company and its seamen came to the surface early in 1975. Sunday sailings had been first introduced for the summer season on 27 May 1973, and for these additional payments were demanded by the National Union of Seamen. Although agreement appeared to have been reached, an unofficial strike of the crews on the *Ulster Prince* and *Ulster Queen* took place in May 1975, when sailings were interrupted for three days.

John Turner retired from the chairmanship of P&O Ferries on 31 March 1975. He had successfully turned Coast Lines around in its closing days and upon his shoulders had lain the heavy responsibility of recommending the P&O approaches to his Board. After the takeover by P&O he had assumed the office of chairman of P&O Ferries with headquarters at Liverpool.

From North Sea Ferries came Ian Churcher to succeed John Turner. His appointment signalled the removal of P&O Ferries' headquarters from Liverpool to London. Even the silver from the management dining room was not spared in the upheaval and had to join in the southward migration to P&O headquarters. What was now, in effect, simply the Belfast Steamship Company's Liverpool staff conducted its business from the buildings at Prince's Dock South West and Reliance House was foresaken although the passenger office was retained as the Liverpool offices of the B & ISP Company. There were to be other and more ominous changes in the immediate future.

The commencement of the Fleetwood/ Larne ro-ro service had immediate repercussions on the Anglo-Irish Transport operation. Londonderry, hard hit by depression and unrest, could no longer support a viable liner service to and from England. Indeed the developing road network from Larne made

The *Cambrian Coast* leaving Belfast Lough. (Captain Grogan)

such an independent service unnecessary and the Preston/Londonderry route was closed down in July 1975. In its time a variety of vessels had served on it, including the *Ulster Merchant*, *Terrier*, *Cambrian Coast*, *Wirral Coast*, *Dorset Coast* and the *Pointer* and *Spaniel*, whose own unit load service from Belfast to Liverpool (latterly South Nelson Dock) had been withdrawn in anticipation of the new service from Fleetwood.

After purchase by Coast Lines, Anglo-Irish Transport had commenced a Preston/Warrenpoint Unit Load Service, later extended to Garston, in succession to the Liverpool/Newry conventional liner service which the Belfast Steamship Company had itself inherited from the B & ISP Company in 1965. Operations to and from Warrenpoint became unattractive to the P&O Group and Anglo-Irish Transport and its services and goodwill were sold to the Coastal Container Group in June 1977.

There was a depressing inevitability characterising an announcement in 1975 that P&O Ferries was to have a 'new image'. A great deal of money was spent in lavish advertising in association with the new image which involved the dropping of the trading name 'Belfast Steamship Company' as well as 'Burns and Laird Lines'. Instead, from 1 October 1975, the trading and travelling public were offered the banal 'P&O Ferries,

Irish Sea Services'. The changes sprang from the reorganisation of P&O in 1972 and in particular from Dr Rodney Leach who headed the European and Air Transport Division including P&O Ferries. It was on his insistence that the individual identities of subsidiary companies were snuffed out. Ian Churcher's statement announcing the changes was well laced with such clichés as 'uniform identity' and 'new corporate image' but brought no indication of what was really needed on the Belfast/Liverpool service – investment in new equipment. The Belfast Steamship Company continued together with Coast Lines, as functionless 'dummies' within P&O. For a time ships continued to be registered in the name of the Belfast Steamship Company at Belfast. When this gave way to registration in the name of P&O Ferries, the port of registration remained unaltered.

The *Ulster Prince* and *Ulster Queen* emerged from their 1976 winter overhauls in unfamiliar and unbecoming colours. The Belfast Steamship Company colours had given dignity to the appearance of these traditionally styled ships, now a blue hull plastered with the legend 'P&O Ferries' and a blue funnel gave an impression of mutton dressed as lamb.

The changes were a psychological mistake which alienated local sympathy for the P&O Group and were a folly that would never have been committed by Sir Alfred Read.

At the time these momentous changes were taking place, the financial spotlight fell uncomfortably on the Ardrossan/Belfast passenger and freight ferry service. Uncertainties over its future had led to a dockers' strike in Belfast on 22 August 1975, which caused the suspension of the Liverpool service on that day at the height of the passenger season. On 30 October P&O announced that the *Lion* would be withdrawn in the following year and replaced by 'a smaller, more suitable vessel'. In fact, she was earmarked for a new venture by P&O from Dover to Boulogne.

On the plea that she had sustained storm damage, the *Lion* was withdrawn on 12 February 1976, earlier than expected. Her chartered replacement offered facilities for ro-ro traffic only and was criticised for being inadequate even in that role. So ended the last vestige of Burns and Laird passenger operations to Belfast.

On 21 June 1977, the *Ulster Prince* had a minor engagement with Royalty in the Mersey. Her Majesty the Queen, on a Royal visit to Liverpool, had embarked on the MV *Royal Iris* for a 50 minute cruise in the Mersey. The *Ulster Prince* embarked 600 passengers for the occasion and was anchored off Seacombe dressed overall. She returned afterwards to Prince's Dock South West.

Despite its unhappy reputation for apparently intractable labour disputes gained in recent years, no one could ignore the strategic position of the port of Liverpool as far as trade with Northern Ireland was concerned. Soon, there would be full implementation of EEC regulations restricting the maximum hours which lorry drivers could spend behind the wheel in any one day and then there would be advantages which no one could dispute for an overnight crossing from the Mersey.

Accordingly, P&O set to work at North West Alexandra Dock, Liverpool, where a ramp and marshalling space for 250 trailers were provided. Pandoro schedules were re-cast and extra tonnage chartered in the form of the four-year-old MV *Union Melbourne* owned by Northern Coasters Limited. From 15 October 1979, nightly ro-ro sailings commenced from Liverpool to Larne with a return daylight service each day. From Fleetwood there were daylight services with return sailings each night.

The *Union Melbourne* came, like the *Bison* and *Buffalo*, from the Hamburg Yard of J J Sietas. She was a little larger, being able to carry 110 trailers instead of the *Bison*'s ninety.

So successful were the new schedules that P&O invested £4 million in their Larne operations. The *Union Melbourne* was purchased and sent to the Tyne Ship Repair Group for alterations to her accommodation. She returned to service in November and was renamed *Puma*. The *Bison* followed her to the Tyne for lengthening and accommodation changes. As a result both vessels could now cater for forty drivers in twenty two berth cabins with private toilet and shower.

The Pandoro operations abstracted most of

One of the buses used latterly to carry passengers and luggage from ship to train at Liverpool. (Coast Lines)

the freight traffic from the Belfast/Liverpool route and they continue in operation to this day. It is clear that the P&O view at the time was to develop the strongest possible freight links with Northern Ireland and they did so at considerable cost. It would be unfair to suggest that they were devoid of understanding for the problems of the Belfast/Liverpool passenger service and the staff involved. But, as we shall see, for various reasons some obvious, some not so, the Northern Ireland passenger business did not seem at the time to be a promising field for investment. The whole P&O Group was plagued by financial problems not directly connected with its Irish Sea operations and had its shareholders to answer to. That does not mean that some of its investment priorities elsewhere are not open to criticism.

Back at Donegall Quay, Harold McMurray had retired as general manager, P&O Ferries, Irish Sea Services, on 30 June 1979. His successor, Derek P Neill, was the sixth and last to occupy the general manager's chair in ninety-two years but was now styled 'senior executive'. He had an unenviable and near impossible task. Without a large regular throughput of freight on the traditional Belfast/Liverpool route the passenger service was not viable. Freight meant ro-ro and demanded the right tools for the job. The

Presentation to R W Berkeley, on board the
Ulster Prince **in 1972, from sea-going staff.**
(Captain P G Lynch)

right tools meant new tonnage without which management was being asked to make bricks without straw. Time was short but P&O was short – of cash.

Labour disputes became tiresome from 1979 onwards and dock workers in particular seemed almost determined to make survival for the route impossible. Coastal dockers struck in Liverpool in July and August 1979 for better bonus payments to match deep sea dockers' earnings. Passenger services were not affected but freight traffic was diverted to Fleetwood with much loss of goodwill and a threat to the new schedules to be introduced in October. However, the goodwill was regained when Fleetwood was strike bound in October 1979 as the result of a manning dispute caused, again, by the new Pandoro schedules.

A particularly frustrating dock dispute in Liverpool succeeded in stopping passenger sailings as well as freight services just before the Easter holiday period of 1980. The strike had nothing whatever to do with P&O services and originated in the suspension of twenty deep sea men for refusing to handle a cargo of export steel which had been 'blacked' due to industrial action in the steel industry.

As if all this was not enough, the services were severely affected by the recession which caused an excess of capacity to arise on Irish Sea routes. At this difficult time an award to the National Union of Seamen of a 24 percent

increase in average wages in January 1980 bore eloquent testimony to the severe inflation from which the national economy was suffering. Only eight months later, in September, a further demand was tabled by the NUS in the shape of a package expected to work out at an average 16 percent increase.

Against this discouraging background, management had to maintain and market the Belfast/Liverpool passenger service. Regular Sunday sailings, instead of simply at peak periods, commenced in January 1979. In the summer of that year daylight sailings at weekends were also introduced and second class was relaunched as economy class.

In the following year the first hints were leaked that firm decisions on new tonnage were not far away, although P&O Ferries were said to be 'playing it close to the chest'.

New ships would mean catering for the ro-ro traffic and greater beam in consequence would demand that the problem of the Liverpool dock entrances be addressed in earnest. Increasing fuel costs would place a premium on economy in the engine room and then there was another problem to be confronted. In the last chapter we alluded briefly to the problems which operators encounter with long overnight cross channel sailings; in the silent hours he was merely conveying the sleeping forms of his fare paying passengers with no further opportunity to maximise revenue from them. Discos, one-armed bandits and cinemas seemed to point the way from the experience with North Sea ferries. It was suggested that '... people are looking for something more to do other than eat, drink and go to their cabins'. Whether this reflected the opinions of the Belfast Steamship Company's loyal but staid following of saloon passengers may be doubted but it might wean away a younger generation from the airport departure lounge.

Optimism seemed to blossom triumphant. The new ships would be ready by 1984. They would need new berthing facilities and there was talk of a £20 million scheme for a new terminal on the reclaimed land at the West Twin with direct motorway links in Belfast. At Liverpool the situation was less promising with the Mersey Docks and Harbour Company, beset with financial problems and rumoured to be anxious to close the Waterloo Entrance. The Mersey Docks and Harbour Company eventually agreed reluctantly that the dock passages could, in fact, be widened but by then it was too late and the Belfast/Liverpool service was already doomed.

An alternative plan was to extend the smaller landing stage that replaced Liverpool's famous Prince's landing stage by degrees in the period 1973-78. The extended stage with ramps would have preserved city centre access as well as being close to the Tunnel entrances and so preferable to a down river berth.

The location of berths at Liverpool was a minor problem for P&O for the whole Group was losing money and rumours had even circulated that it was the possible target of a takeover bid by Far Eastern interests. The Belfast/Liverpool service alone had lost £600,000 in the financial year 1979/80. P&O had let it be known in a report on 26 August 1980, in a local paper, that they would need a government subsidy to build new ships. The Northern Department of Commerce riposted publicly that an intervention fund had been set up by the EEC to help Harland & Wolff with orders for ships and this was available. Even with the aid of the intervention fund, P&O were to find that Harland & Wolff could not match lower prices offered by foreign yards and something more than this was needed.

Speculation about shipboard discos and cinemas and the location of onshore terminals for any new ships was abruptly shattered three days later on 29 August 1980, when Ian Churcher, under pressure from his chairman who, in turn, was under pressure from P&O's bankers, denied that there was any plan to build new vessels for the Belfast/Liverpool service. Instead, priority was to be given by P&O Ferries to a £150 million investment programme which would be devoted to improving their English cross channel services and expanding North Sea Ferries.

In fact, this seemed to be the end of any plan to develop the passenger service. In fairness to P&O, they had expended £96,000 up to 1981 in design studies for new vessels and terminals. As far back as December 1977

the government had been made aware that P&O would face great difficulties in building new ships for the Belfast/Liverpool service. The atmosphere of political and civil unrest in the Province was stifling trade and economic growth and would not allow profit levels sufficient to service fully the capital investment required for new tonnage. Government had responded by forming a working party with P&O and shipbuilding interests to discuss future tonnage requirements for the Belfast/Liverpool passenger service. No subsidies were asked for but P&O submitted that grant assistance and joint participation by the government would be essential for a future service based on new ships. Had the government wished to participate in the control of the service, P&O would have apparently made no objection, even if 'corporate identity' had become a casualty in the process.

Throughout 1980 the Belfast management of P&O made strenuous efforts to economise on shipboard manning levels and cut expenditure, including the closure of the High Street, Belfast, passenger booking office after a relatively short life. Promotion of the route continued with advertising and promotional offers such as 'coach sailers' and 'rail sailers'.

The P&O Group's shipping activities for 1980 had a gloomy tale to tell the shareholders. Catastrophic losses on the English Channel services had cost £1,550,000, £11 million had been written off for jet foil operations whilst the total contribution of shipping to Group finances was a mere 5/6 percent. There could be no mistaking the menace in the warning from the chairman, Lord Inchcape, that for the future the required overall return on all Group activities would be 20 percent and this could only be achieved by cutting back on the dominance of shipping within the Group. For the Belfast/Liverpool route there was only '... A sound as if with the Inchcape Bell, The Devil below was ringing his knell'.

As 1981 opened, the horizon darkened. The NUS had lodged a claim for a 16 percent increase, which was more than the Belfast/Liverpool service could bear. The NUS went on to announce a series of guerrilla actions against owners and a 48 hour stoppage was announced for New Year's Eve. P&O reaction was as swift as it was unexpected by seamen, management and travellers. The strike was described as the 'last straw' and passenger and car ferry services would be discontinued forthwith. A melee of industrial action followed with the *Ulster Prince* and *Ulster Queen* occupied by NUS members at Liverpool and all Pandoro services halted. P&O agreed to resume services from 8 January 1981 in response to urgent representations from the Unions, travel trade and the Northern Ireland Secretary of the day, Humphrey Atkins.

Soon after the service resumed, Ian Churcher made it clear that the reprieve was not unconditional. There would have to be a settlement of the seamens' dispute and a 15 percent increase in usage of the service. Were it not for the 'troubles', 2,000,000 extra visitors could be expected in any one year. New vessels were estimated to cost £32,500,000 each plus £15,000,000 for new terminals. P&O wanted the government, at least, to guarantee loans totalling £80,000,000.

The P&O proposals were neither revolutionary nor unreasonable. The Coast Lines Group had received assistance by way of a loan from the Northern Ireland government in the period 1936/39 when no fewer than seven ships had been built in Belfast with government aid.

That worthwhile government proposals had failed to materialise from the deliberations set in train in 1977 was due to the incompatibility of the philosophies motivating shipowners and politicians. One must plan in the medium or long term if one's business is to survive. The latter is ever at the call of short term expediency. Since 1972, Northern Ireland had no government of its own to lend a sympathetic ear to local problems divorced from what might be expedient in the southeast of England. The General Election of 1979 had produced a change of political colour in the Direct Rule administration and it was soon clear that ideology had ousted pragmatism.

Seamen and dockers did little to assist hopes that the service might be continued. The NUS submitted a claim for increased pay and improved conditions which would amount to an overall increase of 30 percent,

comparable with increases being gained ashore but a near fatal potion for a patient as sick as the Belfast/Liverpool service.

At Liverpool ultra-conservatism on the part of the dockers resulted in iron wheeled trucks with two dockers in charge and many more in attendance. The mere mention of a fork lift truck was liable to 'burst a blood vessel'. The Mersey Docks and Harbour Company struggled through long months of negotiation attempting to persuade the dockers to reduce manning levels, losing £9 million worth of business in the process.

A crisis was clearly approaching in 1981 when losses on the Belfast/Liverpool service were reported to be heavier than in the previous year with the P&O financial director, Oliver Brooks, stating that the figures were 'very bad'. Traffic on all P&O's Irish Sea passenger and freight services was down by 20 percent due to the recession, English Channel services were losing money and the whole P&O Ferries operation was reported to have incurred a loss of £5,200,000 in the first six months of 1981.

At the beginning of October the announcement came that the Belfast/Liverpool passenger and car ferry service would be withdrawn on 12 October 1981. Losses were estimated to reach £1 million by the end of the year, according to a press release. Negotiations with Unions had failed to produce cost effective means to save the service, it went on to say, and the only way for the service to continue would be for the government to assume financial responsibility.

Closure was postponed until 11 November 1981, to enable further representations to be made to the government for short term aid to enable the service to continue and for assistance to be given with the essential task of tonnage replacement. The Lord Mayor of Belfast led a delegation from the city council to David Mitchell, the Minister in charge of the Department of the Environment. Mrs Grace Bannister and her delegation received short shrift from the Minister who told them that 'It was not government policy to subsidise merchant shipping'.

Next day, political differences were laid aside when the present Lord Fitt and Dr Ian Paisley joined others to meet the Northern

Ireland Secretary, James Prior, to plead for the last remaining passenger sea link between the English mainland and Northern Ireland. Alas, Mr Prior's reply, predictably dogmatic and unimaginative, dashed any hopes that remained.

If only the government had been consistent in the application of its policy one might have disagreed without feeling the Ministerial attitudes were tainted with hypocrisy. The government had failed to develop the imaginative proposals set in train by the working party established by its predecessor but it had enthusiastically endorsed and continued that same predecessor's five year programme, announced in 1978, to improve the A75 trunk road from Carlisle which gave access to the short sea terminals of Stranraer and Cairnryan. The programme had been estimated to cost £18,500,000 and whatever its prime purpose, this expenditure amounted to a hefty indirect subsidy for Townsend Thoresen and Sealink. The use of such a long road route from England to Northern Ireland was undesirable environmentally and wasteful in terms of fuel and cost since it requires four times as much fuel to move one tonne of cargo by road as it does by sea. It encouraged less scrupulous hauliers to violate EEC regulations on drivers' hours and so imperil the safety of other road users.

Regrettably, the government saw nothing wrong in the Belfast/Liverpool passenger service continuing to be the victim of most unfair competition from British Airways which they proposed to sell off to the private sector. The airline is known to have practised below cost selling and cross subsidisation to increase sales volume. There were good grounds for believing that these air services lost £1 million in 1980/81 despite carrying 609,000 passengers compared with 359,000 passengers and a loss of £1.3 million in 1977/78.

As if it were not enough to profess a policy of not subsidising merchant shipping, the government saw nothing wrong in abstracting a staple off-season element of passenger traffic from the Belfast/Liverpool route in 1979 and transferring it to British Airways. The traffic concerned was the carriage of military personnel and their families whom the Belfast Steamship Company and P&O after them carried at 9½ percent discount fares. The Ministry of Defence now claimed that British Airways were giving them a discount of 40 percent. It is hard to see how this could possibly be economic for the airline. If the government justified this on some other ground, then at the very least it should have looked, in all fairness, at the possibility of compensating the sea carrier for a grievous loss at a time when for reasons beyond its control the Belfast/Liverpool route could not attract tourist traffic in sufficient quantity to outweigh the loss.

Whilst the sins of previous Conservative and Labour administrations in the way of subsidising competitors could not be visited directly on the government which Mr Prior represented, it is not always appreciated that keeping the peace is a government responsibility. It was not being kept in Northern Ireland and the Belfast/Liverpool route suffered in consequence. When the government fails in its obligations it ill lies in its mouth to plead a doctrinaire indifference to the serious consequential difficulties which afflict such a capital intensive business as shipping.

The P&O Group must bear some responsibility for the situation which developed. Had Dr Rodney Leach's pursuit of corporate indentity not obliterated the Belfast Steamship Company's name, a more sympathetic climate in Belfast and Liverpool might have ensued. Government with all its faults could hardly be blamed for not feeling over sympathetic to a concern which they saw as part of the mighty P&O Group, indistinguishable from it in name, flag and livery. In 1981 the Group was troubled and asking for government assistance to continue one Irish Sea service, yet at the very same time its main Board was negotiating with the Finnish Wartsila Yard to build a 44,000 ton cruising vessel, the future *Royal Princess*.

In Northern Ireland itself, there was no suggestion that any local financial responsibility or risk should be borne for continuing the service. Wise comment and analysis abounded in the columns of local papers but the dogged Ulster independence and enterprise that called Belfast's merchants together in 1852 and saw the *Telegraph* sail away on her

A strike-bound and woebegone *Ulster Queen* at Prince's Dock South East 1981. (J Y Grogan)

maiden voyage in the following year was sadly absent. Ulster was no longer a place where political and commercial decisions were made and a saviour from outside the Province was expected at all times.

On 6 November 1981, the *Ulster Queen*'s crew refused to sail her to Belfast and commenced a 'sit in'. The *Ulster Prince* arrived from Belfast on the following morning and her crew joined the strike and 'sit in'. That was the end of the Belfast/Liverpool passenger service, at least for the present. It was the end of Prince's Dock's association with the Irish trade and a service commenced almost 129 years before and carried on almost continuously since died without dignity. Sad bystanders could at least feel some satisfaction that the Belfast Steamship Company itself was not tarnished by the sordid events of recent months and slumbered on behind the marketing facade of P&O Ferries (Irish Sea Services).

On a lonely and desolate Donegall Quay at the now ironically named Terminal Building, the surviving sixty headquarters staff held a farewell party. Across the water in Liverpool, 140 embittered and angry men continued to occupy the *Ulster Prince* and *Ulster Queen*. Within a week Pandoro services were at a standstill in sympathy. P&O services from Ardrossan and Aberdeen were halted and there were threats to extend the action to P&O's deep sea services.

Early in December, 'sit ins' ended on an assurance being given to the NUS that another operator was attempting to re-open the route and redundant crews would be given employment if the attempt succeeded.

Later in the same month the *Ulster Prince* and *Ulster Queen* slipped out into the Mersey for the last time and forlornly set sail for Ostend pending disposal. There they lay until September 1982, when both were sold to Greek Cypriot owners with delivery at Piraeus. The *Ulster Prince* became the *Lady M* of Panmar Shipping of Limassol. Her new owners lost no time in making alterations to her original design, such as extending her foc'sle deck aft flush to the bridge superstructure. The *Ulster Queen* went to Pangloss Shipping, also of Limassol, as the *Med Sea*.

Enough has surely been said to show that the Belfast/Liverpool route was not what Professor J K Galbraith would call a 'congenital loser'. Had some loan assistance been given to invest in new tonnage there would, as subsequent experience on the route has shown, have been a return to profitability and the taxpayer would have gained on his investment.

The theories that dominated the thinking of the government in 1981, in the words of Dr Michael Bonavia, '... drew a sharp distinction, often superficial and misleading, between what is social and what is economic in transport', 'transport ... is also a public service that is an essential requirement of any advanced society'. A direct surface passenger link between Northern Ireland and the English mainland is an indisputably essential requirement for the Ulster community. A blind belief in the virtues of market forces will not supply this requirement adequately and this deficiency ... 'must outweigh short term benefits from sporadic competition'.

As it was, a selective application of currently fashionable theories enabled James Prior, in the words again of Professor J K Galbraith, albeit in another context, to evade 'painful thought and action'.

XIV
A New Beginning

Towards the end of January 1982, a ray of hope at last pierced the winter gloom which had lain over Donegall Quay since the lights of the *Ulster Prince* faded into the night for the last time on 6 November 1981. Rumour hardened into fact when Irish Shipping Limited of Dublin announced that a Belfast/Liverpool passenger and freight service would be resumed on the following 31 March by a new company under their auspices.

Contingent promises to displaced crew members might have been given but this was to be unequivocally a new operation and not a mere continuation of an old one under new management. 'We are not taking over anything', declared Aubrey McElhatton, managing director of Irish Shipping's Ferry subsidiary, Irish Continental Line. All would depend upon agreement with the unions afloat and ashore over manning. They could agree 'to jobs or no jobs'. So perhaps the closure by P&O had one beneficial effect for it concentrated the minds of those, especially in Liverpool, who were previously reluctant to make concessions on manning levels. It was a pity, however, that such a catharsis was necessary.

Irish Shipping had been formed during the Second World War with Irish Government sponsorship and had been engaged mainly in liner and bulk carrier operations. Their first involvement with ro-ro operations had been in 1968 when they were associated as agents with a summer only freight and passenger service started in that year from Rosslare to Le Havre. The operators were Normandy Ferries, composed of General Steam Navigation Company, a P&O subsidiary of course, and Société Anonyme de Gérance et d'Armement (SAGA), Paris.

In 1971 Normandy Ferries announced that the service from Rosslare would not operate after that year. As this was the year in which P&O had bought the Belfast Steamship Company it was not surprising perhaps to learn that they proposed to operate all Northern Irish traffic to the continent via England and Southampton in future.

There was no service from Rosslare in 1972 but Irish Continental Lines was born in that year to fill the gap left by Normandy Ferries. At first, 50 per cent of the capital was provided by Lion Ferry of Halmstad, Sweden, and other Scandinavian interests and the balance by Irish Shipping.

On 2 June 1973, the MV *Saint Patrick*, delivered new from the Bremerhaven Yard of Schiffbau Gesellschaft Unterweser AG, sailed on her maiden voyage from Rosslare, opening the new service at the same time. Success was soon attained, with operational profits being made, and Irish Continental Lines later became a fully-owned subsidiary of Irish Shipping.

The new subsidiary to operate the Belfast/Liverpool route was named 'Belfast Car Ferries' and incorporated as a private company in Northern Ireland. The bulk of the capital was supplied by Ocean Bank Developments in which Irish Shipping held 75 per cent of the capital with Allied Irish Banks, the largest independent bank in Ireland, holding the remainder.

The chief executive was, and is, John Hewitt FCA, a former financial controller of the Belfast Steamship Company and P&O Ferries (Irish Sea Services). With a staff of some forty drawn mainly from the former BSS head office, John Hewitt moved into the Donegall Quay Terminal Building which was adapted as headquarters. Cohesion within the Irish Shipping Group was ensured by Aubrey McElhatton, based in Dublin, becoming managing director, but combining this post with his existing managing directorship of Irish Continental Line.

The *Saint Patrick* arrives in Liverpool for dry-docking,

... and is refitted and transformed,

... into the *Saint Colum I.* (all J Y Grogan)

The formation of Belfast Car Ferries was possible as a result of the great success achieved on the Rosslare/Cherbourg and Le Havre services. In 1978, a second ship had been acquired in the shape of the larger Yugoslav-built *Stenna Scandanavica* which was renamed *Saint Killian*. Now in 1982, not only was the *Saint Killian* to be lengthened and become the *Saint Killian II* but the Hamburg-built motor ship *Aurella* was also acquired, releasing the *Saint Patrick* of 1973 for the Belfast/Liverpool route.

It was decided to rename the *Saint Patrick* although in view of the national saint's reputed early association with Slemish Mountain in Co Antrim and burial in Downpatrick, this was surprising.

But the *Saint Patrick* was renamed, becoming the *Saint Colum I* registered in Belfast in the name of Allied Irish Banks and Allied Irish Investment Bank Limited and chartered to Belfast Car Ferries. At least she would be able now to visit her home port, an impossible feat when she bore Wexford on her stern. In her stead at Rosslare the *Aurella* became the *Saint Patrick II*.

In the event, 31 March proved too optimistic as a starting date. The *Saint Colum I* was too large for Prince's Dock and on her projected schedule could ill affort a passage up river to the Waterloo Entrance. So, the ninety-two year long association of the Belfast trade with Prince's Dock ended and a new berth at Langton Dock took its place. There a ramp, passenger terminal and secure area for commercial vehicles had to be constructed. Meanwhile, the *Saint Colum I* underwent an extensive refit at the hands of Seaforth Welding of Liverpool.

Was there any real novelty in the involvement of Dublin financial and banking interests in the route or in a *Saint* plying on it? Not really, for the City of Dublin Steam Packet Company carried Belfast products and Belfast citizens across to Liverpool for a quarter of a century from 1826. Though it was a pure financial technicality, the Belfast Steamship Company's shares had been held by the British and Irish Steam Packet Company of Dublin from 1919 to 1923 when they were transferred to the common 'parent' of both companies, Coast Lines Limited. Over

The *Saint Colum I* on passage. (Belfast Ferries)

fifty years before, the Bank of Ireland had made possible the single most significant capital investment in new tonnage in the history of the service. Nor, indeed, was the *Saint Colum I* the first *Saint* to come sailing in, for the *St Clair* from the 'North Company' had relieved on the station in 1970 and 1971 after which P&O decided to do without a relief ship during the winter overhaul period.

Towards the end of April the *Saint Colum I* set sail for Belfast and entertained the Lord Mayor of the city, Mrs Grace Bannister, and civic dignitaries, before starting work. At last on Wednesday night, 1 May, under the command of Captain James Fullerton of Belfast, the *Saint Colum I*'s whistle sounded the traditional three blasts which echoed and re-echoed around Belfast's empty quays as she slipped and proceeded into the still, calm night.

The *Saint Colum I* is the largest ship ever to sail regularly between Belfast and Liverpool. She is also the fastest, her Blohm and Voss Pielstick engines driving twin controllable pitch propellers giving her a speed of 22 knots. Manoeuvrability is assisted by a bow thrust unit. Originally intended for service in the Baltic she has an ice strengthened bow, and bow and stern loading doors. A white hull, unadorned by logos, red boot topping and a red funnel amidships with a white shamrock motif superimposed make for a well-balanced profile unusual in these functional days.

Egalitarianism dictated by economics has swept away the saloon passenger at last on the service. The *Saint Colum I* accommodates 1,040 passengers, berthing 547 of them. Although she has no single berth rooms as such, exclusive use of the two berth room can be offered. She can carry 210 cars or 30m by 12m freight units or the proportion can be varied. A restaurant, cafeteria, two lounge bars, a cinema, discotheque and a gift shop complete her passenger facilities.

Annual overhauls for the *Saint Colum I* have brought from time to time the *Saint Killian II* and the *Saint Patrick II* northwards to maintain the service. The *Saint Killian II*, incidentally, is the largest vessel on the Irish register.

The *Saint Colum I* commenced a punishing schedule, sailing seven nights a week from Belfast and seven days a week from Liverpool. Unfortunately, she has suffered more than her fair share of mechanical problems in the first year of the service. Such are the economics, however, of the 1990s, which demand from a ship responses deemed impossible twenty years ago. Lacking a consort, mechanical failure of any kind means total disruption of the service until it is put right and an undue and unfair ration of opprobrium from the news media as a result. It is not generally appreciated that in four weeks, the *Saint Colum I* covers almost the equivalent in nautical miles of a voyage from Liverpool to

A two berth cabin de-luxe on *Saint Colum I*. (Belfast Ferries)

Copelands Restaurant, *Saint Colum I*. (Belfast Ferries)

New York and back, spending only 168 fragmented hours alongside in which to embark and disembark passengers, cars and commercial vehicles which she would do fifty-six times, as well as locking in and out of the Mersey, a further fifty-six times in all weathers.

Some criticism was levelled at management by local politicians at the outset because it appeared to them that the ship was being based in Liverpool rather than Belfast. The pattern of operation gave no choice, for the *Saint Colum I* had 4 hours alongside at Liverpool as opposed to 2 hours at Belfast. It was convenient to locate marine and catering superintendents along with the operational

manager in Liverpool but this is open to review when circumstances change. It is firm company policy to utilise Northern Ireland firms for the supply and support of the ships wherever possible.

The first management task was to try to win back the ro-ro freight traffic now flowing through Larne as well as the passenger traffic that had gone to other routes since November for competitors had not been idle in the interregnum. Sealink had enticed passengers to its routes from Dun Laoghaire and Rosslare with the slogan, 'Britain's quicker the short way round' and consoling jaded motorists with the promise of duty free facilities on board. The British and Irish Steam Packet Company proclaimed that there was 'No better way to Britain' than by its services, slyly indicating that its Dublin terminal was 'Just off the main road to Belfast'.

In the second year of operation 183,000 tonnes of freight were carried. The new service had established itself, proving that in the event the P&O Board's decision not to invest in more suitable tonnage for the route but to close it down instead was an unduly pejorative one.

Also in the second year came a new venture, 'Belfast Freight Ferries', with capital provided by Messrs Scrutton, whom we have met before, and management was entrusted to Belfast Car Ferries. Using chartered ro-ro tonnage, daily sailings were provided to and from Heysham.

Alas, in Belfast Car Ferries' third year they were to suffer an undeserved blow. Irish Shipping Limited had run into severe financial problems as the result of charters entered into in association with the Reardon-Smith Line which had proved disastrously uprofitable. Amid a storm of public controversy, Dr Garrett Fitzgerald's coalition government placed Irish Shipping in the hands of a liquidator in 1984. Irish Continental Lines and Belfast Car Ferries were both trading profitably, nevertheless in the eyes of the liquidator they were merely assets to be realised and both were put up for sale and the task of finding a buyer entrusted to the Allied Irish Investment Bank and the Investment Bank of Ireland.

The position was especially frustrating

The *Saint Patrick II* at Liverpool. (Belfast Ferries)

The *Saint Killian II*.

since Belfast Car Ferries had traded profitably from commencement on an issued share capital of £100,000 and a £400,000 convertible loan. Worse than frustration was the loss of the management contract for Belfast Freight Ferries. Such was the uncertainty over the future that Scruttons decided to withdraw from the arrangement with Belfast Car Ferries and place the management of Belfast Freight Ferries with the Isle of Man based Wallem Ship Management.

Fortunately, after a protracted period of uncertainty during which the service had to be maintained, successful bidders emerged in the summer of 1987 for Irish Continental Line. Three financial institutions, including Allied Irish Investment Bank, put together a deal which included Belfast Car Ferries and involved the payment of IR£4 million to the liquidator and the assumption of some IR£12 million worth of debts.

Organisational changes soon followed, Aubrey McElhatton resigned as managing director and his place was taken by Paddy Murphy, former head of strategic development at Aer Lingus, the Irish State airline. In November 1987 Irish Continental Lines was floated as Irish Continental Group plc on the Irish stock exchange. An issue of IR£6 million worth of shares was over-subscribed, the majority of the shares being held by leading Irish financial institutions. Some well-known United Kingdom names are represented including, as a link with the past, the former financial advisors to the Coast Lines Group.

Irish Continental Group plc is simply a holding company with two subsidiaries; Irish Ferries which operate from Rosslare to Cherbourg and Le Havre and Belfast Ferries, formerly Belfast Car Ferries, operating the Belfast/Liverpool route.

Plans were announced at the same time for the sale of the *Saint Colum I* and she was withdrawn prior to handing over to her new owners who proposed to use her for cruising in the Caribbean. The *Saint Patrick II* came north to the Belfast/Liverpool station whilst a vessel similar in size to the *Saint Killian II* was sought as her replacement at Rosslare.

Unfortunately, the sale of the *Saint Colum I* foundered on the financial difficulties of her prospective purchasers who had been caught by the depreciation of the dollar against sterling. Further negotiations for her sale to a different purchaser came to nought when it was realised that expensive modifications would have been necessary to the ship which the Group proposed to purchase for service from Rosslare and the sale price of the *Saint Colum I* would not have been sufficient to justify completion of the sale. Instead, the *Saint Colum I* had a refit costing £1 million and returned to Belfast in April 1988 and the *Saint Patrick II* sailed southwards again to Rosslare. Early in 1989 Marine Investments of Luxembourg acquired a 20 percent stake in the Irish Continental Group for IR£2,260,000. The whole group is now valued at IR£11,000,000.

What, then, of the future? The overnight sailings from Belfast are well supported by ro-ro vehicles, passenger accompanied cars and foot passengers. There is less support by commercial traffic for the day service from Liverpool despite the opportunities offered to lorry drivers to use the voyage for the rest periods prescribed in the so called 'Tachograph Regulations'. Ideally, a second passenger car ferry is the answer. Failing this, another possibility would be to buy or charter a trailer ferry, similar to the vessels used on the Pandoro services to Larne, which could offer a night sailing for Liverpool for ro-ro traffic and a return daylight service from Belfast. There is every reasons to believe that a greater slice of the available market could be diverted to Belfast.

On the most optimistic assessment, ie that a second passenger car ferry could be obtained, two ships would make nightly crossings possible from both terminals and make possible again the truth of the former slogan, 'Travel by night and save a day'. Should this optimism be translated into reality, profitable operations would hinge on the skilful utilisation of the ships during daylight hours. From Belfast, the mouth of the Clyde beckons invitingly. There is Ardrossan, where ramps exist and good rail connections and the motorist and lorry drivers would be saved the long slog to remote Cairnryan or Stranraer, not to mention the benefit to the environment of less heavy traffic and polluting fumes on the roads of southwest Scotland. From the

Mersey, Douglas, Isle of Man, is a possibility for a daily service on a year round basis but future ownership of the linkspans at Douglas could be a problem here. A further possibility might be Dublin, a link abandoned by the B & ISP Company in 1987 and where a partnership already exists with Sealink.

The building or purchase of new tonnage is the crucial problem for any operator. Banks and other financial institutions have become accustomed to expecting short-term high returns on their investments and there is little money to be made from liner shipping in these days. It is only in cruising where returns of 25 to 30 percent on capital are apparently possible in this so far insatiable market. Capital apart, intensive utilisation of a second ship can only produce a profit if her earnings can exceed the additional crew, fuel, maintenance, depreciation and hull insurance costs. A good turn of speed is required to maintain intensive day and night schedules and to leave a margin in hand to make up time on voyage and turnround delays. High speed is expensive; at 1988 prices alone, it is a sobering thought that for 'every minute saved £10 is added to the vessel's fuel bill at today's costs …'.

Whilst extra tonnage for the route remains, for the moment, as aspiration, management has plans to develop the existing service to cater for more passengers and cars as well as for the particular needs and requirements of the businessman. There is a widespread belief that today's executive jets relentlessly hither and thither but the fact is that some prefer the few short hours away from the incessant demands of the office and its intrusive communications systems which a sea crossing affords. Here is a chance to relax, reflect, make plans and reach decisions. The exploitation of this market in the future might call for an onboard conference room with secretarial and ship-to-shore telephone for those who seek to combine the relaxation of a sea crossing with the use of some of the time for business. To avoid space wasting the room could double as a private dining room when not required for conferences, a decided asset in a one-class ship. There is a precedent from the North Sea in the Zeeland Steamship Company's motor ship *Koningen Wilhelmina* built in 1960 for the Harwich/Hook daylight service. Here ten people could be seated around a lozenge-shaped table in comfortable leather chairs with typewriter facilities and ship-to-shore telephone.

Any future plans have to take into account the fact that Belfast Ferries must operate for the present in an unsympathetic political environment where the Merchant Marine and its men are only remembered by the government in national emergencies and when these pass they are forgotten. Thus, barely a year after an emotional memorial service in Liverpool Cathedral on 11 June 1982 for those who lost their lives in the Cunard vessel *Atlantic Conveyor* in the Falklands conflict, a Junior Minister told the shipping industry to 'stop deluding itself by chasing objectives it was not going to get, namely, more subsidies and protection'. Given such a governmental attitude, what can be done?

One remedy is a combination of improved technology, reduced manning and the active pursuit of joint ventures with overseas partners. This is difficult for coastal and short sea operators who invest courageously in new technology but can hardly share the venture with overseas partners. An exception is the case of Belfast Ferries who are in partnership with Irish Ferries.

If competition is to be the fashionable prescription for efficient service then at least it must be fair. In the previous chapter we noted the high degree of indirect subsidy being given to road haulage operators using the Loch Ryan ports and Larne which also amounts to a subsidy to the shipping companies operating on those routes. This is strangely inconsistent with current government thinking, apart from its undesirable environmental effects. The reasons for coastal shipping failing to compete effectively with long distance road haulage and for the difficulties which the Belfast/Liverpool service has experienced in the past when faced with this competition via the short sea route to Larne include 'market distortion by government intervention', ie building more roads and not charging the users for them. In South Africa, investment by coastal owners has been met by sympathetic reductions in harbour dues whilst in Taiwan there has actually been

The *Buffalo* of 1975. (J Y Grogan)

funding of harbours and ships to relieve serious road congestion. There is competition enough from Belfast. Belfast freight ferries have increased their service to Heysham to three sailings per day in 1989. Then there is the Coastal Container Group. Hitherto not a serious competitor for ro-ro operators, bigger and better steel containers and flats combined with increasing costs in the road haulage industry, may soon give ro-ro operations a competitive edge. Coastal Containers started to operate from Belfast to Liverpool's Seaforth container terminal in 1989.

Whilst one awaits major government intervention in the environment field, as for example by reducing heavy long distance road haulage where the job can be better done by sea, government environmental policies at a local level can aggravate traffic congestion and consequent pollution. Regrettably, the plans themselves can be well intentioned but outdated in concept. Such a plan is the well meant effort to clean up Belfast's River Lagan. Part of this plan would involve banishing Belfast Ferries' terminal from Donegall Quay where it is reasonably convenient to passengers, especially those on foot, and sending it way down channel to a new terminal possibly at Belfast's West Twin. The result will be inaccessibility added to increased traffic congestion and additional fuel consumption. The opportunity to take advantage of a new cross river bridge for rail and road traffic to provide an interchange for sea travellers will be thrown away.

For some reason or other the passage of ships up and down river to a terminal at Donegall Quay, bringing life and activity to a

Saint Colum I **with company flag painted on funnel. (J Y Grogan)**

city that has seen so much death and decay, seems anathema to the planner – better, apparently, a lifeless river lined with tidy grass plots like a municipal cemetery.

At Liverpool, Belfast Ferries moved in 1987 from Langton Dock to the terminal at North Brocklebank Branch Dock which had been purpose-built for the B & ISP Company, after the closure of the Waterloo Entrance in December 1983. This had dictated a move from their existing berth at Carriers Dock but the Dublin/Liverpool passenger service itself was not fated to survive the move for long and it ended as the result of a rationalisation operation in 1987. In April 1988, Sealink UK Limited commenced a Liverpool/Dun Loaghaire passenger car ferry service with the MV *Earl William* which complemented the

Belfast service as the *Earl William* sailed from Liverpool each night and returned during daylight hours. Belfast Ferries' Liverpool staff provided some agency services for Sealink Limited for looking after their passengers and freight and assisting when requested with the requirements of the ship. This Sealink service had an uncertain start and was withdrawn in January 1990.

There is an imaginative plan in the Mersey for a new landing stage with ramps moored off the Prince's Dock wall. This development, which would not be for the exclusive use of Belfast Ferries, would be underwritten by the European Regional Development Fund which can make infrastructure grants for such purposes. If it comes to fruition this would bring the Belfast Terminal out of seclusion in down-river Bootle to a river berth close to the city centre. The motorist and lorry driver would once more be close to the Mersey Tunnel entrances whilst the ongoing foot passenger would be conveniently placed for bus and rail facilities. A publicity spin off would be the public interest gained from the comings and goings of a large modern passenger vessel in full view of ferry passengers and 'promenaders' from Seacombe to New Brighton.

It is unfortunate that the position is unclear

'The Leaving of Liverpool'. (J Y Grogan)

on whether or not the European Regional Development Fund can be made available to assist in the building or purchase of tonnage. This seems anomalous when railways can benefit by receiving grants towards the improvement of their permanent way and structures, their most costly element, because they are classed as infrastructure. A shipping company has no comparable permanent way yet it does not damage 'the sea surface' in the same way that heavy haulage vehicles damage the road. When it is realised that its services from Ireland to the United Kingdom and the Continent are the only internal trunk shipping services in the EEC (with the exception of those to Orkney and Shetland which are already government assisted) and that these will become crucial to the economy of Ireland, north and south, on the completion of the Channel Tunnel, the anomaly is even more glaring. A recent report suggests that P&O is to seek a 50 per cent cash injection from the European Regional Development Fund for a new vessel on its Aberdeen/Shetland service. If this is correct there is an even more overwhelming case for Brussels to think again on the whole question of Irish Sea shipping services. The prosperity, even survival, of manufacturers and traders in both parts of Ireland will depend increasingly upon the existence of an adequate, efficient and cheap 'sea bridge'.

Throughout the long history of the Belfast Steamship Company, commercial challenge was seldom far below the apparently serene exterior implied by continuity and quality of service. The challenges were unfailingly answered by the skill and ingenuity of management loyally supported by its directors until the final period of P&O control. Belfast Ferries face the most daunting of challenges. But energetic marketing of the 'product' has produced support from shipper and traveller. More support will be forthcoming as facilities are developed even if the pace is not as rapid as management would wish. It is the support of the public which can in its turn persuade financial institutions that the Belfast/Liverpool service will repay investment and therein lies a firm hope for the future.

Acknowledgements

I am deeply grateful to: Reginald Berkeley, CBE, JP; Derek P Neill, MCIT, FICS, FCIS; Arthur Moore; Harold McMurray, MCIT; Frank Olohan, ACWA; my late friend Hugh O'Donnell, who sailed long ago in the *Magic* and *Logic*; Roger T Robinson, MA formerly a Director of Coast Lines; John Turner, last Managing Director of the Coast Lines Group; The late Dr Ernest Reader; The late Mr Robert McDowell; Mrs Mary Langtry who has undertaken erudite research into the origins and fortunes of the Langtry family; Mr John Grogan and Captain William Grogan both of Liverpool; Captain R V E Case, DSO, DSC, RD, RNR, formerly Chief Marine Superintendent of Coast Lines Ltd; The late Captain J B Wright, RNR; the late Captain Joseph Wilson, BBE; The late Captain John Hawthorn, OBE; Captain P G Lynch, RNR; Captain W W Lucas; Captain Frank Forde; Mr Dennis O'Brien, RNR, unfailing in his help and encouragement; Mr Trevor Roach; Mr Alfred Dennis; Mr Alfred Humphries; Mr R J Heslam; Mr P G Grice; Mr C D C McNeil, VRD; Mr W Andrews; Mr H Jones; Mr W E Williams; Mr W Roberts; Mr Harold Machin; Mr A O'Sullivan, formerly of the B & ISP Co; John W D Allison; Ralph Austin; The Revd G Brady; Tom Byrne; Mrs E Craine; Michael Costelo for help with Donaghadee Sound; Canon R Daintith; Jack Dakers; Basil Devenish-Mears; the Revd P P Devereux; Arthur Flynn; Cmdr Claude Herdman; G A Jones; Graham E Langmuir, MA, LLB; J McGannon for helping me with *Lady Connaught*'s wartime career; Mr R Mageean; Mr Alexi Napier; Sir Richard Pim; The late Mr Henry Rea; Mrs Dorothy Rodmell; Mr Thomas Ross.

Belfast Ferries Ltd, especially John Hewitt FCA, Chief Executive, Berkeley McMonagle and Donald Mercer; Belfast Harbour Commissioners and Mr R Yates for permission to reproduce paintings and for access to their records in the PRO (NI); Belfast Public Libraries; The British Library, Wetherby, Yorks; The National Library of Ireland; The library of the Ulster Folk and Transport Museum; the Linenhall Library and the Liverpool Record Office; Cork City Libraries; The County Library, Carlisle; The Portsmouth Library and the City of London Library. Messrs Coastal Containers and Mr G Maxwell; Messrs Harland & Wolff and Mr Trevor

Neill; The British Film Institute; Glasgow Museum and Art Gallery; The Hydrographer of the Navy; The Registrar of Merchant Shipping, Belfast; The Northern Bank; Messrs Racal Decca Marine Navigation Ltd; The Imperial War Museum; The Chartered Institute of Transport; Larne Harbour Company; Londonderry Port and Harbour Commissioners; Lloyds Register of Shipping; The Naval Historical Branch and Naval Historical Library; Messrs James Maxton & Co; The Department of Foreign Affairs of the Government of Ireland; The P&O Group and Mr Stephen Rabson for permission to consult BSS and Coast Lines records; The RFD Group Ltd; The Royal Society of Marine Artists; Messrs Scruttons plc; Department of Trade and Industry and the Shipping Policy and Marine Directorate Sections of the Department of Transport. My wife typed the manuscript and gave support and encouragement without which I could not have persevered.

Photographs

Every effort has been made to comply with the provisions of the Copyright Act. In many cases in the McRoberts and W Grogan collections the photographer is unknown.

I am grateful to Dr Alan Scarth of the Merseyside Maritime Museum for permission to make use of the McRoberts Collection; to Miss Eileen Black of the Ulster Museum for permission to use prints from their collection; and to the Public Record Office of Northern Ireland for permission to reproduce photographs from the Belfast Steamship Company Collection.

Unpublished sources

In the National Maritime Museum, Greenwich, London
Minutes of annual and half-yearly meetings of the Belfast Steamship Co 1852–1919.
Minutes of Directors' Meetings of the Belfast Steamship Co December 1915–February 1937.
Minutes of Powell, Bacon & Hough Lines 1 October 1913–4 April 1917.
Minutes of Coast Lines Ltd, 24 April 1917–1968.
The above are the property of the P&O Group to whom, with the

National Maritime Museum, Mr Geoffrey Stow and Miss Daphne Pipe, I am grateful.
Collection of deeds, documents, papers and Minutes of the Joint Committee (established in 1927) from Belfast Steamship Co Head Office now in the Public Record Office for Northern Ireland, Belfast, and classified PRO/NI/D/3605/C. Also held by PRO (Northern Ireland) Harbour Master's Berthing Books of Belfast Harbour Commissioners extant for 1919.
BSS Head Office scrap book kindly made available by Derek P Neill.
Scrap book kept by Samuel Lawther and made available to me by Arthur Moore.
List of transactions relating to ships, property and staff kept by the late E V Romayne of Coast Lines Head Office staff for 35 years from 1919, to which I was given access.
Minutes of Irish and British Traffic Conference held by The Public Record Office of Ireland, Four Courts, Dublin 7.
Written account of financial crises and other matters in Coast Lines affairs by the late Dr Ernest R Reader. These were prepared despite failing eyesight.
Diary of Charles Stewart (see Chapter 1) kindly made available by T P McDevitt, well-known Ulster author and broadcaster.
Records of Mersey Docks and Harbour Board relating to the allocation of berths in Princes Dock made available through the courtesy of A V Nute, Assistant Secretary to the Mersey Docks and Harbour Co.
Affidavits and reports of the mining of the *Lady Connaught* 26 December 1940, made by Captain Peter Mullan, and made available by his son Captain Peter Mullan, lately Harbour Master at Cork.
Economic Policy in Perspective – An American View, Professor J K Galbraith. 15 June 1987. Lecture given to the Chartered Institute of Transport in Ireland, made available by Tom Reid, Director.
A masterly concise background to Sir Alfred Read's antecedents and personal impressions of Sir Alfred by his grandson, J B Wioner-Lotimer.
Personal records of the late William Grogan.

Bibliography

Shipping and Transport

Beck, Keith M, *The Great Western North of Wolverhampton*, Ian Allan, 1986.
Behrens, C B A, *Merchant Shipping and the Demands of War*, HMSO, 1955.

Belfast Harbour Commissioners, *Belfast Port*; Bicentenary handbook, 1985.
Bennett, Derek, *Telford's Britain*, David & Charles, 1987.
Beth, Hader & Cappel, *Twenty-five Years*

of World Shipping, Fairplay, 1984.
Beesly, Patrick, *Room 40*, Hamish Hamilton, 1982.
Bisset, Sir James, *Commodore*, Angus and Robertson, 1961.

Black, Eileen, Paintings, Sculptures and Bronzes in the collection of the Belfast Harbour Commissioners, 1983.

Bonavia, Dr Michael, *The Four Great Railways*, David & Charles, 1980.

Bonavia, Dr Michael, *Twilight of British Rail?*, David & Charles, 1985.

Brown's Signalling, Brown, Son & Ferguson, 1956 Ed.

Bushell, T A, *Royal Mail – A Centenary History, 1839/1939*, Trade & Travel, 1939.

Chandler, George, *Liverpool Shipping, A Short History*, Phoenix House, 1960.

Chappell, Connery, *Island Lifeline*, T Stephenson, 1980.

Cuthbert, Alan D, *Clyde Shipping Co – A History*, Maclehose, 1956.

Dakres, Jack, *The Last Tide – A History of the Port of Preston*, Carnegie Press, 1986.

Davidson, A S, *Marine Art and Liverpool – Painters, Places and Flag Codes*, Waine Research Publication, 1986.

Duckworth & Langmuir, *Clyde and other Coastal Steamers*, Brown, Son & Ferguson, 1939.

Forde, Captain Frank, *The Long Watch*, Gill and Macmillan, 1981.

Forwood, Sir William, *Reminiscences of a Liverpool Shipowner*, Henry Young, 1920.

Goodwin, A M, *Eight Decades of Herysham/Douglas*, Manx Electric Railway Society, 1985.

Goodwyn, A M, *Is This Any Way To Run a Shipping Line? – The Crisis in Manx Shipping Affairs*, Manx Electric Railway Society, 1986.

Green & Moss, *A Business of National Importance – The Royal Mail Shipping Group, 1902–1937*, Methuen, 1982.

Hollett, D, *From Cumberland to Cape Horn*, Fairplay, 1984.

Howarth, David and Stephen, *The Story of P&O*, Weidenfeld & Nicolson, 1986.

Hyde, Francis E, *Liverpool and the Mersey – The Development of a Port 1700–1970*, David & Charles, 1971.

Jefferson, Hubert, *Viscount Pirrie of Belfast*, Magowan.

Jeffery, A E, *History of Scruttons*, Scruttons.

Joyce, Herbert, *History of the Post Office*, Richard Bentley, 1893.

Kennedy, John, *The History of Steam Navigation*, Charles Birchall, 1903.

Kludas, Arnold, *Great Passenger Ships of the World*, Patrick Stephens, 1976.

Liverpool Nautical Research Society, *A Merseyside Maritime History*, Transactions and Research, 1988.

Maddock, John, *Rosslare Harbour Past and Present*, Harbour Publications, Rosslare, Co Wexford, 1986.

Mallett & Bell, *The Pirrie-Kylsant Motorships*, M & B Publications, 1984.

Marmion, Anthony, *The Ancient and Modern History of the Ports of Ireland*, W H Cox, 1860.

Maxton, Graham, *The Only Way to Cross*, Patrick Stephens, 1972.

McHaffie, Fraser G, *The Short Sea Route*, T Stephenson, 1975.

McNeil, D B, *Irish Passenger Steamship Services*, David & Charles, 1969.

Nockolds, Harold, *Rescue From Disaster – The Story of the RFD Group*, David & Charles, 1980.

Oldham, W J, *The Ismay Line*, Journal of Commerce, 1961.

Owen, D J, *A Short History of the Port of Belfast*, Mayne, Boyd & Son, 1917.

Pearsall, A W H, *North Irish Channel Services*, Belfast Museums and Art Galleries, 1962.

Reader, Dr Ernest R, *Ulster Prince* (Brochure), BSS Co, 1946.

Reader, Dr Ernest R, *Linking Belfast and Liverpool*, BSS Co, 1950.

Ritchie Noakes, Nancy, *Liverpool's Historic Waterfront*, HMSO, 1984.

Roskill, Captain, *The War at Sea*, HMSO, 1954.

Savage, C I, *History of the Second World War – Inland Transport*, HMSO, 1957.

Schofield, B B, *The Arctic Convoys*, Macmillan & James, 1977.

Smyth, Hazel P, *The B & I Line*, Gill and Macmillan, 1984.

Stevens, Edward F, *Shipping Practice*, 1978.

Sturmey, S G, *British Shipping & World Competition*, Athlone Press, 1962.

Thornton, R H, *British Shipping*, Cambridge University Press, 1939.

Watson, Edward, *The Royal Mail to Ireland*, Edward Arnold, 1917.

Wilson, Timothy, *Flags at Sea*, HMSO, 1986.

Wrigley, Captain T F, *MV Ulster Monarch – The Story of a Proud and Gallant Ship*, BSS Co, 1946.

General Works

Bardon, Jonathon, *Belfast*, Blackstaff, 1982.

Beckett, J C and others, *Belfast – The Making of the City*, Appletree, 1982.

Benn, George, *History of Belfast*, Marcus Ward, 1880.

Burn, W L, *The Age of Equipoise*, George Allen & Unwin, 1964.

Chambers, George, *Faces of Change*, Northern Ireland Chambers of Commerce and Industry, 1984.

Friar's Bush Press, *Industries of the North 100 Years Ago* (Reprint), 1986.

Galbraith, J K, *A Life in Our Times*, Houghton Mifflin Co, 1981.

Gash, Norman, *Lord Liverpool*, Weidenfeld & Nicolson, 1984.

Gray, John, *City in Revolt*, Blackstaff, 1985.

Greaves, C Desmond, *Irish Transport and General Workers' Union – The Formative Years*, Gill and Macmillan, 1982.

Green, E R R, *The Lagan Valley*, Faber & Faber, 1949.

Hobsbawn, E J, *The Age of Capital, 1848–1875*, Weidenfeld & Nicolson, 1976.

Lee, Joseph, *The Modernisation of Irish Society, 1848–1918*, The Gill History of Ireland, Gill and Macmillan, 1973.

Liverpool Heritage Bureau, *Buildings of Liverpool*, Liverpool City Planning Department, 1978.

McNeill, Mary, *The Life and Times of Mary Ann McCracken*, Allen Figgis, 1960.

Southey, Robert, *The Inchcape Bell – A Choice of Robert Southey's Verse*, Faber and Faber, 1970.

Official Reports

Captain H C Denham's Reports on Passenger Accommodation on Steamers between Ireland and Liverpool, May 1849. H of C Papers, 5 June 1849. Vol 51, p. 397.

Tribunal of Inquiry into Cross-Channel Freight Rates, Report 1959, (PRL 5068) Government Publications, Molesworth Street, Dublin 2.

Shipping Services between Great Britain and Northern Ireland, Report of the Committee, HMSO, 1963 (House Committee).

Sea Transport to the Scottish Islands, Highlands and Islands Development Board, 1980.

The Future of Ferry Services in the Highlands and Islands, A Development Strategy, Highlands and Islands Development Board, 1980.

Periodicals

Sea Breezes, especially articles December 1979, 'Career of the Ettrick', Michael A Houghton; Sept 1981, 'The Southern Railway Southampton Fleet', John de S Winsor; August 1987, *Russian Convoys* by R G Robertson.

Ships Monthly, June 1985, 'The Post-Dunkirk Evacuation', John de S Winsor; Sept 1988, 'Atlantic Islands Operation', John de S Winsor.

Annual Reviews of the *Journal of Commerce and Shipping Telegraph*, 1967, 'The Seamans' Strike', a day-by-day record by C H Milsom.

Shipbuilding and Shipping Record, Sept 1946, 'Ship Salvage', by G R Critchley on refloating the *Ulster Queen*.

Journal of the Institute of Transport.

Railway Magazine, June 1950, 'Liverpool Riverside Station', H Longbottom; March/April 1948, 'The Last Decades of the Midland', R E Charlewood.

The Illustrated London News, 9 December 1854 and 6 October 1856.

Index